I0202646

A COMPREHENSIVE ANALYSIS AND AN ABSURD READING OF
WAITING FOR GODOT BY SAMUEL
BECKETT ALONG WITH THE TEXT

SUBHAJIT BHADRA

TRUE SIGN
PUBLISHING HOUSE

Published by True Sign Publishing House
Address: SY. No. 21/2 & 21/3, Sonnenahalli,
Krishnarajapura, Bengaluru,
Karnataka - 560049 India
E-mail: truesignbooks@gmail.com
Website: www.truesign.in

Copyright © 2023 by True Sign

**A Comprehensive Analysis And An Absurd Reading Of
Waiting For Godot By Samuel Beckett Along With The Text**

Author: Subhajit Bhadra

ISBN: 978-93-5584-857-4

First Edition: 2023

All Rights Reserved. No part of this publication may be reproduced,
stored in a retrieval system, or transmitted, in any form, or by any means,
electronic, mechanical, photocopying, recording or otherwise,
without the prior permission of the publishers.

CONTENTS

1   Life and Career of Samuel Beckett

Birth and Early life

Samuel Beckett was born in Dublin, Ireland on April 12, 1906. His parent belonged to the Middle-class Protestants. His father, William Frank Beckett worked in a construction business and his mother Maria Jones Roe was a nurse. Samuel Beckett attended Earsfort House School in Dublin. When he was 14, he joined the Portora Royal boarding school in Enniskillen, County Fermanagh, where he excelled in both academics and sports. In 1923 he entered Trinity College in Dublin to specialize in French and Italian and received his Bachelor's degree in 1927. His academic record was so distinguished that upon receiving his baccalaureate degree in 1927, he was awarded a 2-year post as lecteur (assistant) in English at the École Normale Supérieure in Paris. Referring to his childhood, Samuel Beckett, once remaking, "I had little talent for happiness." This was evidenced by his frequent bouts of depression, even as a young man. He often stayed in bed until late in the afternoon and hated long conversations. As a young poet he apparently rejected the advances of James Joyce's daughter and then commented that he did not have feelings that were human. This sense of depression would show up in much of his writing, especially in Waiting for Godod where it is a struggle to get through life.

Besides academic education Samuel Beckett was a well-rounded athlete. He excelled especially in cricket, tennis, and boxing in his school days. Though he continued with sports, his attention turned increasingly to academics when at 17 he entered Trinity College, choosing French and Italian as his subjects. Beckett enjoyed the vibrant theater scene of post-independence Dublin, preferring revivals of J.M. Synge plays. Moreover, he had the opportunity to watch American films and discover the silent comedies of Buster Keaton and Charlie Chaplin that would crucially influence his interest in the vaudevillian tramp.

Early writing

After receiving his BA from Trinity College, he moved to Paris and found a welcome home at Paris. In Paris he first met James Joice who would become a close friend and a seminal influence in his literary career. He soon respected the older writer so much that at the age of 23 he wrote an essay defending Joyce's magnum opus to the public. In 1927, one year later, he won his first literary prize for his poem entitled "Whoroscope." The essay was about the philosopher Descartes meditating on the subject of time and about the transiency of life. Shortly after, he published his brief but groundbreaking Proust, a study of the recently deceased author whom Beckett admired so much; the work at once illuminated its subject but also helped the fledgling and unsure artist shape his own aesthetic. When he returned to Dublin later that year to lecture at Trinity, Beckett was writing his first stories- which would later comprise More Pricks Than Kicks (1934).

Beckett could not manage himself to settle his mind at a fixed career and place. He was too restles in his teaching posts too and his reluctance to settle down in a respectable career worried his family, especially his mother from whom he became estranged for several years. He Returned again to Paris in 1932, he wrote his first novel, Dream of Fair to Middling Women. While reminiscent in its digressive tendencies of Fielding and Sterne, Dream was also highly autobiographical, a powerful indication that Beckett was emerging from Joyce's shadow and developing his own voice. Out of money, he went back to Dublin and then moved temporarily to London where he worked on much of his next novel, Murphy. Still without a steady source of income (his works were not selling, and Murphy, which had been turned down by dozens of publishers, would not appear until 1938), he moved constantly for the next few years before settling permanently in Paris in 1937.

Beckett journeyed through Ireland, France, England, and Germany, all the while writing poems and stories. On his journey to different country he did some odd jobs to support himself financially. It is no doubt that in the course of his journey, he came into contact with many tramps and vagabands who later emerged in his writing, such as the two tramps Estragon and Vladimir in Waiting for Godot. Whenever he happened to pass through Paris, he would call on Joyce, and they would have long visits, although it was rumored that they mostly sit in silence, both suffused with sadness

In 1937, Samuel Beckett settled in Paris. Shortly thereafter, he was stabbed by a pimp after refusing his solicitations. While recovering in the hospital, he met Suzanne Dechevaux-Dumesnuil, a piano student in Paris.

The two would become life-long companions and eventually marry. After meeting with his attacker, Beckett dropped the charges, partly to avoid the publicity.

Before entering the most productive part of his literary career, He produced few minor works. He wrote More Pricks than Kicks (1934), a volume of short stories derived which recounts episodes from the life of Belacqua, a ne'er-do-well Irish reincarnation of Dante's Divine Comedy procrastinator of the same name who lived beneath a rock at the Gates of Purgatory. A blood brother of all Beckett's future protagonists, Belacqua lives what he calls "a Beethoven pause, " the moments of nothingness between the music. But since what precedes and what follows man's earthly life (that is, eternity) are Nothing, then life also (if there is to be continuity) must be a Nothingness from which there can be no escape. All of Belacqua's efforts to transcend his condition fail.

Beckett's friendship with James Joyce continued but with a distance. Beckett's first novel, Murphy (1938), which Joyce completely misunderstood, is evidence of the distance between them. Deep beneath the surface of this superbly comic tale lie metaphysical problems that Beckett was trying to solve. As Murphy turns from the repugnant world of outer reality to his own inner world, always more and more circumscribed until it becomes a "closed system"—a microcosm where he finds a mystical peace—Beckett ponders the relationship between mind and body, the Self and the outer world, and the meaning of freedom and love.

World War II and Resistance fighter

During World War II Beckett joined the underground movement in Paris to resist the Germans. He served in the Resistance movement until 1942, when he was obliged to flee from the German Gestapo into unoccupied France, where he worked as a farmhand until the liberation of Paris in 1945. He only returned in 1945 after Paris was liberated from the Germans. After the war, Samuel Beckett was awarded the Croix de Guerre for bravery during his time in the French resistance. He settled in Paris and began his most prolific period as a writer. During these years he wrote another novel, Watt, published in 1953.

Watt, like each of his novels, carries Beckett's search for meaning a step further than the preceding one, or, as several critics have said, nearer the center of his thought. In many respects Watt's world is everyone's world, and he resembles everyone. And yet his strange adventure in the house of the mysterious Mr. Knott—whose name may signify: not, knot, naught, or the German Not (need, anxiety), or all of them—is Beckett's attempt to clarify the relationship between language and meaning. Watt, like most people, feels comfort when he is able to call things by their names; a name gives a thing reality. Gradually Watt discovers that the words men invent may have no relation to the real meaning of the thing, nor can the logical use of language ever reveal what is illogical and irrational: the infinite and the Self.

Novels and theatre

In 1945, Beckett made a brief visit to Dublin. During his stay, he had a revelation in his mother's room in which his entire future literary direction appeared to him. This experience was later fictionalized in the play Krapp's Last Tape (1958). In the play, Krapp's revelation is set on the East Pier in Dun Laoghaire during a dark and stormy night. Some critics have identified Beckett with Krapp to the point of presuming Beckett's own artistic epiphany was at the same location, in the same weather.

During the 1950s Beckett wrote his famous novel trilogy (Molloy, Malone Dies, The Unnamable). In these Three Novels, the reader can trace the development of Beckett's mature style and themes. He would also write all of his later work in French. Although Beckett was a native English speaker, he chose to write in French because, as he claimed, French was a language in which it was easier to write without style. (Many argue, however, that he simply abandoned English writing to distance himself from his literary idol, Joyce). Molloy has many of the characteristics of a conventional novel: time, place, movement and plot. Indeed, on one level it is a detective novel. In Malone Dies, movement and plot are more or less dispensed with, but there is still some indication of place and the passage of time. The 'action' of the book takes the form of an interior monologue. Finally, in The Unnamable all sense of place and time has also disappeared. The essential theme seems to be the conflict between the voice's drive to continue speaking so as to continue existing and its almost equally strong urge to find silence and oblivion. It is tempting to see in this a reflection of Beckett's experience and understanding of what the war had done to the world. Despite the widely-held view that Beckett's work is essentially pessimistic, the will to live seems to win out.

The trilogy of novels Molloy (1951), Malone Dies (1951), and The Unnamable (1953) deals with the subject of death; however, here it is not death which is the horror or the source of absurdity (as with the existentialists), but life. To all the characters, life represents an exile from the continuing reality of themselves, and they seek to understand the meaning of death in this context. Since freedom can exist only outside time and since death occurs only in time, the characters try to transcend or "kill" time, which imprisons them in its fatality. Recognizing the impossibility of the task, they are finally reduced to silence and waiting as the only way to endure the anguish of living. Another novel, How It Is, first published in French in 1961, emphasizes the solitude of the individual consciousness and at the same time the need for others; for only through the testimony of another can one be sure that one exists. The last of his French novels to be published was Mercier and Camier. This work demonstrates Beckett's interest in wordplay, especially in its use of French colloquialisms. Written in 1946, it was not published until 1974.

Samuel Beckett's first play was Eleutheria published by Satre's magazine Les Tepms Modernes in 1946. The play presents a man's efforts to cut himself loose from his family and social obligations. This has often been compared to Beckett's own search for freedom.

Beckett is most renowned for his play Waiting for Godot. Becket worked on the play between October 1948 and January 1949. It was published in 1952 and premiered in 1953 at the Theatre de Babylone. Although critics labeled the play "the strange little play in which 'nothing happens,'" it gradually became a success as reports of it spread through word of mouth. It eventually ran for four hundred performances at the Theatre de Babylone and was heralded with critical praise from dramatists such as Tennessee Williams, Jean Anouilh, Thornton Wilder, and William Saroyan. An interesting production of Waiting for Godot took place when some actors from the San Francisco Actor's Workshop performed the play at the San Quentin penitentiary for over fourteen hundred convicts in 1957. The prisoners immediately identified with both Vladimir and Estragon about the pains of waiting for life to end, and the struggle of the daily existence. The production was perhaps the most successful ever.

Beckett's second masterpiece. Endgame, premiered on April 3, 1957 at the Royal Court Theatre in London.

Becket wrote his second masterpiece play Endgame and continued to write some more. Krapp's Last Tape, and Happy Days are some other best known plays. He involved himself in various productions of his plays across Europe and in the United States, wrote his first radio plays, and created remarkably innovative prose fiction, including the epic How It Is (1961) and the haunting The Lost Ones (1970). Worldwide appreciation of his work growing, he received in 1969 the Nobel Prize (the third Irishman of the century to be so honored). Characteristically, he was unhappy with the increased public attention that accompanied the prize and in response to a demand for a new work chose instead to release the still unpublished Mercier and Camier. At this time, he also underwent successful operations on his eyes to correct the cataracts that had been plaguing him for years.

Later Writing

The 1970s were a less prolific period, though he managed some new projects, including television plays for the BBC, and continued to interest himself in producions of his theatrical works. In 1977 he began the autobiographical Company and in the early 1980s crafted more prose pieces (including Ill Seen Ill Said and Worstward Ho) as well as more plays (including Rockaby and Ohio Impromptu). His last major work, the prose fiction Stirrings Still, was written in 1986.

Death

In the same year, Beckett began to suffer from onsetting emphysema. After his first hospitalization, he wrote in bed his final work, the poem 'What is the Word'. Moved into a nursing home, Le Tiers Temps, his deteriorating health prevented him from writing, and his efforts were given instead to translation of his works. Suzanne died on 17 July 1989, and Beckett followed her on 22 December. He is buried in Montparnasse Cemetary in Paris.

2   Chronology of Beckett's Works

The following is a selective chronology of Beckett's life with the dates of publication or first performance of principal works.

1906	Born at Foxrock, near Dublin, allegedly on Good Friday, 13 April
1920 - 3	Portora Royal School, Ulster
1923 - 7	Trinity College, Dublin. Read Modern languages (English, French and Italian)
1927 - 8	Taught for two terms at Campbell College, Belfast
1928	Began two-year exchange fellowship at l'Ecole Normale Superieure as Lecteur d'anglais.

Met James Joyce

1929	Published short story 'Assumption' in transition,
16 - 17;	and first criticism, 'Dante . . . Bruno. Vico . . . Joyce', in Our Exagmination
1930	Published Whoroscope (poem on Descartes), which won a £10 prize from Hours Press
1931	Published Proust in London (criticism). MA Trinity College, Dublin, and resigned from post of Assistant in French there
1932	After six months in Kassel began a period of wanderings in Germany, France, England and Ireland. Began Dream of Fair to Middling Women, which draws on these journeys
1933	Father died, leaving Beckett a £200 annuity. Lived for about two years in Chelsea, London, supplementing his annuity by reviewing and translation

1934	Published More Pricks than Kicks (short stories). Began analysis at Tavistock Clinic
1935	Published Echo's Bones (collection of thirteen poems)
1937	Settled in Paris
1938	Published Murphy in London (a novel in English, begun in 1934 - rejected by forty-two publishers before acceptance by Routledge) Stabbed in a Paris street, 7 January. Visited in hospital by pianist Suzanne Dumesnil, who later became his wife
1939	Returned to Paris, from a visit to Dublin, at the outbreak of the Second World War
1941 - 2	Worked in the French Resistance with his friend Alfred Peron
1942	The Gestapo arrested Peron; Beckett and Suzanne Dumesnil fled from Paris to Roussillon in unoccupied France. Began writing Watt
1945	Worked for Irish Red Cross in Normandy. Received Croix de Guerre and Medaille de la Resistance for his service in war-time France. Visited Ireland, and finished Watt in Dublin
1946	Began his most creative period, writing in French, with Mercier et Camier (novel) and Nouvelles ('La Fin', 'L'Expulse', 'Le Calmant' and 'Premier Amour' - stories)
1947	Completed Molloy and Eleutheria (unpublished play)
1948	Completed Malone Meurt
1949	Completed En attendant Godot - in January Published Three Dialogues with Georges Duthuit in transition
1950	Completed L'Innommable. The trilogy of novels was accepted for publication by Editions de Minuit in November. Beckett returned to Dublin before his mother's death in August
1952	En attendant Godot published in Paris
1953	En attendant Godot first performed at the Theatre de Babylone, Paris.

1955	Waiting for Godot produced in London. Began Fin de Partie {Endgame)
1956	Waiting for Godot published in London
1957	All that Fall broadcast by BBC Third Programme. World premiere of Fin de Partie (in French) in London
1958	World premiere of Krapp's Last Tape in London
1961	World premiere of Happy Days in New York. Comment c'est {How It Is) published in Paris 1963 World premiere of Play (in German) in Ulm
1969	Awarded the Nobel Prize for Literature, 23 October. Accepted the award but did not attend the prize-giving ceremony in Stockholm
1970	Lessness published in London
1972	World premiere of Not I in New York
1976	That Time and Footfalls premiere at the Royal Court Theatre to celebrate Beckett's seventieth birthday
1977	Ghost Trio and . . . but the clouds broadcast on BBC Television
1981	Ill Seen III Said published in New Yorker. World premiere of Rockaby and Ohio Impromptu in Buffalo and at Ohio State Beckett Symposium respectively
1982	World premiere of Catastrophe at Avignon Festival
1984	Collected Shorter Plays of Samuel Beckett published in London
1986	Beckett's eightieth birthday celebrated with conferences in Paris, New York, and Stirling, unattended by Beckett

3   Samuel Beckett as a Dramatist

Introduction

Samuel Beckett (1906-1989) is a one of the most creative writers of the twentieth century. He has created a new stream in the dramatic movement of modern theatre—theatre of the Absurd. In the hand of Samuel Beckett, the modern theatre finds a new way to paint the fragmented world. This new movement came to be known as the theatre of the Absurd. The Theatre of the Absurd perceives and presents the human condition as fundamentally absurd and meaningless. After the World War II, the modern man is left fragmented and quite disrupted. They lose the meaning of what they have achieved and what they are looking for. Beckett experiments with new techniques to present the human absurdity and meaninglessness. His negation refers to man's failure in achieving a true confidence different from all that were tried before. In a depression after world wars, Beckett's plays presented a picture of the world fragmented and disrupted. His thought is always occupied with the subjects like alienation, identity, mystery of the self and loneliness.

Samuel Beckett, an Iconoclast

Samuel Beckett is also a realist but in different way. He presents the reality of the distorted mind after the World Wars. Beckett's path-breaking innovative literature presented the parodies of pointlessness of human actions and thoughts in the world. This new dramatic style catapulted Beckett to the centre stage of modern drama, though it should be mentioned that he may not have been influenced in this without the prevailing climate of ideas. The prevailing literary attitude of Modernism indicates that the modern world is irrational and incoherent. Consequently, the conventional play imitated reality could have no more value, for _reality' itself in its conceptual underpinnings was increasingly problematic. To mirror this, a new kind of theatre was needed. Prior to modern period, the focus was mostly confined to professional reviewing of a play in technical matters relating to performance, literary criticism of themes, characters and language, in other words, playwrights and theatre goers were looking at the plays strictly as a genre of literature following Aristotle's conventions of playwriting and its performance. In contrast, along with the fact that Modernism occurred in a restless century, drama has progressively grown dismissive about the old forms of traditional methods. The transition from the traditional method to the modern one happened because the emergence of this century was accompanied by disorder and lack of confidence in life. As an outcome of World War I, every confident aspect of life was questioned and man has been subjected to look inward for a better understanding. Consequently, by discarding nearly all Aristotelian tradition in drama, modern drama dwelt on the subject of man in his society and man in his private world.

Samuel Beckett, last of the modernists

Samuel Beckett is often taken as one of the last figures of the modernism. He has the spirit of the restless modern age. Like most of the prominent dramatists of the modern era—Henrik Ibsen, Bernard Shaw, August Strindberg, Anton Chekhov, Luigi Pirandello, Beckett has been a rebellious artist. Beckett in his own peculiar way found his way to God, society, life, world and existence itself. One may not find a good story in any of their plays, for the playwrights themselves have little interest in telling such stories. This is not to say that they are not deeply felt, deeply emotional plays, but that this emotion is a response to a condition of human experience, not to the events of the narrative. his plays are not knit by the allegedly necessary properties of time and space. Beckett's tramps could be anywhere, anytime; however, at the same time, the modern drama is not ignorant of history or tradition. The modern playwrights have a deep familiarity with Christian tradition or of Western philosophy and literature; but these references are a means of expressing a common human suffering, and not for providing a particular historical referent.) Beckett's Lost Self Subsequent to all prominent playwrights mentioned here, it would not be wrong to take Samuel Beckett as the last modernist when we see Waiting for Godot with no plot, no climax, no denouement, no beginning, no middle and no end. If modernism liberated the writer from conventional storytelling and ordinary psychology, Beckett's play took modernism just as far as it could go. Ibsen and Beckett represent opposite poles of modernism both in time and in spirit. In literary movement of modernism, Beckett is well known for his 'the Theatre of the Absurd', a new movement in modern drama which does not open in any satisfactory clue on the part of human life. Following all contributions of modern dramatists, modern drama encounters with Becketian drama wherein life is simply or merely lived while acknowledging the inherent absurdity of the existence. Beckett's plays features illogical and purposeless activity in plot, and the endless contradiction of language and action in dialogue on a bare stage. Creating such innovative drama, perfectly different from the conventional drama of representing the characters in defined regulation and frame, Beckett's purpose was to discover the limits of drama and to challenge audiences to move away from their complacent and comfortable roles of being as spectators in the theatres. Beckett's dramatic art was designed, wittingly or unwittingly, to give the audience a good shake. Feeling like an outsider in his own life, Beckett was haunted by a feeling of an absence of identity and the sense of alienation in his own world. He was captivated by the notion of never having been born. Right from the beginning, as evident in his drama, he saw birth and death as parts of a single band, with life as a long day's dying. "They give birth astride of a grave, the light gleams an instant, then it is night once more," (Waiting for Godot 82) Pozzo says near the end of Waiting for Godot. Vladimir echoes him: "Down in the hole, lingeringly, the gravedigger puts on the forceps". (Waiting for Godot 83) In such 'meta-theatrical' aspect of modernism, Beckett should be pursued in his creation of 'the aesthetics of silence'. The fragmentary, the inarticulate, and the incoherent and non-verbal aspect in theatrical intercourse are all shown beautifully in his representation of silence. Through both earlier and later plays of Beckett, the characters permanently fall silent, amazed or terrified and their feeling of silence is beautifully conveyed, through the context of play, to the audience. "This is deadly" (Endgame 25) Likewise in Waiting for Godot, in the second dialogue about sand, Estragon breaks the silence first and says: ESTRAGON: In the meantime nothing happens. POZZO: You find it tedious? ESTRAGON: Somewhat. POZZO: (to Vladimir). And you, Sir? VLADIMIR: I've been better entertained. (Silence) (Waiting for Godot 46) The silence that pervades Beckett's drama distinguished the author's work from traditional style of playwriting. Traditional plays begin with some actions or events that result in dramatic conflict, an imperative element to Aristotelian dramatic theory. However Beckett's drama, known as one of the most controversial works of twentieth-century drama, is known for its minimal approach to dramatic form, for its powerful imagery, and for its brief, fragmented, and repetitive dialogue. Waiting for Godot, for instance, begins with no deliberate movement. That is only an abstract struggle involving the passage of time. Vladimir and Estragon, two tramps, wait on a desolate piece of land to keep an appointment with someone called Godot.

Samuel Beckett, an early postmodernist

He is also considered one of the early postmodernists as he pioneered many of the postmodernist tenets through his plays. Beckett used darkness, voice, repetition, and silence to heighten the feeling of damnation, hopelessness, and introspection in much of his work which turned to be dominating subjects of the postmodernist writers. During the years of his stay in Paris, Beckett was able to write everything that made him later well known. In such productive period of writing, he realized that his art must be subjective, in a way being derived wholly from his own inner world. It was, in fact, Beckett's turn from the external world into his within that his goal got an infinite realm. He devoted his time to write about his experience of internal searching, the way by which he is probably best remembered today. During the fifteen years subsequent to the war, Beckett produced four major full-length stage plays: En attendant Godot (written 1948–1949; Waiting for Godot), Fin de partie (1955–1957; Endgame), Krapp's Last Tape (1958), and Happy Days (1960). These plays, which are often considered to have their roots in the Theatre of the Absurd, deal in a very black humorous way with themes similar to those of the roughly contemporary existentialist thinkers of the postmodern era, though Beckett himself cannot be categorized as an existentialist. Broadly speaking, these plays deal with the subject of despair and the will to survive in spite of that despair in an uncomprehending and, indeed, incomprehensible world. Such themes are illustrated in different ways in Beckett's art. Waiting for Godot portrays two tramps in an isolate area, waiting for an unknown figure while doing some works for passing the meaningless moments of their existence.

.Moreover, these late plays deal with the theme of despair in self-searching and observed as a voice comes from the protagonist's mind, as is evident in A Piece of Monologue. The minimalist style dominated Beckett's plays during the last period of his writing career. Come and Go, a bleak drama with three female characters and a text of 121 words; the even more minimal Breath (1969), a 30-second play consisting only of a pile of rubbish, a breath, and a cry; and Not I, a brief, fragmented, disembodied monologue delivered by an actor of indeterminate sex of whom only the _Mouth' is illuminated. Not I lasts only fifteen minutes and all we see is a shadowy auditor and a woman's mouth from which words flow out in a stream.

CONCLUSION

In fact Beckett is a modernist as well as a pioneer of the postmodernism. In his plays the absurdity of life is perceived in the depth of this space, Time becomes unreal; identity of the Self is not attainable; no course of event can be predicted; anything may happen; no intrinsic relationship between cause and effect; there is no achievement in life; life becomes meaningless and purposeless; everything that occurs is due to chance; the universe becomes a chance universe, and the language that reflects it becomes quite incoherent. Since the reality of the irrational world has to be reflected in language, the structure of the language has to be disintegrated, dislocated and disjoined which means the language needs to be _fractured'. In many of his literary works, Beckett gives such an image of a fractured space from the very beginning of his play. Being confined in such an image, nothing is deserved to be acted as Beckett opens his masterpiece by this motif: "Nothing to be done." (Waiting for Godot 1in fact, though Beckett could not rid of the features of the fractured space in his early steps, he succeeds in his later attempts, where one sees that the discovery of the Self is the only hope for him. In his attempt to pass into a realm beyond the fractured space, he finds that his real identity is the only truth by which the ambient absurdity is overcome and crossed. The author finds that his inner self is his only sacred space as his literary work depicts stage by stage the author's contemplative journey toward the Self.

4   Major Works of Samuel Beckett

Novels

1. Molloy

M olloy is first of his novel trilogy; the two others are Malone Does and The Unnamable. Molloy was written in French and published in 1951. The English version was published in 1955.

The plot of the novel consists of two inner monologues. The first monologue is split into two paragraphs. The first paragraph is less than two pages long; the second paragraph lasts for over eighty pages.

The first part or the first monologue is done by Molloy, a former vagrant, who is now living "in mother's room" and writing to "speak of the things that are left, say goodbyes, finish dying." He describes a journey he had taken some time earlier, before he came there, to find his mother. He spends much of it on his bicycle, gets arrested for resting on it in a way that is considered lewd, but is unceremoniously released. From town to anonymous town and across anonymous countryside, he encounters a succession of bizarre characters: an elderly man with a stick; a policeman; a charity worker; a woman whose dog he kills running over it with a bike (her name is never completely determined: "a Mrs Loy... or Lousse, I forget, Christian name something like Sophie"), and one whom he falls in love with ("Ruth" or maybe "Edith"); He abandons his bicycle (which he will not call "bike"), walks in no certain direction, meeting "a young old man"; a charcoal-burner living in the woods, whom he murders with a hard blow to the head; and finally a character who takes him in, to the room.

The second monologue starts with a private detective by the name of Jacques Moran, who is given the task by his boss, the mysterious Youdi, of tracking down Molloy. He sets out, taking his recalcitrant son, also named Jacques, with him. They wander across the countryside, increasingly bogged down by the weather, decreasing supplies of food and Moran's suddenly failing body. He sends his son to purchase a bicycle and while his son is gone, Moran encounters a strange man who appears before him. Moran murders him (in manner comparable to Molloy's), and then hides his body in the forest. Eventually, the son disappears, and he struggles home. At this point in the work, Moran begins to pose several odd theological questions, which make him appear to be going mad. Having returned to his home, now in a state of shambles and disuse, Moran switches to discussing his present state. He has begun to use crutches, just as Molloy does at the beginning of the novel. Also a voice, which has appeared intermittently throughout his part of the text, has begun to significantly inform his actions. The novel ends with Moran delineating how the beginning of his report was crafted. He reveals that the first words of the section were told to him by this nascent voice, which instructed him to sit down and begin writing.

'It is midnight. Rain is beating against the window.' It was not midnight. It was not raining.

Thus, Moran forsakes reality, beginning to descend into the command of this "voice" which may in fact mark the true creation of Molloy.

Due to the succession of the book from the first part to the second the reader is led to believe that time is passing in a similar fashion; however, the second part could be read as a prequel to the first.

2. Malone Dies

Malone Dies is the second novel of Beckett's trilogy. The novel was first published in French in 1951 as Malone Meurt, and later translated into English by the author. Though the novel is second in the trilogy, it should be read as a prequel to the first novel Molloy. In these novels the reader does not get a sense of plot, character development, or even setting in this novel, as with most of his subsequent writing.

The novel revolves around Malone, an old man who lies naked in bed in either asylum or hospital--he is not sure which. Most of his personal effects have been taken from him, though he has retained some, notably his exercise book, brimless hat, and pencil. He alternates between writing his own situation and that of a boy named Sapo. When he reaches the point in the story where Sapo becomes a man, he changes Sapo's name to Macmann, finding Sapo a ludicrous name. Not long after, Malone admits to having killed six men, but seems to think it's not a big deal—particularly the last, a total stranger whom he cut across the neck with a razor.

Eventually, Macmann falls over in mud and is taken to an institution called St. John's of God. There he is provided with an attendant nurse—

an elderly, thick-lipped woman named Moll, with crosses of bone on either ear representing the two thieves crucified with Jesus on Good Friday, and a crucifix carved on her tooth representing Jesus. The two eventually begin a stumbling sexual affair, but after a while she does not return, and he learns that she has died.

The new nurse is a man named Lemuel, and there is an animosity between the two. Macmann (and sometimes Malone drifts into the first-person) has an issue with a stick that he uses to reach things and Lemuel takes it away.

At the end of the novel, Lemuel is assigned to take his group of five inmates on a trip to a nearby island on the charitable dime of a Lady Pedal. His five inmates are Macmann and four others. They are described by Malone as: a young man, the Saxon ("though he was far from being any such thing"), a small thin man with an umbrella, and a "misshapen giant, bearded." Lemuel requests "excursion soup"--the regularly served broth but with a piece of fat bacon to support the constitution—from the chef at the institution, though after receiving the soup he sucks each piece of bacon of its juice and fat before depositing it back into the soup. Lemuel takes his group out on the terrace where they are greeted by a waggonette driven by a coachman and Lady Pedal, along with two colossi in sailor suits named Ernest and Maurice.

They leave the grounds of St. John's and take a boat to the island to picnic and see Druid remains. Lady Pedal tells Maurice to stay by the dinghy while she and Ernest disembark the boat to look for a picnicking site. The bearded giant refuses to leave theboat, leaving no room for the Saxon to get off in turn. When Lady Pedal and Ernest are out of sight, Lemuel kills Maurice from behind with a hatchet. Ernest comes back for them and Lemuel kills him, too, to the delight of the Saxon. When Lady Pedal sees this, she faints, falls, and breaks a bone in the process. Malone as narrator is not sure which bone, though he ventures Lady Pedal broke her hip. Lemuel makes the others get back in the boat. It is now night and the six float far out in the bay. The novel closes with an image of Lemuel holding his bloodied hatchet up. Malone writes that Lemuel will not hit anyone with it or anything else anymore, while the final sentence breaks into semantically open-ended fragments:

3. The Unnamable

The novel The Unnamable was published in French in 1953. It is the third and final novel in Beckett's "trilogy" of novels.

The novel contains a disjoined monologue from the perspective of an unnamable and immobile protagonist. The reader finds no concrete plot, no setting. The novel begins with "Where now? Who now? When now?" (opening sentence); the speaker cannot be silent; he speaks out of nothing, and speaks of Malone 'his mortal likeness'; Malone has gone past, so he is at the centre, or may be in motion instead; hears sounds; remembers visitors, though how can be visited, being nowhere himself?; a visitor called Basil has imposed on him; Murphy, Molloy, Malone are all tracings; nothing to be said of that; the narrator is like a talking ball; believes silence would be better; Basil returns as Mahood; Mahood invents stories of narrator's childhood, falsifying details; the narrator is a trunk of jar near shambles opposite a steak-house, which is emptied weekly by proprietoress, using his filth on lettuces; possible identity of Mahood and Unnamable discussed; emergence of Worm, possibly a stage of development towards Unnamable; threatens (hopes) to go silent; fears to be punished; fixates on a 'small voice'; desires to be punished; imagines he will recover senses (sight, hearing, &c; reduce to pure narrative, variable and speculative fictions (I'm still in it, I left myself behind in it, I'm waiting for me there, [...] perhaps it's a dream [...], a dream of silence, full of murmurs'); feels abandoned; feels himself carried to the 'threshold of his story' amid self and silence, distant cries and the threatening nameless other; can he go on?: 'I can't go on, you must go on, I'll go on ... you must go on, I can't go on, I'll go on' [End.].

Plays

1. Waiting for Godot

Waiting for Godot is Beckett's most celebrated play. It was originally written in French in 1954, as En Attendant Godot and was translated in English by the author himself.

It is a tragic play with two acts depicting the unbearable miserable condition of modern man through the two trams Vladimir (Didi) and Estragon (Gogo). They meet near a tree. They while away the hours, talking philosophy, bodily functions, and sharing a few measly turnips, all while waiting for a man named Godot -- who never seems to come. They are joined by the oafish, bombastic Pozzo, his leashed human slave, Lucky, and eventually by a young boy, who informs them that that although Godot will not come today, he surely will tomorrow. In Samuel Beckett's wickedly funny, frequently moving existential play, Didi and Gogo wait, and wait, and wait. Their plight and the desolate landscape they inhabit was inspired by Beckett's experience during World War II, in which he spent many years in hiding as a member of a betrayed French Resistance group. Though tragic in theme and sweeping in scope, Waiting for Godot is a delectable combination of witty dialogue and physical comedy, and the roles have been embraced by actors such as Ian McKellen and Patrick Stewart, Robin WIlliams and Steve Martin, Nathan Lane and Bill Irwin, and many more. Waiting For Godot is theatre at its best -- surprising, charming, and compulsively watchable.

2. Endgame

This is another most important play of Beckett. It is a one-act play with four characters. The play revolves around Hamm, an aged master, who is blind and can't stand up, and his servant Clov, who can't sit down. They exist in a tiny house by the sea, although the dialogue suggests that there is no exterior to the house beyond stage left -- no sea, no sun, no clouds. The two characters, mutually dependent, have been fighting for years, and continue to do so, as the play progresses. Clov always wants to leave, but never seems to be able. Also present are Hamm's legless parents, Nagg and Nell, who live in rubbish bins, upstage, and argue.

3. Krapp's Last Tape

Krapp's Last Tape is a one-act play written in English. The action of Krapp's Last Tape occurs on "a late evening in the future" in the title character's den. Specifically, the play takes place on Krapp's sixty-ninth birthday. Every year since he was twenty-four, Krapp a would-be writer who has failed as such has recorded his impressions of the previous year and then catalogued the resulting tape's number and contents in a ledger, which he keeps locked in his desk. The play depicts Krapp listening to a tape from thirty years ago (recorded when he was thirty-nine) and then recording this year's tape.

When the play begins, Krapp is sitting at his desk, consulting his watch to confirm that the exact time of his birth is approaching this is when he will record this year's impressions. There is a great amount of silent stage business, as Krapp fumbles with the keys to his desk drawers, removes a reel of tape, opens another drawer, removes a banana and eats it. Krapp leaves the stage (as he will do several times) to drink; the audience hears a "loud pop of cork" to confirm that Krapp is consuming some sort of alcoholic beverage.

Krapp returns to his desk and consults his ledger, looking for the number of the tape that contains the recording made on his thirty-ninth birthday.

He reviews his notes on the tape (as found in the ledger), loads the spools on his recorder and begins listening. The audience then learns about the thirty-nine-year-old Krapp: he was (as he is now) alone and he felt himself to be at "the crest of the wave" in terms of his talent as a writer. The voice on the tape also comments on another tape that the audience does not hear: this one made when Krapp was twenty-nine. At this young age, Krapp was living with a girl named Bianca a relationship that the middle-aged Krapp on the tape calls a "hopeless business." The thirty-nine-year-old Krapp mocks his younger self's resolutions to drink less and participate in a "less engrossing sexual life." The audience further learns that Krapp's father died when Krapp was twenty-nine. At this point, Krapp switches off the tape, leaves the stage, and "pops" three more corks from their bottles.

Krapp returns to his desk, singing and coughing. He turns on the tape recorder again and listens to his voice tell of the death of his mother. While Krapp's mother faced her death, Krapp sat outside her house and toyed with a dog and black rubber ball. The tape reports that his year "of profound gloom" continued, until the night Krapp "suddenly" saw "the whole thing," and had some kind of artistic "vision" at the end of a jetty. Because of this "vision," Krapp denied himself the love of an unnamed woman, to whom he said goodbye after a (presumably sexual) encounter in a boat. The older, listening Krapp becomes disgusted with the voice on the tape and switches it off. He leaves the stage for the last time to steel himself with more alcohol.

Krapp returns and is now ready to make his last tape. He begins his new recording with, "Just been listening to that stupid bastard I took myself for thirty years ago, hard to believe I was ever as bad as that." He reveals that his bowel troubles (first mentioned on the previous tape) still plague him and that he has only sold seventeen copies of his "opus magnum." His life has been reduced to that of a shut-in the only human contact he experiences is that involving Fanny, an "old ghost of a whore." Despite his desire to remain aloof from his old memories, however, Krapp begins speaking of the previously-mentioned scene in the boat. He then removes the reel from the recorder, "throws it away," and replays the tape of him describing the woman in the boat, whose love he denied in order to produce what he thought would be his masterpiece. The play ends with Krapp listening to the end of that tape, staring into silence; the tape's last words, "Perhaps my best years are gone. . . . But I wouldn't want them back. Not with the fire in me now," hang in the air as Krapp sits motionless, staring into space.

5   Waiting for Godot: An Introduction

Introduction

Though difficult and sometimes baffling to read or (even) view, Waiting for Godot is nonetheless one of the most important works of our time. It revolutionized theatre in the twentieth century and had a profound influence on generations of succeeding dramatists, including such renowned contemporary playwrights as Harold Pinter and Tom Stoppard. After the appearance of Waiting for Godot, theatre was opened to possibilities that playwrights and audiences had never before imagined.

Initially written in French in 1948 as En Attendant Godot, Beckett's play was published in French in October of 1952 before its first stage production in Paris in January of 1953. Later translated into English by Beckett himself as Waiting for Godot, the play was produced in London in 1955 and in the United States in 1956 and has been produced worldwide. Beckett's play came to be considered an essential example of what Martin Esslin later called "Theatre of the Absurd," a term that Beckett disavowed but which remains a handy description for one of the most important theatre movements of the twentieth century.

"Absurdist Theatre" discards traditional plot, characters, and action to assault its audience with a disorienting experience. Characters often engage in seemingly meaningless dialogue or activities, and, as a result, the audience senses what it is like to live in a universe that doesn't "make sense." Beckett and others who adopted this style felt that this disoriented feeling was a more honest response to the post World War II world than the traditional belief in a rationally ordered universe. Waiting for Godot remains the most famous example of this form of drama.

Characters in Waiting for Godot wear bowlers, play musical hats, fall down, and try to help each other up, only to all fall down in slapstick fashion, reminiscent of variety theater in Beckett's day. In fact, before becoming an expatriate in Paris in 1928, Beckett regularly attended variety in Dublin. Its antecedent was the music hall, which gave way to "variety" after World War I, though the two terms have often been used interchangeably. An amalgamation of acts, music hall harked back to 1852, the opening of Canterbury Hall, a type that would soon become widespread. By the end of the century, music hall featured animal acts, dancers, serious singers of stirring patriotic tunes and ballads, and the most popular act of all, the comics. There were solo comics who appeared as character types—an egg salesman, for example, the humor stemming not from jokes but from the character sketch. Strong social satire in the early days of music hall gave way to performers who seemed to"preach ironic acceptance of a hard life" during the decline of this form of entertainment (1913-23) and the rise of variety (Wilmut, p. 14). Variety would endure for roughly 40 years (1919-60), enduring difficult times for much of the 1930s, during the economic depression, but rallying at the end of the decade. In revue-like style, variety featured a series of unconnected routines whose performers composed a momentary ensemble, only to afterwards part company and move on to other locations, where they would appear with totally new sets of performers. Variety saw the rise of the double act: two comedians teamed up, one delivering the funny lines, the other acting as his stooge, the dialogue between the straight man and funny man becoming known as"cross talk." The two"often indulged in 'turns, ' borrowing each other's hats, boots and even trousers, or doing slapstick with ladders and chairs" (Cronin, p. 57). They engaged in a rhythmic type of patter with each other: the straight man would question what the comic said by repeating it and then the comic would repeat it again. There is dialogue in Beckett's play that echoes this sort of patter, just as the relationship between the two main characters echoes the distinctive comedy of the double act.

In writing the play, Beckett at first gave one of the tramps a Jewish name. Lévy, evoking the persecution of World War II, but then made their two names Vladimir and Estragon. The tramps have other appellations—Didi and Gogo. respectively, which could bo cryptic ways of mutual recognition by members of the French underground. Each name has four letters, or two syllables, the latter repeating the former, an apt way of generating a sign and the countersign. In addition, the setting of the play—a country road with a solitary tree—typifies a landmark for a clandestine location; at such a site members of a circuit could conduct their rendezvous safely and apart from outside surveillance. Also the meeting of Vladimir and Estragon may reenact a rendezvous of two members of a circuit at a location from which they anticipate departure under the direction of a guide—Godot, perhaps also a code name. When Godot dot not arrive, Vladimir and

Estragon separate for the night, then return to the same setting on the following eve to wait. This activity mimics procedures that would compartmentalize members of a circuit, reducing their knowledge of one another's whereabouts, and minimizing the damage to the circuit as a whole from the capture of a single member.

Integrated into Waiting for Godot is both song and dance. Opening Act 2, the song "A dog came in" tragically recounts how a dog, having stolen a crust of bread, is beaten to death by a ladle-wielding cook. Tending to their own, other dops assemble to dig a grave for the victim: Then all the dogs came running / And dug the dog a tomb— / And dug the dog a tomb (Godot, p. 64). Likewise, dance assumes tragic overtones in the play, when one character entertains the others with his lessthan-fancy footwork:

POZZO: He used to dance the farandole, the fling, the brawl, the jig, the fandango, and even the hornpipe. He capered. For joy. Now that's the liest he can do. Do you know what he calls it?

ESTRAGON: The Scapegoat's Agony.

VLADIMIR: The hard stool.

POZZO: The Net. He thinks he's entangled in a net.

KEY LITERARY ELEMENTS
SETTING

Beckett's own script notes can best describe the setting of "Waiting for Godot": "A country road. A tree". There is an otherworldly alienation in this sparse setting. It could be anywhere, in any country of the world. No visible horizon exists; no markers of civilization are present. The setting is constant; the only change occurs between Act I and Act II, when the barren tree of Act I gives birth to five or six leaves in Act II.

The historical setting is unspecified. The time frame is most likely two days, one of which is probably a Saturday. The only visible reference to the passage of time occurs at the end of Act II when the sun sets and the moon rises. There are verbal references to the passing of time, such as when the characters make mention of yesterday and the previous evening.

LIST OF CHARACTERS

Major Characters

Estragon (Gogo)

A tramp with a sore foot. He wears boots and a bowler hat. He is obsessed with his needs, his health and his hunger.

Vladimir (Didi)

Estragon's companion. He is a philosopher, overly concerned with the state of his life. When Estragon appears consumed by physical suffering, Vladimir is preoccupied with metaphysical suffering - the cruelty of life, the injustices of the world. Like Estragon, he wears slightly oversized boots and a bowler hat.

Pozzo

An extravagant traveler and harsh slave master whose arrogance and pride annoys the two tramps. Later in the play, he suddenly becomes blind.

Lucky

Pozzo's unfortunate servant. He is led around on a rope. In the second act, he becomes mute.

A Messenger Boy

He is sent by Godot to tell the tramps he will not arrive today. The messenger boy periodically reveals bits of information about the mysterious Godot.

Godot

An unseen person for whom Vladimir and Estragon are waiting. All that is known about Godot is that he has goatherds and shepherds and a long white beard. He does nothing all day, and has asked the tramps to meet him by the tree on Saturday. He never appears.

CONFLICT

Protagonist

Vladimir is a somewhat philosophical tramp, spending a lot of time thinking about the state of his life in general. He is usually committed to waiting for Godot, and constantly reminds Estragon that they must wait rather than kill themselves or move on. He likes to talk about the past, and has vague recollections about Bible stories which he periodically shares; he enjoys good conversation and becomes frustrated with Estragon when he does not keep up with him. At times, he displays some pride, such as when he does not want Estragon to beg a bone from Pozzo. Estragon looks to him for intellectual guidance. Together, the two tramps become the central focus of the play; despite their absurd bantering and burlesque appearance, they seem at the mercy of the universe, and as such are almost sympathetic characters who just want a better life.

At the most superficial level, the two tramps can be called the protagonists in the play. However, they represent the whole of mankind. They correlate actions of the other characters to the general concerns of mankind. Even though it is not definite, there are implications that Vladimir knows more about Godot and is the one to remind Estragon of their destiny-that is, that they must wait for Godot.

Antagonist

Pozzo is a wealthy man, commanding attention. He treats his servant, Lucky, with contempt and heaps abuses on him. Pozzo represents the adverse, absurd circumstances of life. He also represents the master, the controlling being. He is thus a sort of antagonist in the play. At times, God or fate, or whatever master of the universe exists, might also be an antagonist, bearing down on the two tramps and making their lives unbearable.

Climax

There is no real climax in the play. Act I happens, followed by a parallel and nearly identical Act II. Life goes on for the two characters, and there is no indication that the third day will be any different than the first two. The absurdist point is that nothing really changes. The circular structure of the play lends itself well to this eternal stasis.

Outcome

The outcome of the play is yet to be determined. There is every indication that had Beckett chosen to write Act III, it would have been very similar to Acts I and II. This unusual structure is an integral part of Beckett's theme.

SHORT PLOT SUMMARY (Synopsis)

Two tramps named Estragon and Vladimir meet on the road, beside a tree. They are very happy to see each other, having been separated for an unspecified amount of time. Estragon has a sore foot and is having trouble taking his boot off. He tells Vladimir that he was beaten the previous evening.

The two men remember that they are supposed to wait under a tree on a Saturday for a man named Godot. It appears they do not remember the man named Godot very well, but they think he was going to give them an answer. They cannot remember the question. While they are waiting, Estragon falls asleep. Vladimir, suddenly feeling lonely, wakes Estragon. Tired of doing nothing, they begin talking about the tree and the wait, then settle on discussing their sorry condition. They are homeless and penniless, traveling from one place to another. They contemplate suicide by hanging. They nibble carrots and turnips for food. Most of the time, they simply wait for Godot.

After a while, Pozzo and Lucky join them. Lucky carries a heavy bag and is led by his master, Pozzo, with a rope. Pozzo sits on a stool, relaxes a little and enjoys some chicken and wine. He is abusive to his servant by demanding things and being rude. Eventually Lucky dozes off to sleep, but is awakened by jerks on the rope from his master.

A hungry Estragon is eager to gnaw the chicken bones thrown on the ground by Pozzo. Pozzo explains that he has long desired that his slave would go away, but he never does. The master tells the tramps that Lucky is pitiful and old, and he would like to get rid of him soon. On hearing all this, Lucky cries. Estragon tries to comfort him, but is rewarded by a hard kick in the leg from Lucky. At this point, Pozzo instructs his slave to dance and think and otherwise amuse the tramps. Lucky's entertainment consists of dancing, which is more like an awkward shuffling motion, and thinking, which is a long and jumbled exercise in rambling. To shut him up, Vladimir takes away his hat. Eventually, the master and slave leave the tramps, and they continue their wait for Godot.

A little later, a young bog brings in a message that Godot might see them the next day, at the same hour and at the same place. Meanwhile, night falls and the tramps decide to leave and come back the next day. Instead, they remain. The act ends.

The next act begins in exactly the same fashion: the two tramps meet on the road after a separation. Nothing has changed except that the bare tree has sprouted five or six leaves. Vladimir is singing a song about a dog that has been beaten. Estragon reveals that he has been beaten as well, again. They resume their wait, though Estragon seems to have forgotten the events of the day before. Vladimir tries to remind him of his wounded leg and the unruly slave who kicked him. Estragon's only memory is a vague one about the bone he was given to chew.

Bored with waiting, Vladimir spots Lucky's hat, and the tramps begin playing with it. For sometime, they initiate Pozzo and his slave. Still bored, they discuss suicide again, call each other names, and wait for Godot. After some time, Pozzo and Lucky re- appear. This time, however, Pozzo is blind and being led by Lucky. They are still bound by a rope, though this one is even shorter. Pozzo falls to the ground and cannot get up. In the process of helping him, Estragon and Vladimir also fall to the ground. The scene deteriorates into a burlesque, with characters trying to get up but only managing to become even more entangled. Finally they are able to get up. Pozzo claims never to have met them before and shocks them by claiming that Lucky is mute. He becomes insulted and departs, stumbling away with Lucky.

The sun sets and the moon rises. A messenger boy enters, claiming not to be the same boy as from the day before. His message, however, is the same. Godot will not come today, but will try to come tomorrow. He leaves and the two men again contemplate suicide. This time, they actually attempt it, but the suspender cords they try to use breaks and Estragon ends up with his pants around his ankles. They decide to come back the next day with a rope, and if Godot does not arrive, they will hang themselves. They decide to move on, but as in the previous act, they stay where they are and the act ends.

MOOD

The play opens on a totally surreal note, with a tramp trying to pull off his boot on a lonely road under a leafless tree. There is no horizon, no sign of civilization. For a moment, this scene might even be considered comic. Eventually, however, the action unfolds and a mood of despair and futility settles over the stage. The surreal feeling never changes, it is merely added to by a host of other feelings. Characters are beaten, cursed, wounded-all without any sign of relief. The few moments of comedy are dampened by an overwhelming sense of tragedy and gloom. In the end, the eternal hopelessness of life permeates every aspect of both acts of the play.

BACKGROUND INFORMATION - BIOGRAPHY

SAMUEL BECKETT

Samuel Barclay Beckett was born on April 12, 1906 (Good Friday), in Foxrock, Ireland. He was the second son of his parents, Mary and William Beckett. At the age of five, he began attending kindergarten. A year later, he began studying languages and learned to play the piano. As a youth, he participated in many sports and also began writing. In 1920, he began publishing stories in a school newspaper. Eventually, he attended Trinity College in Dublin, studying literature.

After securing his B.A. degree in 1927, he took up a two-year fellowship at L'Ecole Normale Superieure in Paris. He befriended the writer James Joyce there. His fiction and criticism was published in Transition. In 1930, he won his first prize in a poetry contest. That same year he translated the "Anna Livia Phirabelle" section of Joyce's Work in Progress into French with Alfred Peron. The next year, with George Pelorson, he wrote Le kid. It was a parody based on Corneille's Cid. He was attacked by the Trinity College newspaper for this piece of work. During this time, he was working as an Assistant in French in the Trinity College. In December 1931, he took his M.A. degree, and a month later resigned from the college. After returning to Paris from Germany in March 1932, he began writing on Dream of Fair to Midding Women. Simultaneously, he translated surrealist poems into English. He returned to Foxrock and a few months later his father died. His brother assumed control of his father's firm.

In 1934, he published More Pricks Than Kicks, a work which was later banned. He also began working on Murphy. Four years later, he traveled to Paris and renewed his friendship with his long time friend Joyce. He wrote his first poems in French. He somehow never appreciated the Nazi oppression of Jewish intellectuals. During the Second World War, he joined the resistance network. He fled to the free areas of France and survived mainly by doing agricultural work. He wrote Watt during this period. After a visit to Ireland in 1945, it became difficult for him to return to France.

He joined The Red Cross to help war-affected people and worked as an interpreter and storekeeper in a field hospital. Eventually he made it back to France and lived through what many call his most creative period, in which he wrote such works as Waiting for Godot and Endgame. He was awarded the Nobel Prize for Literature in 1970.

HISTORICAL / SOCIAL BACKGROUND

Waiting for Godot premiered in 1953 at the Theatre de Babylone in Paris. The early twentieth century had been overshadowed by two World Wars that brought about uncertainties, despair, and new challenges to the all of mankind. The poignancy and calamities of the wars found sharp reflections in the writings of the day. The global conflict and the nuclear destruction stamped a lasting impact on the minds of the writers. A pessimistic outlook laced with sadism and tangible violence, as a rich dividend of the aftermath of wars, provided both contour and content to the writings. The search for meaning had begun. With the future still hazy, writers began to search and research the new meaning of existence in a drastically changed world. A spirit of restlessness with a mixture of sardonic bitterness became an inherent feature of the writings. The writers were torn between a wrecked past and an unpredictable future. Their experiences and memories were neither lively and worth recollecting nor peaceful and worth treasuring. Hence, the mental conflict, distress, loneliness, and anxiety that they went through found an overt and dominant expression in their writings.

LITERARY BACKGROUND

Waiting for Godot was a unique outburst on the literary world. It made no claim to have a place in conventional drama; rather, it carried a "fascination" of its own, authenticated by the undercurrent of resentment in accepting the illogical and unreasonable norms of the society.

It was first written in French and called En attendant Godot. The author himself translated the play into English in 1954. The uniqueness of the play compelled the audiences to flock to the theaters for a spectacularly continuous four hundred performances. At the time, there were two distinct opinions about the play; some called it a hoax and others called it a masterpiece. Nevertheless, Waiting for Godot has claimed its place in literary history as a masterpiece that changed the face of twentieth century drama.

LITERATURE OF THE ABSURD

Literature of the Absurd is a term most often used to class together works by such artists as Samuel Beckett, Eugene Ionescoe, Jean Genet, Edward Albee and Harold Pinter. The reason these men formed this rather notoriously elite group of playwrights is rather obvious when one studies each playwright's style and subject. Though none necessarily imitate each other, all share a same subjugation of plot, character, and theme. That is, there is no particular attention spent developing a recognizable plot, no detailed characterization, and no readily definable theme. This bizarre rejection of any recognizable pattern or development gave birth to the term Literature of the Absurd.

Literature of the Absurd followed closely on the heels of two of the twentieth century's most recognizable literary styles: modernism and post-modernism. Modernism was a term widely used to signify the post World War I writings that questioned the traditional modes of religion, morality and also traditional ways of conceiving one's own existence. A prominent feature of modernism was its avant-garde contributors. A small group of writers and artists created a new form of style and expression and concentrated on hitherto neglected or forbidden matters. They were seen as free-spirited and unconventional, shocking and on the edge. Simultaneously, another artistic movement called surrealism was launched in France. Surrealism was a revolt against restrains, promoting free creativity violating norms and control over artistic expression and process. It was a revolutionary movement in all arts including literature. Post-modernism belonged to the post World War II phase. The implacable unrest due to destruction, totalitarianism and devastation in the name of progress became apparent in literature that became more and more separated from conventional art.

Literature of the Absurd was simply a later development of these innovative writing styles. It focused sharply on the irrationality and absurdity of the world. The writers exhibited an unreserved contempt and scorn for hypocrisy in the world. It was an intellectual reproduction of reality, rather than a physical or even practical one. The psychology of the work mirrored the helplessness and emptiness of human life as its creators saw it.

Samuel Beckett, the eminent and influential writer of this mode, wrote enormously in French and later translated his works into English. His plays depict the irrationalism of life in a grotesquely comic and non-consequential fashion with the element of "metaphysical alienation and tragic anguish."

Beckett's Philosophy

An avid reader of philosophy, Beckett declared that he himself was no philosopher, yet his literature resounds with ideas peculiar to his time.

Various related philosophies flourished during the World War II era, particularly in France, where they manifested themselves in such works as Albert Camus's novel L'Étranger (1942; The Stranger) and his essay Le Mythe de Sisyphe(1942; The Myth of Sisyphus). Camus saw humanity as confronting a universe that is unintelligible. In his view, the universe provides no answers to profound questions about where one comes from or where one is going, a situation he considered absurd.

Drama too gave expression to philosophies of the era, with Jean-Paul Sartre's Huís dos (1945; In Camera, also titled No Exit) featuring existential philosophy. Coined by French journalists in the World War II era, existentialism became a popular term for a family of philosophies of despair, though much in existential writing did not fit this definition. The philosophies aimed to interpret human existence. A human being has no God-given or nature-given essence, taught the existentialists; instead each being makes himself or herself to be what he or she is through his or her choices and actions. Building on prior philosophers (such as Søren Kierkegaard and Martin Heidegger), the existentialists became preoccupied with ideas like 1) nothing truly exists, 2) even if something does exist, it cannot truly be known, and 3) even if it can be known, it cannot be truly communicated to others. Taken together, these ideas comprise the skeptical extreme known as"nihilism." Existentialism became preoccupied too with death and suicide. One must face death, taught Heidegger, to enter into"authentic" being. Sartre addressed the subject of a person's social responsibility. Human consciousness, he taught (in Existentialism and Humanism, 1946), gives rise to the freedom of the individual, and freedom, to social responsibility. The individual, said the existentialists, is not a detached observer in this world but a participant—again, humans define themselves by the choices they make, the way they act. Actually the existentialists were philosophers of creation. One can better take their full measure by distinguishing between their diagnosis of humanity's current condition and the possibilities for an ethical life that their diagnosis opened up. As shown, Sartre's view does not ultimately lead to despair but to engagement, pointing to the responsibility of the individual to make life worth living.

Beckett did not identify himself with any of these thinkers per se; in fact, he "distanced himself from existentialism" (Kern, p. 170). Yet Beckett's literature addresses many of these same subjects, as well as those posed by other philosophers, such as Arthur Schopenhauer (1788-1860), whom

Beckett avidly read and whose teachings support his view that suffering is the norm for humanity. Beckett did not, how ever, prefer one philosopher to the exclusion of others or develop a system of philosophy separate from his drama and fiction. He nevertheless has been regarded as a philosophical writer, and his works mined for ideas of modern life, perhaps because of his overall intent. Beckett aimed, he said,"to imitate the universal mess. ... To find a form that accommodates the mess, that is the task of the artist now" (Beckett in Cormier and Pallister, p. 118). In the process, he evokes"existential" and other ideas about existence—the condition of irremediable solitude, the experience of cosmic absurdity, the failure to communicate.

Of course, historical events as well as philosophy impinged on Beckett's outlook. His, it should be remembered, was a lifetime that before the brutalities of World War II had witnessed the bloody carnage of the First World War and of the Irish Civil War, whose"cumulatory effect ... was a general cynicism and disbelief in either virtue or decency, in goodness or uprightness or honesty" (Gordon, p. 20). However, Beckett's personal theater, or field of battle, was neither the Irish Civil War nor the First World War but rather the civilian underground in World War II France, and it did not present him with unrelieved human depravity. There were the activists in the Resistance—everyday teachers, farmers, and parents—who risked life and limb to combat the Nazis. Also, to the south of Beckett's rural refuge, Roussillon, was another village, Le Chambón, a Protestant town whose ordinary citizens took bold yet unobtrusive action, sneaking into the protective folds of their homes hundreds of Jewish children and raising them as their own. Such valiance paled beside the butchery of millions in the Nazi gas chambers, or the torture of Resistance agents captured by the Nazis, or the passive attitudes toward Nazi evils adopted by many other citizens. Still, it existed, validating the idea of"suffering redeemed through camaraderie" that"would resound throughout [Beckett's] work and life," and that would surface in the not unrelieved despair of Waiting for Godot (Gordon, p. 17).

Sources and literary context

Beckett's sources for Waiting for Godot are multiple and various, ranging from his own real-life experience in World War II and as a fan of the music hall (described above) to paintings and readings. According to Beckett himself, the visual setting of the play stemmed from a painting he saw by

Caspar David Friedrich. At the end of each act in the play, Vladimir and Estragon stand by the tree as the moon rises, forming silhouettes against the evening sky. The image resembles two paintings by Friedrich—Two Men Contemplating the Moon (1819) and Man and Woman Observing the Moon (1824). Exactly which one inspired Beckett remains

Reception

Waiting for Godot opened in France at the Theatre de Babylone 5 January, 1953. The curtain fell, reported Sylvain Zegel in Liberation, before a confused audience that nevertheless realized they had just seen an important play. Preeminent French playwright Jean Anouilh cemented its success with his review in Arts-Spectacle. "Godot" he said is "a masterpiece that will cause despair for men in general and for playwrights in particular" (Anouilh in Cronin, p. 421). Dazzled by the reviews, crowds stormed into the playhouse for every performance but often left after the first act, confused by it and, many of them, bored. Yet the praise from critics continued; a month after the play's opening Alain Robbe-Grillet observed that though "made out of nothingness," Waiting for Godot flowed forward seamlessly "without an empty space" (Robbe-Grillet in Cronin, p. 423).

Outside France, Waiting for Godot was a resounding success. The audience in Ireland appears to have been more steadfast about staying for the duration. In The Irish Times (February 18, 1956), Vivian Mercier contended that Beckett has "achieved a theoretical impossibility—a play in which nothing happens, that yet keeps audiences glued to their seats" (Mercier in Andonian, p. 95). In England's The Spectator (August 12, 1955), Anthony Hartley described Waiting for Godot as "a play of great power and skill (the dialogue is masterly)" (Hartley in Andonian, p. 92). Brooks Atkinson, who reviewed the American production on Broadway for the New York Times, sensed "an illusion of faith flickering around the edges of the drama. It is as though Mr. Beckett sees very little reason for clutching at faith, but is unable to relinquish it entirely" (Atkinson, p. 21). The play prompted not only such comments but also a flurry of interpretation. All the interpretation distressed Beckett, who thought it reflected a fundamental misunderstanding of the intent of Waiting for Godot. "The end, ' Beckett said, 'is to give artistic expression to something hitherto almost ignored—the irrational state of unknowingness where we exist... which is beyond reason'" (Beckett in Cronin, p. 457

6   Waiting for Godot: Plot Overview

Waiting for Godot revolves around the two characters, Vladimir and Estragon, wait for the arrival ofsomeone named Godot who never arrives, and while waiting they engagein a variety of discussions and encounter three other characters.[Waiting for Godot is Beckett's translation of his own original Frenchversion, En attendant Godot, and is subtitled (in English only) "a tragicomedy in two acts".The original French text was composedbetween 9 October 1948 and 29 January 1949. The première was on 5January 1953 in the Théâtre de Babylone, Paris. The English languageversion was premiered in London in 1955. In poll conducted by the BritishRoyal National Theatre in 1990 it was voted the "most significant Englishlanguage play of the 20th century".

The play opens on an outdoor scene of two bedraggled companions: thephilosophical Vladimir and the weary Estragon who, at the moment, cannot remove his boots from his aching feet, finally muttering, "Nothingto be done." Vladimir takes up the thought loftily while Estragonvaguely recalls having been beaten the night before. Finally, his bootscome off, while the pair ramble and bicker pointlessly. When Estragonsuddenly decides to leave, Vladimir reminds him that they must stay andwait for an unspecified person called Godot—a segment of dialogue thatrepeats often. Unfortunately, the pair cannot agree on where or when theyare expected to meet with this Godot. They only know to wait at atree, and there is indeed a leafless one nearby.

Eventually, Estragon dozes off and Vladimir rouses him but then stopshim before he can share his dreams—another recurring activity betweenthe two men. Estragon wants to hear an old joke, which Vladimir cannotfinish without going off to urinate, since every time he starts laughing, akidney ailment flares up. Upon Vladimir's return, the increasingly jadedEstragon suggests that they hang themselves, but they abandon the ideawhen the logistics seem ineffective. They then speculate on the potentialrewards of continuing to wait for Godot, but can come to no definiteconclusions. When Estragon declares his hunger, Vladimir provides acarrot (among a collection of turnips), at which Estragon idly gnaws,loudly reiterating his boredom.

"A terrible cry"heralds the entrance of Lucky, a silent, baggage-burdened slave with a rope tied around his neck, andPozzo, his arrogant and imperious master, who holds the other end and stops now to rest. Pozzo barks abusive orders atLucky, which are always quietly followed, while acting civilly though tersely towards the other two. Pozzo enjoys a selfishsnack of chicken and wine, before casting the bones to the ground, which Estragon gleefully claims. Having been in adumbfounded state of silence ever since the arrival of Pozzo and Lucky, Vladimir finally finds his voice to shout criticisms atPozzo for his mistreatment of Lucky. Pozzo ignores this and explains his intention to sell Lucky, who begins to cry. Estragontakes pity and tries to wipe away Lucky's tears, but, as he approaches, Lucky violently kicks him in the shin. Pozzo thenrambles nostalgically but vaguely about his relationship with Lucky over the years, before offering Vladimir and Estragonsome compensation for their company. Estragon begins to beg for money when Pozzo instead suggests that Lucky can"dance" and "think" for their entertainment. Lucky's dance, "the Net", is clumsy and shuffling; Lucky's "thinking" is a long-winded and disjointed monologue— it is the first and only time that Lucky speaks. The soliloquy begins as a relativelycoherent and academic lecture on theology but quickly dissolves into mindless verbosity, escalating in both volume andspeed, that agonises the others until Vladimir finally pulls off Lucky's hat, stopping him in mid-sentence. Pozzo then hasLucky pack up his bags, and they hastily leave.

Vladimir and Estragon, alone again, reflect on whether they met Pozzo and Lucky before. A boy then arrives, purporting to bea messenger sent from Godot to tell the pair that Godot will not be coming that evening "but surely tomorrow".DuringVladimir's interrogation of the boy, he asks if he came the day before, making it apparent that the two men have been waitingfor a long period and will likely continue. After the boy departs, the moon appears and the two men verbally agree to leaveand find shelter for the night, but they merely stand without moving.

It is daytime again and Vladimir begins singing a recursive round about the death of a dog, but twice forgets the lyrics as hesings. Again, Estragon claims to have been beaten last night, despite no apparent injury. Vladimir comments thatthe formerly bare tree now has leaves and tries to confirm his recollections of yesterday against Estragon's extremely vague,unreliable memory. Vladimir then triumphantly produces evidence of the previous day's events by showing Estragon thewound from when Lucky kicked him. Noticing Estragon's barefootedness, they also discover his previously forsaken bootsnearby, which Estragon insists are not his, although they fit him perfectly. With no carrots left, Vladimir is turned down inoffering Estragon a turnip or a radish. He then sings Estragon to sleep with a lullaby before noticing further evidence toconfirm his memory: Lucky's hat still lies on the ground. This leads to his waking Estragon and involving him in a frenetic hat-swapping scene. The two then wait again for Godot, while distracting themselves by playfully imitating Pozzo and Lucky,firing insults at each other and then making up, and attempting some fitness routines—all of which fail miserably and endquickly.

Suddenly, Pozzo and Lucky reappear, but the rope is much shorter than during their last visit, and Lucky now guides Pozzo,rather than being controlled by him. As they arrive, Pozzo trips over Lucky and they together fall into a motionless heap.Estragon sees an opportunity to exact revenge on Lucky for kicking him earlier. The issue is debated lengthily until Pozzoshocks the pair by revealing that he is now blind and Lucky is now mute. Pozzo further claims to have lost all sense of time,and assures the others that he cannot remember meeting them before, but also does not expect to recall today's eventstomorrow. His commanding arrogance from yesterday appears to have been replaced by humility and insight. His partingwords—which Vladimir expands upon later—are ones of utter despair. Lucky and Pozzo depart; meanwhile Estragon hasagain fallen asleep.

Alone, Vladimir is encountered by (apparently) the same boy from yesterday, though Vladimir wonders whether he might bethe other boy's brother. This time, Vladimir begins consciously realising the circular nature of his experiences: he evenpredicts exactly what the boy will say, involving the same speech about Godot not arriving today but surely tomorrow.Vladimir seems to reach a moment of revelation before furiously chasing the boy away, demanding that he be recognised thenext time they meet. Estragon awakes and pulls his boots off again. He and Vladimir consider hanging themselves oncemore, but when they test the strength of Estragon's belt (hoping to use it as a noose), it breaks and Estragon's trousers falldown. They resolve tomorrow to bring a more suitable piece of rope and, if Godot fails to arrive, to commit suicide at last.Again, they decide to clear out for the night, but, again, neither of them makes any attempt to move.

Summary & Analysis

Act I

Sitting on the side of a country road by a tree, Estragon tries repeatedly to pull off one of his boots. Vladimir enters and Estragon exasperatedly tells him there's "nothing to be done." Vladimir agrees and asks Estragon where he spent the last night. Estragon says he slept in a ditch.

The general statement, "nothing to be done," can refer to Estragon's inability to pull off his boot, waiting for Godot, or the characters' lives in general—even the human condition itself.

Vladimir asks if "they" beat Estragon while he was sleeping there and he says that they did. Vladimir says, "It's too much for one man," but then reasons that there's no point in giving up now. Estragon tells Vladimir to stop talking and help him get his boot off. Vladimir asks if the boot hurts, and Estragon balks at the question. Vladimir reminds him that he's not the only one who suffers, and points out to Estragon that his fly is unbuttoned.

The beginning of the play introduces the audience to the characters' bleak world, which is filled with all kinds of suffering, from the more trivial (a boot that is stuck on) to the more serious (an anonymous "they" who beat Estragon mercilessly). Beckett mixes this suffering with abrupt humor, here in the form of Estragon's unbuttoned fly.

Estragon again asks for help, but Vladimir ignores him, taking off his hat, looking in it, and shaking it upside down, as if hoping for something to fall out. Nothing does, and he says, "nothing to be done." Estragon finally gets his boot off and then looks inside it and shakes it upside down, apparently also hoping to find something inside it. Vladimir says, "show me," but Estragon tells him there's nothing to see.

The characters' absurd behavior (looking inside their hats and boots) is never explained. Vladimir ignores Estragon's pain, and repeats Estragon's assertion that there is nothing to be done: they are not only bored, but crippled by their inability to do anything at all.

Vladimir wonders what would happen if he and Estragon repented. Estragon asks what they would be repenting for and Vladimir doesn't say. Estragon suggests repenting being born, which makes Vladimir laugh. Estragon tells him not to laugh, and instead only to smile.

The Christian idea of repentance no longer has any real value for Vladimir and Estragon. Estragon's comment underscores the uneasy quality of the play's humor. Should the audience heed his warning too, or is it okay for us to laugh?

Vladimir asks if Estragon has ever read the Bible and if he remembers the Gospels. Estragon remembers only colored maps of the holy land. As Estragon describes the colorful maps, Vladimir jokes that he should have been a poet. Estragon says he was one. Vladimir asks how Estragon's foot is doing. It's swollen.

In somewhat typical Postmodern fashion, Estragon's stance toward Biblical tradition is devoid of any reverence or specialness. It is unclear whether Estragon's absurdly abrupt statement that he was a poet is to be taken seriously or not.

Vladimir tells Estragon about the two thieves crucified alongside Jesus in the Bible. One of the two thieves was damned to hell, while the other was saved. "Saved from what?" asks Estragon. Vladimir says from hell. Vladimir wonders why only one of the four Evangelists writes of the one thief being saved. Estragon is bored by the conversation.

The Biblical story introduces the idea of salvation into the play. But in the Modern-Postmodern world of the play there is no God by whom the characters hope to be saved—only Godot. Estragon, meanwhile, is bored even by his friend's conversation.

Vladimir continues to wonder about the two thieves, and whether one was saved or not. Estragon doesn't follow Vladimir's thinking and is confused. Vladimir asks why they should believe the one Evangelist who says a thief was saved, when the other three disagree. Estragon asks who believes that one of the thieves was saved and Vladimir says that everybody does. Estragon says people are "bloody ignorant apes."

Vladimir is skeptical of the Bible and points out its self-contradictions. Estragon's comment shows the bleak status of humanity in the play. While he nonchalantly compares humans to apes, Vladimir will be greatly pained throughout the play by his lack of dignity.

While Estragon gets up and looks around, Vladimir looks in Estragon's boot but doesn't find anything. Estragon suggests they go somewhere, but Vladimir tells him they can't, because they are waiting for someone named Godot. Estragon asks if Vladimir is sure that they are in the right place, and Vladimir says that it must be, because of the tree at the side of the road.

Estragon will ask this question repeatedly over the course of the play, due to his absurd lack of memory. The promise of some kind of help from Godot is actually an insidious form of control and entrapment, as it forces Vladimir and Estragon to stay put, waiting indefinitely.

Estragon asks where the tree's leaves are and Vladimir says it must be dead, or else it's not the right season for leaves. The two agree that the tree is more like a bush or shrub. Vladimir doubts whetherGodot will really come. Estragon asks what they will do if he doesn't come, and Vladimir says they'll come back to the same place the next day, and the next day, and so on, until Godot arrives.

Vladimir and Estragon absurdly deny that the tree on-stage is really a tree. Vladimir's plan to wait for Godot indefinitely shows how he and Estragon are trapped here in a kind of prison of their own making: they are free to leave but kept here by their hope for Godot's arrival.

Estragon says they came to this place yesterday, but Vladimir disagrees. Estragon asks if Vladimir is sure that they are at this spot on the right day. Vladimir thinks so (it is Saturday), but looks through his pockets to see if he wrote down somewhere on which day they were supposed to come. Estragon doubts what day it is and worries that maybeGodot came yesterday and they weren't there to meet him.

Unlike Vladimir, who has a somewhat stable sense of time, Estragon is completely temporally disoriented, and has no idea what day it is, let alone a sense of what he and Vladimir did yesterday.

The two take a break from talking andEstragon falls asleep. Vladimir wakes him and Estragon asks why he won't let him sleep. Vladimir says he was lonely. Estragon says he had a dream and begins to tell Vladimir about it, but Vladimir angrily shouts at him not to describe the dream. He tells Estragon to keep his nightmares private.

Vladimir has an intense fear of loneliness. He feels painfully alone even when Estragon simply stops talking to him and falls asleep.

Estragon wonders if it would be better for he and Vladimir to go their separate ways. He is reminded of a joke about an Englishman at a brothel that he tells to Vladimir, who stops him in the middle of the joke and leaves the stage. Vladimir returns and Estragon asks if he has something to tell him. Vladimir says he has nothing to say.

Estragon's unfinished joke and Vladimir's having nothing to say to Estragon lend an absurd tone to the scene. Vladimir says he has nothing to say, but just saying this proves that he did, in fact, have something to say.

Estragon apologizes and the two embrace. Estragon jumps back, though, because Vladimir reeks of garlic. Vladimir asks what they should do now. Estragon suggests they wait. Vladimir asks what they will do while they wait and Estragon suggests they hang themselves. They go over to the tree, but neither wants to be hanged first.

Estragon's jumping back from the garlic smell of Vladimir undercuts their tender embrace with abrupt humor. Estragon's nonchalant suggestion of suicide is uneasily absurd and uncomfortable for the audience, as it is both comical and deeply troubling.

Estragon says Vladimir should hang himself first because he is heavier. If Estragon hanged himself first, and then Vladimir tried but the branch broke under his weight, Vladimir would be all alone. Vladimir asks if he is really heavier than Estragon and then asks, "Well? What do we do?" Estragon says it's safer to do nothing at all. Vladimir suggests they wait and see what Godot says.

The characters' calm consideration of the details of how they might hang themselves continues the eerily absurd quality of the play. In the end, though, they decide simply to keep on waiting, doing nothing at all.

Vladimir says he is interested to hear what Godot will offer them. Estragon asks what they asked Godot for and Vladimir says nothing very specific; it was just a vague sort of prayer. Estragon asks what Godot's reply to the prayer was and Vladimir reminds him that Godot said he would wait and see. Estragon remembers and adds that Godot said he couldn't promise anything.

The promise of some kind of salvation through Godot is anything but certain. Not only are Vladimir and Estragon not sure that Godot will come, but they don't even know if he would really help them if he did. Nonetheless, they keep waiting for him.

Estragon asks, "Where do we come in?" and Vladimir is confused at first, then responds, "on our hands and knees." Estragon asks if they don't have rights any longer and Vladimir tells him they got rid of them. Suddenly, Vladimir tells Estragon to listen, as if he hears something. The two listen, but neither actually hears anything. They sigh in relief.

Vladimir's comment that they would approach Godot on their hands and knees might suggest a parallel between Godot and God. However, this subservient posture might also suggest that Godot is not some kind of savior, but merely a new, oppressive master.

Vladimir says he thought he had heard Godot. Estragon says he's hungry and Vladimir offers him a carrot, but then all he can find in his pockets are turnips. At last, he finds a carrot and gives it to Estragon, who excitedly eats it.

Estragon is desperate for food. Vladimir's confusion over whether he has a carrot or not and adds some humorous levity to the characters' suffering.

Estragon asks Vladimir if they are "tied." Vladimir asks what he means and Estragon asks if they are tied to Godot. Vladimir says they are, at least for the moment. Estragon asks if they are sure that this person is named Godot, and Vladimir says he thinks so. Estragon finishes his carrot and says again, "nothing to be done."

Waiting for Godot has become such an obligation that Vladimir and Estragon are "tied" to him, trapped though apparently free to leave. Estragon repeats his earlier assertion of boredom and nihilism: there is nothing for them to do, and perhaps there is really nothing ever to be done.

The two are interrupted by a horrible scream off-stage. They run to the edge of the stage. Estragon stops and runs back to get his boot, then runs back toVladimir. They huddle together, frightened by the noise.

In the face of their fear and suffering, Vladimir and Estragon huddle together. They are each other's only companions.

Pozzo and Lucky enter. Pozzo drives lucky like an animal with a rope around his neck. He carries a whip to drive him along, while Lucky carries a folding stool, a bag, a picnic basket, and a coat. Pozzo whips Lucky as they pass across the stage and just as they are leaving the stage, he stops Lucky suddenly, causing him to drop all his things. Vladimir goes to help Lucky, but Estragon stops him. Pozzo tells the two of them to be careful, as Lucky is dangerous.

Pozzo's horrible treatment of Lucky and Lucky's physical suffering are, at the same time, tragic and (with Lucky's slapstick clumsiness) and somewhat comical. The audience or reader is unsure whether to laugh or cringe.

Estragon asks Vladimir if this is Godot, but then Pozzo introduces himself by name and asks if they are not familiar with him. Estragon mishears him and ponders out loud if he knows a Bozzo. Pozzo angrily corrects him. Estragon apologizes, saying they are not from here, but Pozzo says, "you are human beings none the less," and ironically says they are all made in God's image.

Pozzo's ironic reference to the Bible emphasizes the undignified position of suffering humans in this environment. The mix-ups with Pozzo's identity and name further the sense of unstable identities in the play.

Pozzo asks who Godot is. Vladimir says he's an acquaintance, but Estragon says they hardly know him. Pozzo asks if they were waiting for Godot here, on his land, but then he admits that the road is free land. He changes the conversation and jerks the rope that is tied around Lucky'sneck, calling him "pig." He continues to pull Lucky around by the rope around his neck, then asks Lucky for his coat.

Pozzo's treatment of Lucky, whom he simply calls "pig," is the most blunt and obvious form of dehumanizing suffering that Beckett displays on-stage. And Estragon and Vladimir, for now at least, seem not at all interested in trying to help Lucky.

Pozzo asks Lucky for his stool, which Lucky places on the ground for Pozzo to sit on. He orders Lucky around some more, ordering him to bring his basket, from which he takes out a piece of chicken and a bottle of wine. He eats and drinks, as Vladimir and Estragon inspect Lucky, who is exhaustedly falling asleep as he stands.

Pozzo continues to maltreat Lucky as his slave. Vladimir and Estragon inspect Lucky, but more out of curiosity than empathy or pity for his suffering.

Vladimir and Estragon continue to examine Lucky, noticing how the rope chafes his neck and how tired he looks. They examine Lucky's appearance, with eyes "goggling out of his head." Vladimir suggests they ask Lucky a question and Estragon begins to speak to him, when Pozzo stops them, telling them to leave Lucky alone. He calls for his basket again and when

Lucky doesn't move, Pozzo yanks the rope again. Lucky takes the bottle of wine and puts it back in the basket.

Again, Vladimir and Estragon observe Lucky's suffering, but don't seem to sympathize with his pain. Their indifference to his suffering allows Pozzo to continue to treat him so horribly.

Estragon looks at the chicken bones that Pozzo has thrown on the ground and tentatively asks if he can have them. Pozzo says he doesn't need the bones, but that they should go to Lucky, so Estragon should ask Lucky if he can have them. Estragon asks and Lucky doesn't reply. Pozzo yells at Lucky to answer, but when he says nothing Pozzo tells Estragon the bones are his.

Estragon stoops so low as to beg for the leftover bones of Pozzo's meal, displaying both how his suffering has robbed him of his dignity and how insensitive Pozzo is to the suffering of others. He could have offered some actual food to the nearly starving Estragon, after all.

Vladimir suddenly shouts out, "It's a scandal!" Pozzo asks what he is talking about, and Vladimir says that it is a scandal to treat Lucky in such a way. Pozzo asks how old Vladimir is (he does not respond) and then says he must be leaving. He thanks Vladimir and Estragon for their company. But then he debates smoking some more from his pipe before he leaves.

Vladimir finally protests against Pozzo's treatment of Lucky, but doesn't actually do anything about it. The ease with which Pozzo moves on in the conversation after Vladimir's accusatory outburst is uncomfortably absurd.

Vladimir tells Estragon they should leave, but Pozzo stops them. He yanks Lucky's rope again and has him move the stool. He sits back down and refills his pipe. Vladimir wants to leave, but Pozzo tells him, "wait a little longer, you'll never regret it," and Estragon admits they are "in no hurry."

Estragon's humorous comment that he and Vladimir are "in no hurry," encapsulates their predicament. They will keep waiting "a little longer," for quite a long time.

Vladimir still wants to go, and Pozzo tells him to think carefully, asking what would happen if Vladimir missed his "appointment" with Godot. Pozzo says he would like to meet Godot as well, since, as he says, "the more people I meet the happier I become." Estragon asks Pozzo why Lucky doesn't put down his bags and Vladimir encourages Estragon to ask Lucky himself. Lucky doesn't reply, but Pozzo says he will tell them.

Pozzo is perhaps also lonely, eager to encounter new people. Vladimir wants to leave, but feels obligated to stay and wait for Godot (though no one is forcing him to).

Pozzo prepares to speak and makes sure everyone is listening (jerking the rope around Lucky's neck to make him pay attention). He pauses to think and then asks what the question was. Estragon and Vladimir remind him. Pozzo says that Lucky has the right to "make himself comfortable," so the only reason why he doesn't must be that he doesn't want to. He says Lucky doesn't want to, because he wants to impress Pozzo, so that Pozzo will "keep him."

Pozzo makes everyone pay attention but then comically forgets what he was going to say. Pozzo's explanation for why Lucky endures such horrible treatment is absurd, yet it is reminiscent of arguments made by other slaveholders. For instance, Southern slave owners often argued that their slaves were better off for being slaves, or pointed to slave songs as indications of their slaves being happy as slaves.

Vladimir and Estragon are confused, wondering why Pozzo would get rid ofLucky. Pozzo repeats that Lucky wants to show how well he carries things so that Pozzo will keep him. But, Pozzo says, Lucky actually carries things "like a pig." He says that he has plenty of slaves and cries out, "Atlas, son of Jupiter!"

Pozzo inverts the entire logic of slavery, asserting that Lucky acts like a slave because he wants to be Pozzo's slave, which seems ludicrous. Atlas is not the son of Jupiter, suggesting that the knowledge and authority Pozzo projects are based on false premises.

Vladimir again asks if Pozzo wants to get rid of Lucky. Pozzo says he is on his way to the fair to sell Lucky, but that it would be better just to kill him. Lucky begins to weep, and Pozzo says, "old dogs have more dignity." Pozzo gives his handkerchief to Estragon and tells him to wipe away Lucky's tears. Estragon hesitates, so Vladimir says he'll do it. The two fight over the handkerchief.

Pozzo cruelly comments on Lucky's lack of dignity, caused by his suffering at Pozzo's own hands. Vladimir and Estragon absurdly fight over the right to wipe away Lucky's tears—it is never explained why either of them should care who does this.

Estragon walks up to Lucky with the handkerchief, but Lucky kicks him in the shins. Pozzo shouts for the handkerchief, which Lucky picks up and returns to him. Meanwhile, Estragon's leg is bleeding, and he cries out that he can hardly walk. Vladimir says he'll carry Estragon, "if necessary." Pozzo notes that Lucky has stopped crying and jokes that Estragon has replaced Lucky. "The tears of the world are a constant quantity," he says.

Should we see Lucky's kicking Estragon as some light slapstick comedy or as a continuation of the haunting world of suffering that pervades the play? As is typical of Beckett's dark humor, the answer is a mix of both. Pozzo sees the suffering of the world as a constant, unavoidable fact (though this may also just justify his own role in inflicting abuse on others that might create tears).

Pozzo says that "our generation" is no unhappier than any previous one and says that Lucky taught him that. He says that he took Lucky as a slave 60 years ago and Vladimir is astonished that he would turn away "such an old and faithful servant." Vladimir says that Pozzo is throwing Lucky away "like a banana skin."

Pozzo characterizes the unspecified time of the play as no unhappier than any other time. This can be taken optimistically (the present time is just as happy as any other) or more pessimistically (all other times have been as bleak as this one). Vladimir is again upset by Lucky's suffering.

Pozzo mumbles that he "can't bear it" with Lucky and that he is going crazy. Vladimir and Estragon repeat his words, and then Vladimir turns to Lucky accusingly, telling him his behavior is "abominable" toward "such a good master." Pozzo begins to cry, saying that Lucky "used to be so kind... so helpful...and entertaining." Vladimir and Estragon wonder whether Lucky wants a new slave to take his place or not.

Pozzo imposes suffering on Lucky but presents himself as the victim of his own slave's change in behavior. Vladimir abruptly shifts from scolding Pozzo to chastising Lucky, suggesting that Vladimir dislikes abuse but doesn't actually have the ability to separate real abuse from false. This is not to say that Pozzo is faking his sadness, but rather that his sadness is, on some fundamental level, illegitimate.

Pozzo collects himself and says there wasn't "a word of truth" in what he just said. "Do I look like a man that can be made to suffer?" he asks. Vladimir and Estragon comment on how "charming" and "unforgettable" their evening has been. Pozzo tries to find his pipe, which he has misplaced, while Vladimir leaves the stage momentarily.

Pozzo shifts emotions with comic abruptness. His rhetorical question is meant to imply that he cannot be made to suffer, but clearly (as we have just seen) he can.

Pozzo is distraught at having lost his pipe and begins to ask Vladimir if he has seen it, before he notices that Vladimir has left without saying goodbye. Estragon tells Pozzo to get up and look at something. He points off in the distance and says, "it's all over." Vladimir returns, angry, and kicks over Pozzo's stool. He calms down and asks, "will night never come?"

Estragon's vague comment of despair ("it's all over,") is all the more bleak for how vague it is: it could apply to anything, from Estragon's hopes for a better life to all of human history. Vladimir is beginning to get angry from waiting all day for Godot.

Pozzo says he understands and that he wouldn't want to leave before nightfall either if he were waiting for Godot. He says he'd like to sit down on his stool again, but doesn't know how. Estragon offers to help and Pozzo tells him to ask him to sit down. Estragon asks Pozzo to sit down and he does.

Pozzo's inability to sit down unless asked to is absurd and humorous, but is also another example of characters constrained by seemingly nothing, but constrained nonetheless.

Pozzo says he must be going, because of his schedule, though Vladimir says, "time has stopped." Pozzo disagrees, then says he will tell Vladimir and Estragon about twilight. He prepares to speak and asks for everyone's attention. He cracks his whip to get Lucky's attention then throws down the whip, saying it is worn out. Pozzo forgets what he was going to talk about.

Vladimir's comment that time has stopped characterizes the repetitive, recursive way time functions in the play. Pozzo again calls for everyone's attention and then comically forgets what he wanted to say.

Vladimir again suggests he and Estragon leave. Pozzo asks Estragon what his name is, and Estragon says it is Adam. Pozzo remembers that he wanted to talk about the night. He tells everyone to look up at the sky and describes its shifting colors lyrically. Then, he describes how night "burst[s] upon us," saying, "that's how it is on this bitch of an earth."

Whether Estragon is playing with Pozzo or actually thinks his name is Adam, his reply to Pozzo suggests the instability of individuals' identities in the play. Adam, of course, is also the name of the Biblical first man in Eden, a condition that is almost the opposite of Estragon's.

Vladimir says that he and Estragon can simply bide their time and wait. He says they are used to it. Pozzo asks them what they thought of his speech: "Good? Middling? Poor? Positively bad?" They compliment his speaking. Estragon and Vladimir describe their boredom, waiting while "nothing happens."

Pozzo's asking for feedback on his speech is somewhat silly and humorous. After the momentary distraction of some conversation, Vladimir and Estragon are again bored, returning again to the conclusion that "nothing happens."

Pozzo says that since Vladimir andEstragon have been civil to him, he wonders if there is anything he can do to help them, since they are "having such a dull, dull time." Estragon asks for money, though Vladimir is offended and says they are not beggars. Pozzo concludes that he has done enough just by talking to Vladimir and Estragon for some time.

Estragon has no shame in asking for money, whereas Vladimir sees this as beneath their dignity. Pozzo's self-satisfied conclusion that he has given them the gift of his speaking is absurd, but to some degree true—he has distracted them from their "dull, dull" waiting.

Pozzo pulls on Lucky's rope, picks up the whip, and asks whether Estragon andVladimir want Lucky to dance, sing, recite, or think. He says that Lucky can think out loud for hours. Estragon says he'd rather see Lucky dance, but Vladimir wants to hear Lucky think. Estragon suggests they have Lucky dance first, and then think. Pozzo says Lucky only refused to dance once.

Vladimir is apparently no longer troubled by Lucky's suffering, as he is eager to be entertained by his dancing and thinking. The idea of Lucky thinking on command for entertainment is particularly odd and absurd, though Estragon and Vladimir treat it as perfectly ordinary.

Lucky dances. Pozzo says Lucky used to be able to dance better. He asks if Estragon and Vladimir know what Lucky's dance is called. Estragon guesses "The Scapegoat's Agony," while Vladimir guesses "The Hard Stool." Pozzo says the dance is called "The Net," because Lucky thinks he's entangled in a net.

Estragon's guess at the dance's name points to Lucky's status as a scapegoat, the person on whom Pozzo takes out his own unhappiness. Vladimir's guess is a crude pun. Pozzo's suggests the pervasive sense of entrapment that all the characters feel.

Estragon asks about the time Luckyre fused to dance. Pozzo prepares to speak, then forgets what he was going to say. Estragon and Vladimir try to remember, as well. Estragon thinks maybe he was going to say why Lucky doesn't put down his bags. Vladimir says Pozzo already answered that question. In any case, Vladimir notes that Lucky has put his bags down in order to dance.

All three characters are comically unable to remember what they were just talking about. It is this kind of forgetfulness that allows for the play's repetitive sense of time.

Estragon laments the fact that "nothing happens, nobody comes, nobody goes. "Vladimir asks Pozzo to tell Lucky to think. Pozzo says Lucky needs his hat first, which has fallen off during the dance. Estragon doesn't want to give Lucky his hat and asks Pozzo to order Lucky to fetch it, but Pozzo wants someone to give it to him. Vladimir picks up Lucky's hat and offers it to him, but Pozzo says he must place it on Lucky's head.

Estragon and Vladimir periodically return to the blunt fact that nothing happens in their lives. Estragon's comment could easily be spoken by one of Beckett's audience members, watching a play in which nothing happens. Meanwhile, Pozzo and Lucky's absurd antics continue.

Vladimir puts the hat on Lucky's head, but Lucky does nothing. Pozzo jerks the rope around his neck and orders him to think. Lucky begins to speak, but Pozzo stops him and orders him to back up, then turn to face the audience. He orders him to think again. Lucky delivers a long, nonsensical speech marked by repeated syllables ("Acacacacademy") and pseudo-academic language.

The idea of Lucky thinking on command is humorous, but the way in which Pozzo orders Lucky around is cruel. The combination of Lucky's suffering and his ridiculous speech create an uncomfortable absurdity.

As Lucky continues, he begins describing repeatedly mountains, rivers, air, fire, stones, and the sea. He repeats phrases nonsensically, including "in spite of the tennis," and the other three characters begin to find his speech annoying and painful. They throw themselves on top of Lucky to stop him from talking, and Vladimir finally takes his hat away. Lucky falls silent. Pozzo snatches the hat and stomps on it, proclaiming, "There's an end to his thinking!"

Lucky's speech is absurd and mostly unintelligible. It is never explained why Lucky's ability to think out loud is bizarrely dependent on his wearing his hat.

Pozzo kicks Lucky and calls him a pig again. He asks Vladimir and Estragon to help pick Lucky up and hold him steady. They let go of him and he falls, so they pick him up again. Pozzo puts his bag and basket back in Lucky's hands, and Lucky regains his balance, so that Vladimir and Estragon can let go of him. Pozzo thanks the two and prepares to leave, but realizes he has misplaced his watch.

Lucky can only stand when he holds Pozzo's things. He is paradoxically dependent upon his own servitude and suffering. Similarly, Vladimir and Estragon rely upon Godot, who, since he never arrives, is also the source of their torturous boredom.

Pozzo calls for silence and he, Estragon, and Vladimir listen to see if they can hear the ticking of the watch. Pozzo asks which of the two smells so bad and Estragon answers that his feet stink, but Vladimir's breath does. Pozzo decides to leave, reasoning that he must have left his watch "at the manor."

The missing watch could symbolize the absence of a normal system of time in the play. One of the ways Beckett creates his absurd humor is by undercutting serious moments with physical humor like the characters' bad smells, which also highlights that just as Vladimir and Estragon are trapped on stage, people are trapped in their bodies.

The three characters say "adieu" but no one moves. They say it again and politely bid farewell to each other once more. No one moves. Pozzo says that he seems to be unable to leave. Estragon says, "such is life." Pozzo backs away from Lucky, and then, holding onto the rope, cracks his whip and orders Lucky to move. Lucky begins to move, with Pozzo following after.

The characters comically repeat "adieu" over and over again but are inexplicably unable to move. They seem to be somehow trapped by their own free will. "Adieu," literally means "to God," so there may be some ironic wordplay here: is there even a God in this world for the characters to go to?

As Pozzo is about to leave the stage, he calls for his stool and Vladimir gets it and gives it to him. Pozzo, Vladimir, and Estragon say "adieu" again and Pozzo leaves, shouting at Lucky. Vladimir says that this encounter with Pozzo and Lucky passed the time, and Estragon asks what they should do now. Vladimir doesn't know, so Estragon suggests they leave, but Vladimir says they can't, since they are waiting for Godot.

While uneventful, the meeting with Pozzo and Lucky at least distracted Vladimir and Estragon from their boredom. Now they are alone and bored again. Unable to leave, the characters are trapped here by their own sense of hope. Ironically, if they were to give up hope of Godot's arrival, they might be free to leave.

Vladimir comments on how much Pozzo and Lucky had changed. Estragon is confused, because they did not know this pair before, but Vladimir assures him they did and says that Estragon forgets everything. Estragon asks why Lucky and Pozzo didn't recognize them, if they knew each other, but Vladimir says, "That means nothing. I too pretended not to recognize them."

Vladimir is able to recognize people from his past, whereas Estragon's constant forgetfulness means he lives life in a kind of perpetual present. In pretending not to recognize Lucky and Pozzo, Vladimir perpetuates the cycle of characters refusing or failing to acknowledge other people's humanity and identity.

Estragon's one foot with the boot still on begins to hurt, while Vladimir ponders whether Lucky and Pozzo were the same people he knew from before, or different. A boy calls from off-stage and enters. Estragon and Vladimir yell at him to approach. The boy says he has a message from Mr. Godot. Estragon asks why the boy is so late, and the boy says it's not his fault.

Vladimir's confusion over Lucky and Pozzo's identities is linked to a confusion over time: is this day merely a repetition of the previous one, or is it a new day with different people? It is likely the former, as act two will imply (by being very similar to act one).

The boy says he was afraid of Lucky and Pozzo, which is why he is late. Vladimir asks if the boy knows Lucky and Pozzo and whether he is from "these parts." The boy doesn't know them, but is from the area. Estragon doesn't believe the boy and shakes him angrily, but Vladimir tells him to calm down.

Although the boy might be another companion or might at least have a useful message from Godot, Estragon greets him angrily and violently.

Estragon lets go of the boy and covers his face, telling Vladimir that he has been unhappy for longer than he can remember. Vladimir asks the boy to deliver his message and whether he has seen the boy before. The boy says no, and Vladimir asks if it was not him who came the day before. The boy says it wasn't him.

Again, Vladimir is attempting to ascertain to what degree his life is merely repeating itself, with the same people appearing every day and doing the same things.

The boy finally delivers his message: "Mr. Godot told me to tell you that he won't come this evening but surely tomorrow. "Vladimir asks if the boy works for Godot, and the boy says he does; he looks after the goats. He says Godot is good and doesn't beat him, though he does beat the boy's brother, who minds the sheep. He says Godot feeds him well. Vladimir asks if the boy is happy, and the boy is unsure.

Godot's arrival is the entire point of the characters' waiting and of Beckett's play itself. The revelation that he will not come is at once frustrating, funny, and sad. From the boy's description, it is unclear whether Godot is really a way towards freedom or merely another form of domination, as he seems to be the boy's master.

Vladimir tells the boy he can leave, and the boy asks what message he should bring back to Godot. He asks the boy to tell Godot that he saw them. The boy leaves, as night comes. Estragon looks at the moon, saying that it is "pale for weariness." He leaves both his boots on the ground, saying that "another will come, just as...as...as me, but with smaller feet, and they'll make him happy."

Vladimir's message to Godot shows what he desperately wants: some acknowledgment of his identity and humanity. He wants to be recognized, in contrast to all of the times that characters like Lucky and Pozzo don't recognize him, day after day.

Vladimir tells Estragon he can't go on with bare feet, and Estragon says that Christ did. Vladimir thinks Estragon is ridiculous to compare himself to Christ. Vladimir says they have nothing to do here, but says that tomorrow will be better, because Godot will come tomorrow. Estragon says that they should wait here, then, but Vladimir says they must take cover during the night.

Vladimir does not escape the trap of waiting for Godot, as he eagerly looks forward to tomorrow, when he is convinced that Godot will finally come. In the play's Postmodern setting, comparisons to Christ or other Biblical characters are deemed ridiculous.

Estragon looks at the tree and says it's a pity they don't have any rope. He asks Vladimir to remind him to bring rope tomorrow. He asks Vladimir how long they've been together, and Vladimir guesses fifty years. Estragon wonders aloud if they would have been better off alone, rather than together.

The characters' nonchalant consideration of hanging themselves is eerily absurd. By Vladimir's reckoning, he and Estragon have been repeating the same things over and over again for fifty years.

Estragon says he and Vladimir "weren't made for the same road." Vladimir says that it is not certain and tells Estragon that they can still part now, if he'd like to. Estragon says it's not worth it. Estragon asks if they should go and Vladimir says, "Yes, let's go," but neither move.

Vladimir and Estragon ultimately decide to stay together as companions. The act ends with a final absurd gesture, as the characters are inexplicably trapped in their places, despite their willingness to leave now.

Act II

Act 2 begins the next day, at the same time and in the same place. Estragon's boots are still on the ground. Vladimir enters, examines one of Estragon's boots, and then begins to sing. He sings a nonsensical song about a dog who steals a crust of bread from a kitchen and then is beaten to death.

Act two will repeat many of the events of act one, showing how time operates repetitively in the play. Vladimir's nonsensical song is humorous, but also tragic—Lucky and Estragon are not so different from the song's suffering, physically abused dog.

Estragon enters and Vladimir tries to embrace him, but Estragon pushes him away. Vladimir asks where Estragon spent the night and whether "they" beat him. Estragon tells Vladimir not to touch him or ask him questions, but Vladimir tells Estragon to look at him. They look at each other and then embrace.

While Estragon is at first indignant, he soon embraces Vladimir, his only companion amid all his suffering (physical and otherwise).

Estragon remarks, "What a day!" and Vladimir tells him the day isn't over yet. Estragon tells him he heard his singing and Vladimir says, "one is not master of one's moods," and that he has felt good today. He tells Estragon he missed him last night, but was happy at the same time.

Vladimir's assertion that he is not in control of his own moods is both absurd and an evaluation of the radical lack of freedom in the bleak world he inhabits, and, again, a suggestion that people are in some sense controlled by their bodies as opposed to the other way around—that life itself is a kind of prison.

Estragon says he too feels better alone. Vladimir asks him why he keeps "crawling back" then, and suggests it's because Estragon can't defend himself. He says he would have stopped "them" from beating Estragon. Estragon says Vladimir couldn't have stopped them, because there were ten of them.

As Vladimir claims, Estragon is dependent on him. However, he also relies on Estragon. The two companions are codependent and lonely without each other.

Vladimir says that he would have stopped Estragon from doing whatever he did to provoke the beating, but Estragon says he wasn't doing anything, and he doesn't know why he was beaten. Vladimir says that something he was doing or something in the way he was doing it must have caused the beating, but Estragon insists, "I wasn't doing anything."

Estragon was beaten for no reason, in line with the absurd, unexplained suffering of the rest of the play. Such suffering happens for no reason at all; it happens just because you are alive.

Vladimir says that Estragon must be happy now that they are together again. Estragon is not sure but Vladimir has him repeat the words, "I am happy." Estragon then asks, "What do we do now, now that we are happy?" and Vladimir suggests they wait for Godot. Estragon wonders what will happen if Godot doesn't come, but Vladimir says that things are different today than yesterday.

Estragon suddenly and bizarrely shifts emotions and agrees that he is happy. Just as in act one, Estragon again asks Vladimir what they should do and Vladimir again answers that they should do nothing, but simply wait.

Vladimir tells Estragon to look at the nearby tree. Estragon asks if it was there yesterday and Vladimir says it was. Estragon tells him he "dreamt it," but Vladimir says he may have just forgotten about it. He asks Estragon if he forgot about Pozzo and Lucky, as well, and Estragon asks who they are.

Estragon's absurd forgetfulness allows time to repeat itself in the play, as he forgets that he has already been in this same place, doing the same thing (waiting), and encountering the same people.

Estragon remembers "a lunatic" who kicked his shins and a man who gave him a bone. Vladimir tells him those people were Lucky and Pozzo. Estragon asks if this all happened yesterday at this very place and Vladimir is amazed that Estragon doesn't recognize the place. Estragon is suddenly upset, asking, "What is there to recognize?"

Unlike Estragon, Vladimir has a memory of the past and so can realize that they are trapped in a life that keeps repeating itself. Estragon's question implies that there is nothing worth recognizing in the world, a deeply nihilistic sentiment.

Vladimir mentions "the Macon country," but Estragon says he's never been there. He says he's "puked my puke of a life away here...in the Cackon country," though Vladimir says he thought they were together in the Macon country, picking grapes for a man whose name he cannot remember. Estragon says this is possible.

Again, Estragon has no memory of the past. This means that he also lacks a sense of his own identity, of who he is, because he can't remember anything about his life.

Estragon says that things would be better if he and Vladimir parted. Vladimir says that Estragon always says this, but always comes back to him. Estragon tells him it would be best to kill him, "like the other." Vladimir asks who he is referring to, and Estragon answers, "like billions of others." He tells Vladimir that they should talk in the meantime.

Estragon keeps repeating himself, saying that he will leave Vladimir, though he never does. His reference to billions of people killed is absurd because it is never explained or mentioned again, but suggests that suffering is widespread in this world—everyone, after all, dies.

Estragon says that they should talk so they don't hear "all the dead voices," that talk about their lives, making a noise that sounds like feathers, leaves, or ashes. There is a long pause, and Vladimir urges Estragon to say something, "anything at all!" Estragon asks what they should do, and Vladimir again answers that they should wait for Godot.

When Estragon and Vladimir stop talking, they must confront the emptiness of their lives—the fact that they have nothing to do but wait for Godot. Thus they are compelled to fill their time with absurd, often nonsensical conversation.

The two struggle to find something to talk about. Vladimir says "it's the start that's difficult." He asks Estragon to help him find something to talk about, and Estragon tells him he's trying. The two disagree over whether listening prevents one from thinking. Estragon suggests they ask each other questions. Vladimir suddenly asks, "Where are all these corpses from?"

The two characters are ironically talking about how they have nothing to talk about. But Beckett quickly mixes this comedy with Vladimir's deeply troubling and unexplained reference to corpses.

Vladimir says that "to have thought" is the worst thing of all, and the two ponder whether they have ever thought. Estragon comments that they are talking well now, but Vladimir notes that now they need to find something else to talk about. They both concentrate during a long silence.

Just like talking about not being able to talk, thinking about whether one has ever thought is ironic and funny. Vladimir and Estragon desperately seek something to talk about to relieve their intense boredom.

Vladimir asks what they were talking about at the beginning of the evening, and recalls the opening of act two, when they embraced and were happy. He tells Estragon to look at the tree and notes that it has leaves, whereas yesterday it was bare. He is shocked that the leaves appeared overnight, and Estragon sees this as proof that they weren't actually here the previous day.

The tree's sudden leaves further disrupt Vladimir's sense of time, seemingly contradicting the natural cycle of the seasons. This temporal disorientation causes Estragon to continue to misunderstand time and not believe that he was here the day before.

Vladimir accepts, for the moment, that they were not in this place the previous day, and asks Estragon what they did the previous night, then. Estragon says they "blathered," about "nothing in particular." He says this has been going on for fifty years now. Vladimir asks if he remembers the sun and the moon, Lucky and Pozzo. Estragon remembers the bones Pozzo gave him and when Lucky kicked him.

For fifty years, apparently, Vladimir and Estragon have been doing nothing, as well as talking about nothing. (But, given the strangeness of time in the play, it is unclear whether we should take this measure of time literally.)

Vladimir lifts up the legs of Estragon's pants and sees the wound from Lucky's kick, which would suggest that they were here yesterday. He asks Estragon where his boots are, and Estragon doesn't know. He says he threw them away because they were hurting. Vladimir spots the boots and says they are exactly where they were left yesterday.

Unlike Estragon, who accepts his strange disorientation in time and space, Vladimir tries to pin down exactly where and when they are, and whether it's the same place they were yesterday. The boots seem proof of this.

Estragon says the boots are not his, because they are not the right color. Vladimir says someone must have taken Estragon's boots and left these other ones. Estragon says he's tired and wants to leave, but Vladimir says they can't—they have to wait here for Godot. Estragon asks what they will do, and Vladimir says there's nothing they can do.

Yet Estragon's comment that the boots aren't his raises questions: does Estragon even really remember the color of his boots? Did someone simply replace the boots? Is it possible they are in a slightly different reality than they were in act one? Estragon repeats himself again, wanting to leave and Vladimir must remind him that they are stuck here waiting for Godot, with nothing to do.

Vladimir asks if Estragon would like a radish or turnip. Estragon asks if there are any carrots; Vladimir says there are not. He finds a radish in his pocket and gives it to Estragon. Estragon rejects the radish, and says he'll go get a carrot, but he doesn't move at all.

This scene repeats a similar one from act one, but with a radish instead of a carrot. The discrepancy between Estragon saying he will go find a carrot and standing still is humorous.

Vladimir suggests that Estragon try on the boots. He says it would at least pass the time, and that he'll help Estragon put them on. He picks up one of the boots and Estragon raises up his foot. They struggle to get it on, but finally do. Estragon says the boot fits. They put the other boot on, and Estragon says the boots don't hurt, at least "not yet." He says they are too big, but Vladimir responds that he might get socks one day.

Vladimir is willing to help Estragon in order to ease his boredom. His comment about the socks is silly and comical, but at the same time pathetic—the most Estragon can hope for is to find socks someday. Now Estragon can wait for socks just like he waits for Godot.

Estragon sits down and wishes he could sleep. He tries to sleep, but Vladimir tells him to wait and begins singing loudly, repeating the word "bye." Estragon falls asleep, then wakes up and is startled. Vladimir comforts him. Estragon begins to describe his dream, but Vladimir stops him. He tells Estragon to "walk it off," and the two walk around the stage, until Estragon says he's tired. He says he'd rather do nothing than walk.

Vladimir and Estragon both need each other as companions. Here, Vladimir comforts Estragon after his dream. After walking around the stage, the characters return to doing nothing. It is not entirely clear why Vladimir doesn't want to hear Estragon's dream—it may be that such a thing is just too intimate to share in the realm of the play.

Estragon wants to leave, but Vladimir reminds him that they must stay and wait for Godot. Vladimir says Godot will come at nightfall. Estragon says after the night, it will be day again, and asks, "What'll we do, what'll we do!" Vladimir tells him to stop complaining.

Estragon begins to wonder what will happen after Godot arrives, after the thing they have been waiting for happens. Vladimir refuses to engage in such speculation.

Estragon announces that he is going to leave. Vladimir sees Lucky's hat from yesterday lying on the ground. This confirms for him that they are in the right place. He gives Estragon his hat and tries on Lucky's. Estragon puts on Vladimir's hat and gives his own to Vladimir, who puts it on instead of Lucky's, which he gives to Estragon. Estragon puts on Lucky's hat, and Vladimir puts his own hat back on before giving Estragon his hat back. They exchange the hats back and forth.

The exchange of hats back and forth playfully encapsulates the instability of identities in this play where characters fail or refuse to recognize each other and acknowledge other characters' humanity.

Vladimir asks Estragon how he looks in Lucky's hat. Estragon says he looks "hideous," and Vladimir asks if he looks more or less hideous than usual. Estragon says "neither more nor less," and Vladimir says Estragon can keep the hat, then. Estragon says he is going to leave, and Vladimir asks if he wants to "play at Pozzo and Lucky." He imitates Lucky and asks Estragon to act like Pozzo.

The idea that someone in Vladimir's desperate position would care so much about his appearance is rather absurd and comical. Vladimir's idea to act like Pozzo and Lucky raises the question of to what degree any of the characters has a stable identity aside from a similar kind of "playing." It also brings up the question of the power dynamics between any two people, given that the dynamic between Pozzo and Lucky is that of master to slave.

Vladimir encourages Estragon to yell at him like Pozzo. Estragon shouts, "Think, pig!" at Vladimir, who says he cannot. He asks Estragon to command him to dance, but Estragon says he's leaving. Vladimir pretends to be both Pozzo and Lucky. Estragon leaves for a moment and then comes back. They embrace and Vladimir says, "There you are again at last!"

When Estragon leaves even for just a moment, Vladimir becomes intensely lonely. While he earlier asserted that Estragon needed him, we now see that the two companions need each other. They are "tied" to each other.

Estragon says "they" are coming but doesn't know who they are or how many of them there are. Vladimir excitedly says that it must be Godot. He shouts, "We're saved!" Vladimir pulls Estragon toward the edge of the stage, but Estragon leaves by himself. He returns immediately and the two embrace again. Estragon says that "they" are coming, and Vladimir says he and Estragon are surrounded.

Vladimir is again lonely when Estragon leaves for hardly any time. The anonymous "they" keep Estragon and Vladimir in a state of fear and paranoia, though it is not clear who they are (or if they are even real).

Vladimir tells Estragon his only hope is to disappear. He tells Estragon to hide behind the tree. Estragon hides behind it, but realizes the tree does not cover him completely. Estragon asks Vladimir what to do, and he answers, "there's nothing to do."

Estragon's lame attempt at hiding behind the tree is comical. There is nothing for Vladimir and him to do in this situation, or in general.

Estragon brings Vladimir to the right edge of the stage and tells him to be on the lookout. He does the same at the left edge. He asks if Vladimir sees anything coming. Neither of them does. They try to speak at the same time and each politely tell the other to speak first. Their back-and-forth politeness turns into an argument, and Estragon enthusiastically suggests that they pass the time insulting each other

The characters' exaggerated politeness is absurd and funny, as well as an abrupt change of mood. They suddenly don't seem very worried about the people Estragon thought he heard coming. Are they really in danger? The audience doesn't know what to take seriously and what to laugh at.

They insult each other back and forth and then Estragon decides it's time to make up. They embrace. "How time flies when one has fun!" muses Vladimir. Estragon asks what they should do now, and Vladimir suggests they continue waiting. He says they could do some exercises. They hop from one foot to the other, standing in place. Vladimir suggests they "do the tree," balancing on one foot.

Vladimir and Estragon bizarrely have fun throwing insults back and forth. But, after this brief entertainment they return to their usual activity of waiting and doing nothing. Their desire to be doing anything at all leads to their absurd activities, like "doing the tree."

Pozzo and Lucky enter. Lucky has the rope around his neck as before, and is carrying the same things, but now Pozzo is blind, following closely behind Lucky. Lucky stops when he sees Estragon and Vladimir, and Pozzo continue walking until he bumps into Lucky. Pozzo asks who it is, and Lucky falls down, bringing Pozzo down with him.

Pozzo and Lucky arrive, just like yesterday, though now Pozzo is blind. While Lucky is under Pozzo's control, Pozzo now relies on Lucky, since he can't see. Their codependent relationship is comparable to the companionship of Vladimir and Estragon.

Estragon asks if this is Godot. Vladimir says, "Reinforcements at last!" He says that now they will surely make it through the evening. Pozzo asks for help. Vladimir says that he and Estragon are finally no longer alone, and that now time "flows again already." Estragon says he knew it was Godot, but Vladimir corrects him: it's Pozzo. Pozzo, meanwhile, is still lying on the ground, asking for help. Estragon wants to leave, but Vladimir tells him they are still waiting for Godot.

Vladimir sees the arrival of Pozzo and Lucky as an opportunity to be distracted from his boredom. With them, time seems to "flow again." Estragon does not recognize Pozzo and ignores his plea for help. Vladimir must remind Estragon yet again that they have to stay and wait for Godot.

Vladimir says that Pozzo might have another chicken bone for Estragon, and suggests that they help him up. Estragon asks why Pozzo can't get up and Vladimir says he doesn't know. Pozzo writhes on the ground, unable to stand up. Estragon suggests that they ask Pozzo for a bone before helping him. Vladimir agrees, but worries that Lucky might "get going," and stop them from taking advantage of Pozzo in this way.

Pozzo's inability to get up is somewhat comic as well as tragic and pathetic. Whereas Vladimir was sympathetic to Lucky in act one, here he and Estragon are indifferent to Pozzo's suffering and seek to get something out of helping him up.

Confused, Estragon asks who Lucky is, and Vladimir reminds him of how Lucky kicked Estragon the previous day. He points to Lucky, who is motionless. Estragon asks if they should beat Lucky, and Vladimir says that sounds like a good idea, but he isn't sure if Lucky is asleep or not. He says it would be better "to take advantage of Pozzo's calling for help."

Estragon fails to recognize Lucky's identity. Vladimir and Estragon have gone from doing nothing to stop the suffering of Lucky and Pozzo to plotting to help continue their suffering.

Pozzo continues to cry out for help. Vladimir says that he and Estragon should "do something, while we have the chance." He ponders the situation and whether he and Estragon are needed. He wonders aloud what they are doing here, and then says that the answer is that they are waiting for Godot, or at least for nightfall. He says he and Estragon have kept their appointment. Pozzo again cries out for help.

Vladimir rightly concludes that all he and Estragon are doing is waiting. His absurd, rambling thoughts take precedence over helping a fellow suffering human. Waiting for Godot interferes with helping a fellow in trouble.

Vladimir continues to talk, so Pozzo shouts that he'll pay someone to help him. Estragon asks how much. He says he'd pay one hundred francs, and Estragon says this isn't enough. Pozzo offers two hundred francs. Vladimir says they are "bored to death." He doesn't want to let this potential "diversion" go to waste, so he tries to help Pozzo up, but fails several times and falls down. He asks Estragon to help, but Estragon says he's leaving.

Vladimir thought taking money from Pozzo was beneath his dignity in act one, but now he is ready to take money in return for helping Pozzo, if only so he has something to do while he is "bored to death." In trying to help, Vladimir falls down himself, a pathetic but darkly comic development.

Vladimir begs Estragon not to leave. He and Pozzo both ask Estragon for help. Vladimir promises that he will leave with Estragon if he will help Pozzo and him. Estragon asks if they can leave and never come back. Vladimir says they can go wherever he wants, if he helps.

Vladimir is so desperate not to lose Estragon (and to get up from the ground) that he even promises to abandon waiting for Godot.

Estragon again says he's going to leave. Vladimir says he'll just get up himself, but he is unable to. Estragon asks if Vladimir is going to stay here, and finally extends a hand to help him up. Vladimir pulls on Estragon's hand while trying to get up, and Estragon falls, as well.

Vladimir's unexplained inability to get up is absurd, but can also be seen as a comment on Postmodern life, with Vladimir trapped, but yet constrained by no one in particular. And any effort to help, as Estragon does, results in even more people getting trapped.

Pozzo asks who Estragon and Vladimir are, and Vladimir answers that they are men. Vladimir asks Estragon if he can get up, and he says he doesn't know, but he can't at the moment. Estragon suggests they sleep while they're stuck on the ground. Pozzo continues to cry out, "Pity! Pity!" and Vladimir hits him to shut him up. Pozzo begins to crawl away, and then collapses. Estragon asks, "What do we do now?"

Like Estragon, Pozzo does not remember yesterday and thus fails to recognize Estragon and Vladimir. Pozzo's crawling around on the ground is a strange mix of slapstick comedy and pathetic suffering. Vladimir responds to this suffering violently.

Vladimir says he could crawl over to Pozzo, but Estragon doesn't want Vladimir to leave him. They both call over to Pozzo, but he doesn't respond. Estragon asks if Vladimir is sure that Pozzo is the right name. Vladimir says he thinks Pozzo is dying. Estragon says it would be fun to try calling out different names, to see if Pozzo might respond, but Vladimir says that he is sure the man's name is Pozzo.

Now it is Estragon who irrationally fears losing Vladimir, showing that the two rely on each other mutually. Estragon is comically enthusiastic about trying different names for Pozzo, whom he still fails to recognize from the previous day.

Estragon shouts, "Abel! Abel!" and Pozzo cries out for help. Estragon thinks Abel is the right name. He thinks Lucky might be called Cain, and shouts this name out loud. Pozzo shouts for help again. Estragon suggests he and Vladimir find a new topic of conversation, but neither can think of anything to talk about. Estragon suggests they try to get up, and they both get up easily. Pozzo shouts for help yet again.

Estragon's name mix-up, with its reference to Cain and Abel of the Bible, is absurd and shows the ironic distance between the western tradition of the Bible and this Postmodern world. The absurdity continues with Estragon and Vladimir again talking about having nothing to talk about and then suddenly being able to stand up.

Estragon wants to leave, but Vladimir reminds him yet again that they are waiting here for Godot. Estragon asks what they will do in the meantime, and Vladimir says they could help Pozzo get up. They help Pozzo stand up, but when they let go, he falls down again. They help him up again and hold him steady between them.

Estragon repeats his desire to leave yet again, but he and Vladimir are still kept here waiting. Pozzo's inability to stand is darkly comic—humorous, but pathetic at the same time.

Pozzo asks who Vladimir and Estragon are, because he is blind and cannot see them. Estragon wonders if he can see into the future, since he is blind. Pozzo asks if they are his friends, and Vladimir says they have proven that they are, by helping him up. Pozzo begs them not to leave him, and Vladimir says they won't. "For the moment," Estragon specifies.

Pozzo seems just as desperate for company as Estragon and Vladimir. While he is Lucky's master, he seems hardly any better off than Lucky. Everyone seems to suffer in the bleak world of Beckett's play.

Pozzo asks what time it is, and Estragon and Vladimir look at the sky, guessing seven or eight o'clock in the evening. Estragon isn't sure whether it's the evening or dawn, but Vladimir is sure it's evening. Pozzo again asks what time it is, and Vladimir assures him it's evening, in spite of what Estragon may think.

Estragon and Vladimir disagree over the time. While Vladimir seems correct, given the strange functioning of time in the play, one can't be entirely sure. The audience is left in a state of temporal disorientation.

Estragon asks how long he and Vladimir will have to hold up Pozzo for. Pozzo says he used to have excellent sight, and that he woke up one day completely blind. He says he's not sure if he's still asleep or awake. Vladimir asks if this happened yesterday, and Pozzo angrily replies that "the blind have no notion of time."

Like Estragon, Pozzo lacks a normal sense of time. He is content to stay in this disoriented state, whereas Vladimir struggles to establish a stable chronology of events. Vladimir is always looking to explain what may not be explainable, suggesting the limits of reason and rationality,

Estragon says he is leaving. Pozzo asks where they are, and Vladimir says he doesn't know. Pozzo asks if they are at the place called the Board, which Vladimir hasn't heard of. Pozzo asks Vladimir to describe their surroundings. Vladimir says, "It's indescribable. It's like nothing. There's nothing. There's a tree." Pozzo says that it is not the Board, then.

Not only do the characters not know when they are, but they also don't know where they are. Vladimir's attempt to describe the place is rather nihilistic: ultimately, there's nothing much to see here.

Pozzo asks where Lucky is, and why he isn't responding to his call. Vladimir says Lucky seems to be sleeping, but might be dead. Pozzo asks Vladimir or Estragon to go check on Lucky and see if he is okay. Estragon doesn't want to go, since Lucky kicked him, but Pozzo asks for Estragon to go, because he stinks.

The more serious elements of the play are counterbalanced by moments of simple humor, like Pozzo wanting Estragon to go check on Lucky because he smells bad. Again, though, such physical disgust is a reminder that the body is physical, and that all life is trapped in this physicality.

Estragon doesn't move. Vladimir asks Estragon what he is waiting for, and Estragon answers that he is waiting for Godot. Pozzo tells Estragon to pull on Lucky's rope to get his attention. If that doesn't work, he suggests kicking him. Estragon asks what would happen if Lucky were to defend himself, but Pozzo says Lucky never defends himself. Estragon approaches Lucky.

Estragon comically misinterprets Vladimir's question and thinks that Vladimir has forgotten that they are waiting for Godot. Pozzo's cruel suggestion of kicking Lucky and assurance that Lucky won't defend himself show how Lucky has been robbed of his dignity.

Estragon checks if Lucky is still breathing (he is) before starting to kick him repeatedly. He hurts his foot in the process and limps away. Lucky begins to move. Estragon tries to take off one of his boots, but gives up and sits down to sleep.

In causing Lucky pain, Estragon ends up hurting himself. This is both comical and an encapsulation of how causing suffering harms both the victim and the perpetrator.

Pozzo asks what has just happened, and Vladimir explains. Vladimir asks him if he and Lucky are the same Pozzo and Lucky from the day before. Pozzo says he doesn't remember meeting anyone yesterday. But, he says, he won't remember meeting Vladimir today, so he might have. Vladimir reminds him of the previous day, and how Pozzo was bringing Lucky to a fair to sell him away.

Vladimir is now starting to doubt his understanding of time and recognition of Pozzo and Lucky.

Pozzo shouts, "Up pig!" and Lucky gets up and gathers his things. Vladimir asks where Pozzo is going, and he simply says, "On." Lucky puts the rope that is tied around his neck in Pozzo's hand, and gives him his whip. Vladimir asks Pozzo what's in the bag Lucky carries. The bag is filled with sand. Vladimir asks what Pozzo does when he falls and no one is around to help. Pozzo says he waits until he can get up, and then he continues walking.

Lucky's bag that he lugs around with him is filled with nothing but sand. As a darkly comic touch, there is no purpose to his suffering in carrying it around. Equally absurd is Pozzo's random and unexplained inability and ability to get up at different times.

Vladimir asks Pozzo to have Lucky sing, think, or recite something. Pozzo says Lucky is mute, and "can't even groan." Pozzo is frustrated with all of Vladimir's questions related to time, which he insists does not matter. He and Lucky leave the stage. Vladimir walks over to Estragon and wakes him.

Vladimir still tries to establish a normal sense of time, but Pozzo will have none of his time-related questioning.

Estragon asks why Vladimir won't let him sleep. Vladimir says he was lonely. Estragon begins to describe his dream, saying that he dreamt he was happy, but Vladimir angrily tells him not to describe his dream. He wonders whether Pozzo was really blind.

Vladimir is again lonely when Estragon sleeps and leaves him by himself.

Estragon says, "let's go," but then remembers they can't. He asks if Vladimir is sure that Pozzo wasn't actually Godot. Vladimir says he's certain, but then he says, "I don't know what to think any more." Estragon tries to get his boots off and asks Vladimir for help.

Estragon keeps on forgetting that he and Vladimir are bound to stay and wait for Godot. Vladimir now doubts his own knowledge of people's identities—the rationalist begins to doubt his ability to understand the world. Estragon relies on Vladimir's help for even minor things like taking off a boot.

Vladimir wonders if he himself is sleeping at this very moment. He ponders what he will say of this day tomorrow and laments the fact that Estragon will not remember this day and they'll have to go through the same conversations all over again. He says he can't go on, but then stops and asks, "What have I said?"

Vladimir's questioning of reality and confusion of reality with a dream is a common feature of Postmodernism. The constant repetition of time in the play is beginning to wear on Vladimir.

The boy from yesterday enters. Vladimir asks if the boy recognizes him, but the boy says he doesn't and that he didn't come yesterday. Vladimir asks if the boy has a message from Godot, which the boy does: Godot will not come this evening, but he will come tomorrow. Vladimir asks if the boy ran into Pozzo and Lucky, and the boy says he didn't see anyone on the way over.

The boy repeats his message from yesterday, keeping Vladimir and Estragon waiting. Despite Vladimir's plea for the boy to remember seeing Vladimir, he fails to recognize him.

Vladimir asks the boy what Mr. Godot does. The boy says Godot does nothing. Vladimir asks whether Godot has a beard and what color it is. The boy says that Godot has a white beard. The boy asks if Vladimir would like to send a message back to Godot. Vladimir tells the boy to tell Godot that he saw Vladimir.

Vladimir repeats his message from the day before, wanting someone to acknowledge and remember him as an individual. According to the boy, Godot does nothing, just like Vladimir and Estragon.

Vladimir grabs the boy and violently asks him, "You're sure that you saw me, you won't come and tell me tomorrow that you never saw me!" The boy runs off, as the moon rises and night comes. Estragon says he's leaving, and Vladimir says he'll leave as well. Estragon asks how long he was asleep for, and Vladimir doesn't know.

Vladimir desperately wants for someone else to affirm his sense of identity and time. He needs some affirmation that the world is objectively as he sees it, and that he has a place in that world. Instead of the constant repetition of people forgetting him.

Estragon wants to go far away, but Vladimir says they can't go far, because they have to come back tomorrow to wait for Godot. Estragon asks if Godot came and whether it's too late for him to come tonight. Estragon asks what would happen if they "dropped" Godot. Vladimir says Godot would punish them. He says everything is dead, except for the tree.

Despite all of the pain caused by waiting for Godot, Vladimir still feels compelled to come back tomorrow and do it again. The events of Beckett's play could repeat indefinitely.

The two go up to the tree and examine it. Estragon suggests they hang themselves, but they don't have any rope. Estragon says they could use his belt, but then there would be nothing to hang Vladimir with. Vladimir asks to look at Estragon's belt. He takes off his belt and his oversized pants fall to the ground. Vladimir wonders whether the belt would be strong enough to hang either of them with.

Estragon repeats his uncomfortably casual suggestion of suicide from yesterday. Yet even the possible dignity of suicide—of making a choice for oneself in the face of the meaninglessness of the world—is mocked when he makes an undignified fool of himself, taking his belt off and his pants fall down.

Vladimir and Estragon pull on either end of the belt to test its strength. It breaks. Estragon asks if they have to come back to this place tomorrow, and Vladimir says they must. Estragon says they should bring some rope with them next time. Then, he says he "can't go on like this," and says that it might be better if he and Vladimir parted. Vladimir says they will hang themselves tomorrow, unless Godot arrives.

There is something humorous in the belt breaking so easily, which jars with the intense sadness of the play's ending. Doomed to keep waiting, Vladimir and Estragon can do nothing—not even kill themselves. They have no control about what will happen or where they can go, or even over whether they will live at all.

Estragon asks if they can leave. Vladimir tells him to pull up his pants. Estragon misunderstands, and asks if Vladimir wants him to pull down his pants. Vladimir repeats himself and Estragon pulls his pants up. Vladimir asks if Estragon is ready to go. He says, "Yes, let's go," but neither of them move.

Just as they ended the last act, Vladimir and Estragon say they are ready to leave but don't move an inch. They end the play as they began it, trapped in this bleak place, with nothing to do.

8   Notes on Characters

Characters

Vladimir - One of the two main characters of the play. Estragon calls him Didi, and the boy addresses him as Mr. Albert. He seems to be the more responsible and mature of the two main characters.

Estragon - The second of the two main characters. Vladimir calls him Gogo. He seems weak and helpless, always looking for Vladimir's protection. He also has a poor memory, as Vladimir has to remind him in the second act of the events that happened the previous night.

Pozzo - He passes by the spot where Vladimir and Estragon are waiting and provides a diversion. In the second act, he is blind and does not remember meeting Vladimir and Estragon the night before.

Lucky - Pozzo's slave, who carries Pozzo's bags and stool. In Act I, he entertains by dancing and thinking. However, in Act II, he is dumb.

Boy - He appears at the end of each act to inform Vladimir that Godot will not be coming that night. In the second act, he insists that he was not there the previous night.

Godot - The man for whom Vladimir and Estragon wait unendingly. Godot never appears in the play. His name and character are often thought to refer to God.

Beckett refrained from elaborating on the characters beyond what he had written in the play. He once recalled that when Sir Ralph Richardson "wanted the low-down on Pozzo, his home address and curriculum vitae, and seemed to make theforthcoming of this and similar information the condition of his condescending to illustrate the part of Vladimir ... I told himthat all I knew about Pozzo was in the text, that if I had known more I would have put it in the text, and that was true also ofthe other characters."

Vladimir and Estragon

Vladimir and Estragon (June 2010 production of theplay at The Doon School, India)

When Beckett started writing he did not have a visual image of Vladimir and Estragon. They are never referred to as tramps in the text, though are often performed in such costumes on stage. Roger Blin advises:"Beckett heard their voices, but he couldn't describe his characters to me. [He said]: 'The only thing I'm sure of is that they're wearing bowlers. "The bowler hat was of course de rigueur for male persons in many social contexts when Beckett was growing up in Foxrock, and [his father] commonly wore one." That said, the play does indicate that the clothes worn at least by Estragon are shabby. When told by Vladimir that he should have been a poet, Estragon says he was, gestures to his rags, and asks if it were not obvious.

There are no physical descriptions of either of the two characters; however, the text indicates that Vladimir is possibly the heavier of the pair. The bowlers and other broadly comic aspects of their personas have reminded modern audiences of Laurel and Hardy, who occasionally played tramps in their films. "The hat-passing game in Waiting For Godot and Lucky's inability to think without his hat on are two obvious Beckett derivations from Laurel and Hardy – a substitution of form for essence, covering for reality," wrote Gerald Mast in The Comic Mind: Comedy and the Movies.

Vladimir stands through most of the play whereas Estragon sits down numerous times and even dozes off. "Estragon is inert and Vladimir restless." Vladimir looks at the sky and muses on religious or philosophical matters. Estragon "belongs to the stone", preoccupied with mundane things, what he can get to eat and how to ease his physical aches and pains; he is direct, intuitive. He finds it hard to remember but can recall certain things when prompted, e.g., when Vladimir asks: "Do you remember the Gospels?" Estragon tells Vladimir about the coloured maps of the Holy Land and that he planned to honeymoon by the Dead Sea; it is his short-term memory that is poorest and points to the fact that he may, in fact, be suffering from Alzheimer's disease. Al Alvarez writes: "But perhaps Estragon's forgetfulness is the cement binding their relationship together. He continually forgets, Vladimir continually reminds him; between them they pass the time." They have been together for fifty years but when asked–by Pozzo–they do not reveal their actual ages.

Vladimir's life is not without its discomforts too but he is the more resilient of the pair. "Vladimir's pain is primarily mental anguish, which would thus account for his voluntary exchange of his hat for Lucky's, thus signifying Vladimir's symbolic desire for another person's thoughts."

Throughout the play the couple refer to each other by the pet names "Didi" and "Gogo", although the boy addresses Vladimiras "Mister Albert". Beckett originally intended to call Estragon "Lévy" but when Pozzo questions him he gives his name as"Magrégor, André" and also responds to "Catulle" in French or "Catullus" in the first Faber edition. This became "Adam"in the American edition. Beckett's only explanation was that he was "fed up with Catullus". Vivian Mercier described Waiting for Godot as a play which "has achieved a theoretical impossibility—a play in whichnothing happens, that yet keeps audiences glued to their seats. What's more, since the second act is a subtly differentreprise of the first, he has written a play in which nothing happens, twice.". Mercier once questioned Beckett on thelanguage used by the pair: "It seemed to me...he made Didi and Gogo sound as if they had earned PhDs. 'How do you knowthey hadn't?' was his reply." They clearly have known better times, a visit to the Eiffel Tower and grape-harvesting by the Rhône; it is about all either has to say about their pasts, save for Estragon's claim to have been a poet, an explanationEstragon provides to Vladimir for his destitution. In the first stage production, which Beckett oversaw, both are "more shabby-genteel than ragged...Vladimir at least is capable of being scandalised...on a matter of etiquette when Estragon begs forchicken bones or money."

Pozzo and Lucky

Although Beckett refused to be drawn on the backgrounds of the characters, this has not stopped actors looking for their ownmotivation. Jean Martin had a doctor friend called Marthe Gautier, who was working at the Salpêtrière Hospital, and he said toher: "'Listen, Marthe, what could I find that would provide some kind of physiological explanation for a voice like the onewritten in the text?' [She] said: 'Well, it might be a good idea if you went to see the people who have Parkinson's disease.'So I asked her about the disease ... She explained how it begins with a trembling, which gets more and more noticeable, untillater the patient can no longer speak without the voice shaking. So I said, 'That sounds exactly what I need.'""Sam andRoger were not entirely convinced by my interpretation but had no objections." When he explained to Beckett that he wasplaying Lucky as if he were suffering from Parkinson's, Beckett said, "'Yes, of course.' He mentioned briefly that his motherhad had Parkinson's, but quickly moved on to another subject."

When Beckett was asked why Lucky was so named, he replied, "I suppose he is lucky to have no more expectations..."

It has been contended that "Pozzo and Lucky are simply Didi and Gogo writ large", unbalanced as their relationship is. However, Pozzo's dominance is noted to be superficial; "upon closer inspection, it becomes evident that Lucky always possessed more influence in the relationship, for he danced, and more importantly, thought – not as a service, but in order to fill a vacant need of Pozzo: he committed all of these acts for Pozzo. As such, since the first appearance of the duo, the true slave had always been Pozzo." Pozzo credits Lucky with having given him all the culture, refinement, and ability to reason that he possesses. His rhetoric has been learned by rote. Pozzo's "party piece" on the sky is a clear example: as his memory crumbles, he finds himself unable to continue under his own steam.

Little is learned about Pozzo besides the fact that he is on his way to the fair to sell his slave, Lucky. He presents himself very much as the Ascendancy landlord, bullying and conceited. His pipe is made by Kapp and Peterson, Dublin's best-known tobacconists (their slogan was 'The thinking man's pipe') which he refers to as a "briar" but which Estragon calls a "dudeen" emphasising the differences in their social standing. He confesses to a poor memory but it is more a result of a biding self-absorption. "Pozzo is a character who has to overcompensate. That's why he overdoes things ... and his overcompensation has to do with a deep insecurity in him. These were things Beckett said, psychological terms he used."

Pozzo controls Lucky by means of an extremely long rope which he jerks and tugs if Lucky is the least bit slow. Lucky is the absolutely subservient slave of Pozzo and he unquestioningly does his every bidding with "dog-like devotion". He struggles with a heavy suitcase without ever thinking of dropping it. Lucky speaks only once in the play and it is a result of Pozzo's order to "think" for Estragon and Vladimir. Pozzo and Lucky have been together for sixty years and, in that time, their relationship has deteriorated. Lucky has always been the intellectually superior but now, with age, he has become an object of contempt: his "think" is a caricature of intellectual thought and his "dance" is a sorry sight. Despite his horrid treatment at Pozzo's hand however, Lucky remains completely faithful to him. Even in the second act when Pozzo has inexplicably gone blind, and needs to be led by Lucky rather than driving him as he had done before, Lucky remains faithful and has not tried to run away; they are clearly bound together by more than a piece of rope in the same way that Didi and Gogo are "[t]ied to Godot". Beckett's advice to the American director Alan Schneider was: "[Pozzo] is a hypomaniac and the only way to play him is to play him mad."

"In his [English] translation ... Beckett struggled to retain the French atmosphere as much as possible, so that he delegatedall the English names and places to Lucky, whose own name, he thought, suggested such a correlation."

The Boy

The cast list specifies only one boy.

The boy in Act I, a local lad, assures Vladimir that this is the first time he has seen him. He says he was not there theprevious day. He confirms he works for Mr. Godot as a goatherd. His brother, whom Godot beats, is a shepherd. Godotfeeds both of them and allows them to sleep in his hayloft.

The boy in Act II also assures Vladimir that it was not he who called upon them the day before. He insists that this too is hisfirst visit. When Vladimir asks what Godot does the boy tells him, "He does nothing, sir." We also learn he has a whitebeard—possibly, the boy is not certain. This boy also has a brother who it seems is sick but there is no clear evidence tosuggest that his brother is the boy that came in Act I or the one who came the day before that.

Whether the boy from Act I is the same boy from Act II or not, both boys are polite yet timid. In the first Act, the boy, despitearriving while Pozzo and Lucky are still about, does not announce himself until after Pozzo and Lucky leave, saying toVladimir and Estragon that he waited for the other two to leave out of fear of the two men and of Pozzo's whip; the boy doesnot arrive early enough in Act II to see either Lucky or Pozzo. In both Acts, the boy seems hesitant to speak very much,saying mostly "Yes Sir" or "No Sir", and winds up exiting by running away.

Godot

The identity of Godot has been the subject of much debate. "When Colin Duckworth asked Beckett point-blank whetherPozzo was Godot, the author replied: 'No. It is just implied in the text, but it's not true.'"Deirdre Bair says that though "Beckett will never discuss the implications of the title", she suggests two stories that bothmay have at least partially have inspired it. The first is that because feet are a recurring theme in the play, Beckett has saidthe title was suggested to him by the slang French term for boot: "godillot, godasse". The second story, according to Bair, isthat Beckett once encountered a group of spectators at the French Tour de France bicycle race, who told him "Nousattendons Godot" — they were waiting for a competitor whose name was Godot. "Beckett said to Peter Woodthorpe that he regretted calling the absent character 'Godot', because of all the theoriesinvolving God to which this had given rise. "I also told [Ralph] Richardson that if by Godot I had meant God I would [have]said God, and not Godot. This seemed to disappoint him greatly." That said, Beckett did once concede, "It would befatuous of me to pretend that I am not aware of the meanings attached to the word 'Godot', and the opinion of many that itmeans 'God'. But you must remember – I wrote the play in French, and if I did have that meaning in my mind, it wassomewhere in my unconscious and I was not overtly aware of it." (Note: the French word for 'God' is 'Dieu'.) However,"Beckett has often stressed the strong unconscious impulses that partly control his writing; he has even spoken of being 'in atrance' when he writes."

Unlike elsewhere in Beckett's work, no bicycle appears in this play, but Hugh Kenner in his essay "The Cartesian Centaur" reports that Beckett once, when asked about the meaning of Godot, mentioned "a veteran racing cyclist, bald, a 'stayer,'recurrent placeman in town-to-town and national championships, Christian name elusive, surname Godeau, pronounced, ofcourse, no differently from Godot." Waiting for Godot is clearly not about track cycling, but it is said that Beckett himself didwait for French cyclist Roger Godeau (1920–2000; a professional cyclist from 1943 to 1961), outside the velodrome in Roubaix.

Of the two boys who work for Godot only one appears safe from beatings, "Beckett said, only half-jokingly, that one of Estragon's feet was saved". The name "Godot" is pronounced in Britain and Ireland with the emphasis on the first syllable, /ˈɡɒdoʊ/ go-doh; in NorthAmerica it is usually pronounced with an emphasis on the second syllable, /ɡəˈdoʊ/ gə-doh. Beckett himself said theemphasis should be on the first syllable, and that the North American pronunciation is a mistake. Georges Borchardt, Beckett's literary agent, and who represents Beckett's literary estate, has always pronounced "Godot" in the French manner, with equal emphasis on both syllables. Borchardt checked with Beckett's nephew, Edward, who told him his uncle pronounced it that way as well.

9   Themes and techniques

Major Themes:

The Absurd

Waiting for Godot is a prime example of what has come to be known as the theater of the absurd. The play is filled with nonsensical lines, wordplay, meaningless dialogue, and characters who abruptly shift emotions and forget everything, ranging from their own identities to what happened yesterday. All of this contributes to an absurdist humor throughout the play. However, this humor is often uncomfortably mixed together with tragic or serious content to make a darker kind of comedy. Estragon refers to "billions of others," who have been killed, and describes being beaten by an anonymous "they." Lucky (whose ill-fitting name is itself darkly comic) is treated horribly and physically abused on-stage. And Vladimir and Estragon talk nonchalantly and pleasantly about suicide. All this has a discomforting effect on the audience, who is not sure how to react to this absurd mixture of comedy and tragedy, seriousness and playfulness. In act one, Vladimir says, "one daren't even laugh any more," and his comment could apply well to the audience of Beckett's play, who don't know whether to laugh or to cringe at the events on-stage. The absurdity caused by the seeming mismatch between characters' tones and the content of their speech can be seen as a reaction to a world emptied of meaning and significance. If the world is meaningless, it makes no sense to see it as comic or tragic, good or bad. Beckett thus presents an eerie play that sits uneasily on the border between tragedy and comedy, in territory one can only call the absurd.

Waiting, Boredom, Nihilism

As Beckett's title indicates, the central act of the play is waiting, and one of the most salient aspects of the play is that nothing really seems to happen. Vladimir and Estragon spend the entire play waiting for Godot, who never comes. Estragon repeatedly wants to leave, but Vladimir insists that they stay, in case Godot actually shows up. As a result of this endless waiting, both Vladimir and Estragon are "bored to death," as Vladimir himself puts it. Both Vladimir and Estragon repeat throughout the play that there is "nothing to be done" and "nothing to do." They struggle to find ways to pass the time, so they end up conversing back and forth about nothing at all—including talking about how they don't know what to talk about—simply to occupy themselves while waiting. The boredom of the characters on-stage mirrors the boredom of the audience. Beckett has deliberately constructed a play where not only his characters, but also his audience wait for something that never happens. Just like Estragon and Vladimir, the audience waits during the play for some major event or climax that never occurs. Audience members might at times feel uncomfortable and want, like Estragon, to leave, but are bound to stay, in case Godot should actually arrive later in the play.

All of this waiting for nothing, talking about nothing, and doing nothing contributes to a pervasive atmosphere of nihilism in the play. Broadly defined, nihilism is a denial of any significance or meaning in the world. Deriving from the Latin word for "nothing" (nihil), it is a worldview centered around negation, claiming that there is no truth, morality, value, or—in an extreme form—even reality. This seems to describe the world of the play, largely emptied out of meaning, emotion, and substance, leading to characters who blather on endlessly in insignificant conversation. Given the play's deep exploration of the absurd humor and feelings of alienation that arise from this nihilistic understanding of the world, one could say that Waiting for Godot is, at its core, about nothing.

Modernism and Postmodernism

Written in 1953, Waiting for Godot was a somewhat late successor to the vibrant experimentation in art and literature of the late 19th and early 20th centuries known as Modernism. Modernist writers saw themselves as dramatically breaking with the past and innovating in all aspects of art, literature, and culture. Beckett's play shares with Modernist works a fascination with pushing the boundaries of literary genre, representation, and etiquette, as well as an interest in language and thought prioritized above action and plot. However, the play can also be seen as somewhat Postmodern, belonging to the literary and artistic period following Modernism. Both Modernism and Postmodernism are rather vague terms, often used differently by different critics. Moreover, it is also debated whether Postmodernism continues the aspirations of Modernism, or is a more radical break with it. In any case, Beckett's play sits on the fence between these two movements.

While Postmodernism is difficult to define exactly, Waiting for Godot displays a number of the defining features of a Postmodern conception of the world. One of these is an alienation from tradition and a questioning of the grand narratives that were previously seen to have some kind of authority. This includes grand narratives of historical progress—that history is the story of human life continually getting better—as well as religious narratives like the Bible. There are some biblical and classical references in the play, but they are only used ironically. Estragon compares himself to Christ in act one, for example, but the comparison is rather ridiculous. And Pozzo invokes "Atlas, son of Jupiter!" but doesn't actually believe in the force of this classical reference (what's more, he gets his mythological family tree wrong). The religious and cultural traditions of the past have lost their authority and centrality in the world of the play. Another Postmodern feature of the play is a pervasive sense of entrapment or enslavement, but a lack of any central authority. Characters are often unable to move or get up from the ground for no apparent reason. Vladimir and Estragon are, in a sense, trapped in their place of waiting, even though no one is forcing them to stay. Pozzo is Lucky's master, but he is far from free or powerful. Everyone in the play seems to be trapped or enslaved in some way, but no one seems to be the master. The characters of Waiting for Godot are also profoundly disoriented: they don't know where, or when, they are. At times, the characters don't even know who they are, as Estragon cannot remember his own past, for example. Finally, some of Beckett's characters feel a separation from reality. Both Vladimir and Pozzo question, in act two, whether they are actually awake or are simply dreaming. This confusion of reality with a dream or a false representation is a central, common feature of Postmodernism.

Seeing Beckett's play as Postmodernist is more than just labeling it as part of a particular literary movement; it gets to the heart of the world Beckett represents, one defined by alienation, entrapment, disorientation, and a questioning of reality. With the play's lack of specifics regarding its place or time, the circumstances of its events, or the particular back stories of its characters, Waiting for Godot can even be seen as a kind of allegory for the Postmodern condition. Beckett wrote his play before Postmodernism really coalesced or was written about as a distinct period or movement. Nonetheless, while in some ways still belonging to Modernism, the play presciently depicts many of the defining aspects of a Postmodern world. In representing these negative features, the play can be seen as either a pessimistic indictment of the present or as a chilling warning of what the future might look like: as how Beckett saw the world to be or as he feared it might become.

Humanity, Companionship, Suffering, and Dignity

Beckett's play is filled with a great deal of physical, mental, and emotional suffering. Vladimir and Estragon (especially Estragon) are starved for food, in physical pain, and "bored to death." Both fear an anonymous "they" who threaten to beat them at night, and are frequently unable to move of their own accord. Estragon mentions "billions of others," who have been killed, but does not elaborate. Lucky, meanwhile, is treated horribly, pulled about by a rope tied around his neck, beaten by Pozzo, and kicked repeatedly by Estragon. All of this suffering has a dehumanizing effect, and robs characters of their dignity. Lucky, for example, is addressed by Pozzo as "pig," and treated like a pack animal. Estragon is reduced to sucking on Pozzo's leftover chicken bones pathetically. And even Pozzo, who imposes suffering on Lucky, is unable to get up from the ground when he falls in act two.

Amid all this, Vladimir and Estragon desperately seek two things throughout the play: some recognition of their humanity, and companionship. When the boy asks Vladimir what message he would like to send to Godot, he simply asks the boy to tell Godot that he saw Vladimir. In other words, Vladimir wants to be acknowledged as a person. This is particularly important to him because the other characters in the play forget and mix up their identities. Pozzo and Lucky don't recognize Estragon and Vladimir in act two, whereas Estragon forgets about Lucky and Pozzo. In this environment where people are so easily forgotten, Vladimir wants some confirmation of his own identity and humanity. Beyond this, Vladimir and Estragon also desire companionship. Although Estragon repeatedly suggests that they go their separate ways, the two stay together out of a mutual fear of loneliness. When Estragon momentarily leaves the stage, Vladimir panics and becomes immediately lonely. And Estragon needs Vladimir as well—whether to have someone to talk to and ask questions of, or to help him put on his boots.

Nonetheless, even as Vladimir and Estragon seek some kind of dignity and companionship in the face of suffering, they are remarkably indifferent to the suffering of others. Vladimir is at first outraged at Pozzo's treatment of Lucky, but soon gets used to it and even encourages Estragon to kick him. Vladimir and Estragon converse nonchalantly while Pozzo is stuck on the ground and crying for help in act two, and they first scheme how they might take advantage of him rather than help him. Vladimir and Estragon value their own relationship, but generally fail to sympathize with Pozzo and Lucky as other potential companions. Beckett suggests that this kind of indifference to the pain of others is what allows the vicious cycle of suffering to continue on indefinitely, as it does in the play.

Techniques:

Symbolism is the technique Beckett uses to highlight the religious context of the book. In the book, Vladimir and Estragon represent the two halves of mankind: Vladimir represents the mental half, while Estragon represents the physical half. This symbolic dichotomy is heavily expressed through the polemic behaviors of Vladimir and Estragon. Estragon is always preoccupied with his physical welfare rather than his spiritual one, which makes as a simplistic character. However, both characters despite their overwhelm differences, they do share one thing in common which is they are both dependent on God to perform miracles in their lives. In the book, the only thing they do is sit under the tree, waiting for "Godot", Godot obviously represents God. He is a person who has never been seen, but who people still believe will make sense of the world and their lives for them. In addition to these characters, there are two other symbolic characters within the book, the boy who represents the Bible and Pozzo, who represents the false prophet. At the end of both acts, this boy delivers a message from Godot; "Mr. Godot told me to tell you he won't come this evening but surely tomorrow" (Beckett 55). This message is very similar to the Book of Revelation 22:12, which states "Look! I am coming soon! I bring my rewards with me. I will reward each person for what he has done." These two messages are parallel in that they both reassure them that God/ Godot is coming, but do not absolutely specify when he will come. Pozzo is an authoritarian figure. He possesses the trait of being decisive, powerful, and very confident in all situations. With these traits, it made Estragon and Vladimir immediately mistakenly thought that he is Godot who the two were expected to arrive at any time. Although it was a misunderstanding as Pozzo himself said he isn't god but does have god-like features, as mentioned in act I; "As far as one can see. Of the same species as myself. Of the same species as Pozzo! Made in God's image" (Beckett 19).

In addition to the symbolism in the characters, Beckett uses the technique of symbolism on the objects within the play. Examples of the objects are Estragon's boots, Pozzo's watch, carrots and turnips, and the tree and its leaves. Referencing act II, Estragon was having a problem putting his boots on. He attempted to put it on and off multiple times but it wasn't at all successful. It was enough for the two to come in conclusion that there is nothing they can do to fix the situation. It makes the boots symbolizes the feeling of hopelessness that occurs after a decent amount of time has passed. The source of hopelessness came from the fact that Godot didn't come and left Vladimir and Estragon hoping for his presence in their lives. Both of the characters are humans. They have feelings and being kept to wait for someone who has never met before for a very long time, surprisingly they kept on waiting although hopelessness started to crept into them. In addition to Estragon's unfit boots, Pozzo's watch is also an indicator for the passage of time. Out of all the characters, Pozzo seems to be one who mostly understands the concept of time and values it. In act I, Pozzo constantly consults his watch to see the time and the passage of time. However in act II he unfortunately lost his watch. Pozzo without his watch makes him a blind person who is not able to keep track of time and lost the concept of time entirely. With this example, it shows that time is very important in our lives. Without time mankind wouldn't function properly. Another example for the importance of time is Beckett's use of small comic trivial dialogue between Vladimir and Estragon about carrots and turnips. The dialogue is very trivial and useless but the fact that it happened was Vladimir and Estragon have nothing to do while waiting for Godot, so the purpose of this conversation is mainly to allow time to pass by. From the two symbols that signify the importance of time, it can be concluded that Beckett is trying to support his viewpoint that we shouldn't just be waiting for God but rather should be self-sufficient and do the tasks that make those miracles attributed to God possible. The last significant symbol in the book is the tree and its leaves. In act I, the tree was described as infertile and has a dead appearance. It was assumed by Vladimir that, "It must be dead" (Beckett 8). Death in many ways signifies hopelessness. However, the unexpected happened. In act II, the leaves started to sprout on the tree. For a dead looking tree which was assumed to be dead to blossom leaves out of nowhere signifies hope. The hope that Godot/God made a miracle and it is the sign he is on his way to meet Vladimir and Estragon. Besides from the symbolism that the tree and its leaves gives, the situation itself lights up the mood of the reader as it gives a sense of hope from within particularly when the characters are in a terrible physical condition. Yet, it is realized that this hope is temporary because Godot did not show up at any point within the play but sent the boy to give the message, "Mr. Godot told me to tell you he won't come this evening but surely tomorrow" (Beckett 55). Also it is possible that when the two characters first seen the tree, it wasn't the season for it to blossom which makes it appear to have a dead looking but in it is the appropriate season the tree blossoms and shed leaves at the end of it.

Beckett is a modernist who believes that time gives the illusion of order, security and structure to mankind. This is because time allows us to know when things are going to happen. By distorting time, it makes humans become victims to time. Control is taken from us and we are left to struggle to find order in the world. In Waiting for Godot, time has been distorted. The examples of time distortion are the random orientation of the day and nighttime, the lack of memory about yesterday and the elusive existence of tomorrow. The random orientation of day and nighttime e.g. the immediate falling of the sun makes Vladimir and Estragon needs to calling the waiting for Godot a day and looking for shelter. For the lack of memory about yesterday and the elusive existence of tomorrow, it happened in the second act of Waiting for Godot. Having Estragon and Vladimir experience these two things shows that Beckett thinks that the concept of time is meaningless because the only thing that is important in our lives is the present. Waiting for Godot to come tomorrow which isn't surely going to come is meaningless in Beckett's idea. He thinks that the most important thing is to do the present in the best of our abilities because nobody knows whether tomorrow will exist or not it is a conceptualized word that indicates a specific time. It is concluded that to the present in the best of our abilities is meant by that we shall not wait for god to perform miracles in our lives tomorrow but is to make the best out of the present and to stop waiting for god as it is meaningless.

In Beckett's Waiting for Godot repetition is considered to be a very essential element to the story's structure and is one of the tools that take the point that we shall be self-sufficient and do the tasks that make those miracles events attributed to God possible across. The two major repetitions in the book are the literature's plot and phrase repetition. For the literature plot, it is structured to be very cyclical in both of the acts e.g. the character's appearance with the book. The character appearance of the book is as the following; Vladimir and Estragon will be waiting for Godot under the tree, Pozzo will walk up to them to talk, although the first act they are healthy while the second act he is dumb and blind and the last appearance is where the boy comes as the messenger to tell the two that Godot will come tomorrow. Using the literature's structure repetition is one way trying to show that time has gone by so fast but the routine of Vladimir and Estragon is still the same which is to wait for Godot. From the plot, nothing has become better for the characters but it became worst. If Vladimir and Estragon has stopped waiting for Godot and start doing other things in their lives, things might have ended in a better way because what they are doing is a vicious cycle of waiting for the unknown existence which in the end hasn't made any different in their lives. For the phrase repetition, the most used phrase is "waiting for Godot" throughout the entire book. As an observation, this phrase is also the book title which makes it very obvious that to wait for Godot one of the main themes of the story itself. The phrase "waiting for Godot" has repetitively been used as a response of the action that Vladimir and Estragon are doing. Using the phrase multiple times shows that this action has been done for a very long time and it has never been accomplished. It is considered to be Beckett's attempt to show that waiting for Godot/God for miracles would not accomplish anything in the end.

The book has shown one of the main themes which is that we shouldn't just be waiting for God, an abstract religious figure to come to make miracles happen. Waiting for someone ot something that doesn't have definitive existence can make us lose hope in doing great things. As at the end of Waiting for Godot , Vladimir and Estragon lost all their hope and were planning to hang themselves. It they have decided to stop waiting for Godot and move on with their lives, thing wouldn't end as anticipated. Although, Waiting for Godot is just a book, but after it has been heavily examined, the book is a good reflection of our lives today. There are many people who are still waiting for miracles to happen with good faith especially in amidst of a natural disaster. Many people have lost their property and love ones, which left them in devastation. Many have turned towards religious figures and wait for miracles to happen with good faith. However, the world today doesn't consist with only good people but there are also bad people with malicious intentions who use the faith in people to take an advantage of like Pozzo who nearly took advantage of Vladimir and Estragon by claiming to be God. In order for people to not be taken advantage of, it is best for the people to be as self-sufficient as possible and make miracles happen in our lives with our own hands, not just solely waiting for God. It has been shown in many people's lives including myself that miracles can happen through self-determination, hard work and self-worth. It is at least something concrete and possible as it is better to do something than nothing at all.

10   Criticism on Waiting for Godot

Since its publication the play has been interpreted in different perspectives and angles. Throughout Waiting for Godot, the audience may encounter religious, philosophical, classical, psychoanalytical and biographical especially wartime references. There are ritualistic aspects and elements taken directly from vaudeville   and there is a danger in making more of these than what they are: that is, merely structural conveniences, avatars into which the writer places his fictional characters. Beckett tired quickly of "the endless misunderstanding". As far back as 1955, he remarked, "Why people have to complicatea thing so simple I can't make out." He was not forthcoming with anything more than cryptic clues, however: "PeterWoodthrope [who played Estragon] remembered asking him one day in a taxi what the play was really about: 'It's allsymbiosis, Peter; it's symbiosis,' answered Beckett."

Political

"It was seen as an allegory of the Cold War or of French Resistance to the Germans. Graham Hassell writes, "[T]heintrusion of Pozzo and Lucky [...] seems like nothing more than a metaphor for Ireland's view of mainland Britain, where society has ever been blighted by a greedy ruling élite keeping the working classes passive and ignorant by whatever means."

Vladimir and Estragon are often played with Irish accents, as in the Beckett on Film project. This, some feel, is an inevitableconsequence of Beckett's rhythms and phraseology, but it is not stipulated in the text. At any rate, they are not of Englishstock: at one point early in the play, Estragon mocks the English pronunciation of "calm" and has fun with "the story of the Englishman in the brothel"

Freudian

"Bernard Dukore develops a triadic theory in Didi, Gogo and the absent Godot, based on Sigmund Freud's Trinitarian description of the psyche in The Ego and the Id (1923) and the usage of onomastic techniques. Dukore defines thecharacters by what they lack: the rational Go-go embodies the incomplete ego, the missing pleasure principle: (e)go-(e)go.Di-di (id-id) – who is more instinctual and irrational – is seen as the backward id or subversion of the rational principle. Godotfulfils the function of the superego or moral standards. Pozzo and Lucky are just re-iterations of the main protagonists.Dukore finally sees Beckett's play as a metaphor for the futility of man's existence when salvation is expected from anexternal entity, and the self is denied introspection."

Jungian

"The four archetypal personalities or the four aspects of the soul are grouped in two pairs: the ego and the shadow, thepersona and the soul's image (animus or anima). The shadow is the container of all our despised emotions repressed bythe ego. Lucky, the shadow, serves as the polar opposite of the egocentric Pozzo, prototype of prosperous mediocrity, whoincessantly controls and persecutes his subordinate, thus symbolising the oppression of the unconscious shadow by thedespotic ego. Lucky's monologue in Act I appears as a manifestation of a stream of repressed unconsciousness, as he isallowed to "think" for his master. Estragon's name has another connotation, besides that of the aromatic herb, tarragon:"estragon" is a cognate of oestrogen, the female hormone (Carter, 130). This prompts us to identify him with the anima, thefeminine image of Vladimir's soul. It explains Estragon's propensity for poetry, his sensitivity and dreams, his irrationalmoods. Vladimir appears as the complementary masculine principle, or perhaps the rational persona of the contemplativetype."

Philosophical

Existential

Broadly speaking, existentialists hold that there are certain fundamental questions that every human being must come toterms with if they are to take their subjective existences seriously and with intrinsic value. Questions such as life, death, themeaning of human existence and the place of (or lack of) God in that existence are among them. By and large, the theoriesof existentialism assert that conscious reality is very complex and without an "objective" or universally known value: theindividual must create value by affirming it and living it, not by simply talking about it or philosophising it in the mind. The playmay be seen to touch on all of these issues.

Martin Esslin, in his The Theatre of the Absurd (1960), argued that Waiting for Godot was part of a broader literarymovement that he called the Theatre of the Absurd, a form of theatre which stemmed from the absurdist philosophy ofAlbert Camus. Absurdism itself is a branch of the traditional assertions of existentialism, pioneered by Søren Kierkegaard,and posits that, while inherent meaning might very well exist in the universe, human beings are incapable of finding it due tosome form of mental or philosophical limitation. Thus humanity is doomed to be faced with the Absurd, or the absoluteabsurdity of the existence in lack of intrinsic purpose. This interpretation has since been viewed by many scholars as narrowand limiting.

Ethical

Just after Didi and Gogo have been particularly selfish and callous, the boy comes to say that Godot is not coming. The boy(or pair of boys) may be seen to represent meekness and hope before compassion is consciously excluded by an evolvingpersonality and character, and in which case may be the youthful Pozzo and Lucky. Thus Godot is compassion and fails toarrive every day, as he says he will. No-one is concerned that a boy is beaten. In this interpretation, there is the irony thatonly by changing their hearts to be compassionate can the characters fixed to the tree move on and cease to have to wait forGodot.

Christian

Much of the play is steeped in scriptural allusion. The boy from Act One mentions that he and his brother mind Godot's sheep and goats. Much can be read into Beckett's inclusion of the story of the two thieves from Luke 23:39–43 and theensuing discussion of repentance. It is easy to see the solitary tree as representative of the Christian cross or the tree of life. Some see God and Godot as one and the same. Vladimir's "Christ have mercy upon us!" could be taken as evidencethat that is at least what he believes.

This reading is given further weight early in the first act when Estragon asks Vladimir what it is that he has requested fromGodot:

VLADIMIR: Oh ... nothing very definite.

ESTRAGON: A kind of prayer.

VLADIMIR: Precisely.

ESTRAGON: A vague supplication.

VLADIMIR: Exactly.

According to biographer Anthony Cronin, "[Beckett] always possessed a Bible, at the end more than one edition, and Bible concordances were always among the reference books on his shelves." Beckett himself was quite open on the issue:"Christianity is a mythology with which I am perfectly familiar so I naturally use it." As Cronin argues, these biblicalreferences "may be ironic or even sarcastic"

"In answer to a defence counsel question in 1937 (during a libel action brought by his uncle) as to whether he was aChristian, Jew or atheist, Beckett replied, 'None of the three'". Looking at Beckett's entire œuvre, Mary Bryden observedthat "the hypothesised God who emerges from Beckett's texts is one who is both cursed for his perverse absence and cursedfor his surveillant presence. He is by turns dismissed, satirised, or ignored, but he, and his tortured son, are neverdefinitively discarded."

Autobiographical

Waiting for Godot has been described as a "metaphor for the long walk into Roussillon, when Beckett and Suzanne slept inhaystacks [...] during the day and walked by night [... or] of the relationship of Beckett to Joyce."

Sexual

Though the sexuality of Vladimir and Estragon is not always considered by critics, some see the two vagabonds, asan aging homosexual couple, who are worn out, with broken spirits, impotent and not engaging sexually any longer. The twoappear to be written as a parody of a married couple. Peter Boxall points out that the play features two characters thatseem to have shared life together for years; they quarrel, embrace, and are mutually dependent. Beckett was interviewedat the time the play was priemiering in New York, and, speaking of his writings and characters in general, Beckett said "I'mworking with impotence, ignorance. I don't think impotence has been exploited in the past." Vladimir and Estragonconsider hanging themselves, as a desperate way to achieve at least one final erection. Pozzo and his slave, Lucky, arriveon the scene. Pozzo is a stout man, who wields a whip and holds a rope around Lucky's neck. Some critics have consideredthat the relationship of these two characters is homosexual and sado-masochistic in nature. Lucky's long speech is atorrent of broken ideas and speculations regarding man, sex, God, and time. It has been said that the play contains little or nosexual hope; which is the play's lament, and the source of the play's humor and comedic tenderness. Norman Mailer wonders if Beckett might be restating the sexual and moral basis of Christianity, that life and strength is found in an adorationof those in the lower depths where God is concealed. Beckett's objection to female actors

Beckett was not open to most interpretative approaches to his work. He famously objected when, in the 1980s, severalwomen's acting companies began to stage the play. "Women don't have prostates," said Beckett a reference to the factthat Vladimir frequently has to leave the stage to urinate.

Commentary by Artists or Critics on the Play

Waiting for Godot's success came as a surprise, even for its author. Becket expected the theater to be half empty for the majority of his shows, and certainly did not strive for the worldwide fame that his work received. Although the first Paris performance in 1953 left audience members "baffled, bored, and irritated" (Graver 9), others were soon inspired to develop various interpretations of the mysterious play.

Critics received the play with several different attitudes and conclusions. Some praised Waiting for Godotas revolutionary art, while others dismissed it as nonsense. In 1953, the playwright Jean Anouilh reviewed the play, remarking that "'nothing happens, nobody comes, nobody goes, it's awful.' This line... provides [the play's] best summary" (Cohn 11). Despite this comedic restatement of one of the lines from the play, Anouilh was among those who were captivated by the work's brilliance, and wrote a praising review of the play. Sylvain Zegel, writing the first review at the Theatre de Babylone in 1953, suggests the Didi and Gogo represent all of humanity with thier lack of understanding and attempts to pass time. They try to "live or give themselves the illusion that they are living... [Godot] might be happiness, eternal life, the ideal and unattainable quest of all men – which they wait for and which gives them the strength to live on" (Cohn 12). Zegel quickly recognized the importance of the play, and accurately predicted it's long term success. John Gielgud, however, wrote in the spring of 1953 that the play was "'a load of old rubbish'" (Graver 13). He was not alone in this opinion. Marya Mannes, a visiting American journalist, expressed her distaste with Beckett by claiming the play was, "'typical of the self-delusion of which certain intellectuals are capable, embracing obscurity, pretense, ugliness, and negation as protective coloring for their own confusions.'" (Cohn 14). For different reasons, the Lord Chamberlain had some objections with the play. The official censor of plays disliked the language and gestures used by the characters, and Becket agreed to make some changes while refusing to alter other aspects of the play. To sidestep the Lord Chamberlain, the London production opened at the private Arts Theatre Club on August 3rd, 1955 (Graver 13).

Among those who praised Waiting for Godot, disagreement over the "hidden" meanings created many interpretations. In 1953, Alain Robbe-Grillet, the young novelist of the Nouveau Romain, insisted that the play was not an allegory that contained all sorts of hidden symbolism, and that Beckett succeeded in his "dramatization of the human condition: the state of 'being there'" (Graver 12). He tells that the characters who are waiting for Godot do not experience a future or past, but are simply there (Graver 12). Beckett himself was not pleased by the success of his play because of the tendency audience and critics had to see religious and philosophical meanings that were not purposely included. Beckett insists that "the key to the play was the literal relations among its surface features, not any presumed meanings that could be deduced from them" (Cousineau 11). In this light, Dina Scherzer suggests that Beckett's resistance to meaning in Waiting for Godot asserts that "language is not an inert substance; rather, it is a material that can be shaped and transformed" (Cousineau 18). Scherzer views the play as a way to express the potentials in language that are normally suppressed. This viewpoint more closely aligns with Beckett's desire for the analysis of literal relations as opposed to symbolism. Waiting for Godot could be Beckett's way of liberating language from its rational entrapment.

Other critics of Beckett sought symbolism and philosophy in the piece of art. G.S. Fraser authored an article in the 1956 Times Literary Supplement suggesting that the play is a metaphor about the nature of human life "'which makes a particular appeal to the mood of liberal uncertainty which is the prevailing mood of modern Western Europe'" (Graver 15). He also insists that it is a modern morality play on permanent Christian themes, and that Didi and Gogo represent the fallen state of man and the contemplative life. Pozzo and lucky represent the life of practical action adopted as an end in itself. The tree stand for the tree of knowledge of good and evil, the tree of life, the cross, and (for hanging) the Judas tree (Graver 15).

Katherine M. Wilson disagrees with G.S. Fraser in 1956, and writes that Waiting for Godot conveys modern life in its full horror so that, "'the audience, finding it unendurable, may be forced to remedy it'" (Graver 16). Wilson suggests that Fraser's analysis leads the audience to blame all our misery on God and fate, excusing us of the responsibility to do anything about it. Taking existentialist views, Wilson feels the need to begin analysis of the play with the human individual. By focusing on the person instead of religion and mystery, the audience members may understand the purpose of the art and become inspired to initiate the change that Beckett desires. Wilson sees the moral of the play as a question: "If this is what waiting for Godot is like, must we wait for him?"

Although critics of Waiting for Godot have written reviews ranging from positive introspection to disgusting confusion, there is no debate on the success and longevity of this play. Other playwrights may have dissected the play in more ways than Beckett believed possible, but the audience may never know Beckett's true intentions. We must accept this ambiguity as part of the play's essence, and not impose heavy-handed interpretations upon Waiting for Godot.

Comment by Brooks Atkinson

Don't expect this column to explain Samuel Beckett's "Waiting for Godot," which was acted at the John Golden last evening. It is a mystery wrapped in an enigma.

But you can expect witness to the strange power this drama has to convey the impression of some melancholy truths about the hopeless destiny of the human race. Mr. Beckett is an Irish writer who has lived in Paris for years, and once served as secretary to James Joyce.

Since "Waiting for Godot" has no simple meaning, one seizes on Mr. Beckett's experience of two worlds to account for his style and point of view. The point of view suggests Sartre--bleak, dark, disgusted. The style suggests Joyce--pungent and fabulous. Put the two together and you have some notion of Mr. Beckett's acrid cartoon of the story of mankind.

Literally, the play consists of four raffish characters, an innocent boy who twice arrives with a message from Godot, a naked tree, a mound or two of earth and a sky. Two of the characters are waiting for Godot, who never arrives. Two of them consist of a flamboyant lord of the earth and a broken slave whimpering and staggering at the end of a rope.

Since "Waiting for Godot" is an allegory written in a heartless modern tone, a theatre-goer naturally rummages through the performance in search of a meaning. It seems fairly certain that Godot stands for God. Those who are loitering by the withered tree are waiting for salvation, which never comes.

The rest of the symbolism is more elusive. But it is not a pose. For Mr. Beckett's drama adumbrates--rather than expresses--an attitude toward man's experience on earth; the pathos, cruelty, comradeship, hope, corruption, filthiness and wonder of human existence. Faith in God has almost vanished. But there is still an illusion of faith flickering around the edges of the drama. It is as though Mr. Beckett sees very little reason for clutching at faith, but is unable to relinquish it entirely.

Although the drama is puzzling, the director and the actors play it as though they understand every line of it. The performance Herbert Berghof has staged against Louis Kennel's spare setting is triumphant in every respect. And Bert Lahr has never given a performance as glorious as his tatterdemalión Gogo, who seems to stand for all the stumbling, bewildered people of the earth who go on living without knowing why.

Although "Waiting for Godot" is an uneventful, maundering, loquacious drama, Mr. Lahr is an actor in the pantomime tradition who has a thousand ways to move and a hundred ways to grimace in order to make the story interesting and theatrical, and touching, too. His long experience as a bawling mountebank has equipped Mr. Lahr to represent eloquently the tragic comedy of one of the lost souls of the earth.

The other actors are excellent, also. E. G. Marshall as a fellow vagrant with a mind that is a bit more coherent; Kurt Kasznar as a masterful egotist reeking of power and success; Alvin Epstein as the battered slave who has one bitterly satirical polemic to deliver by rote; Luchino Solito De Solis as a disarming shepherd boy--complete the cast that gives this diffuse drama a glowing performance.

Although "Waiting for Godot" is a "puzzlement," as the King of Siam would express it, Mr. Beckett is no charlatan. He has strong feelings about the degradation of mankind, and he has given vent to them copiously. "Waiting for Godot" is all feeling. Perhaps that is why it is puzzling and convincing at the same time. Theatregoers can rail at it, but they cannot ignore it. For Mr. Beckett is a valid writer.

Comment by Michael Sinclair

The purpose of human life is an unanswerable question. It seems impossible to find an answer because we don't know where to begin looking or whom to ask. Existence, to us, seems to be something imposed upon us by an unknown force. There is no apparent meaning to it, and yet we suffer as a result of it. The world seems utterly chaotic. We therefore try to impose meaning on it through pattern and fabricated purposes to distract ourselves from the fact that our situation is hopelessly unfathomable. "Waiting for Godot" is a play that captures this feeling and view of the world, and characterizes it with archetypes that symbolize humanity and its behaviour when faced with this knowledge. According to the play, a human being's life is totally dependant on chance, and, by extension, time is meaningless; therefore, a human's life is also meaningless, and the realization of this drives humans to rely on nebulous, outside forces, which may be real or not, for order and direction.

The basic premise of the play is that chance is the underlying factor behind existence. Therefore human life is determined by chance. This is established very early on, when Vladimir mentions the parable of the two thieves from the Bible. "One of the thieves was saved. It's a reasonable percentage" (Beckett, 8). The idea of "percentage" is important because this represents how the fate of humanity is determined; it is random, and there is a percentage chance that a person will be saved or damned. Vladimir continues by citing the disconcordance of the Gospels on the story of the two thieves. "And yet...how is it - this is not boring you I hope - how is it that of the four Evangelists only one speaks of a thief being saved. The four of them were there - or thereabouts - and only one speaks of a thief being saved" (Beckett, 9). Beckett makes an important point with this example of how chance is woven into even the most sacred of texts that is supposed to hold ultimate truth for humanity. All four disciples of Chirst are supposed to have been present during his crucifixion and witnessed the two thieves, crucified with Jesus, being saved or damned depending on their treatment of him in these final hours. Of the four, only two report anything peculiar happening with the thieves. Of the two that report it, only one says that a thief was saved while the other says that both were damned. Thus, the percentages go from 100%, to 50%, to a 25% chance for salvation. This whole matter of percentages symbolizes how chance is the determining factor of existence, and Beckett used the Bible to prove this because that is the text that humanity has looked to for meaning for millenia. Even the

Bible reduces human life to a matter of chance. On any given day there is a certain percent chance that one will be saved as opposed to damned, and that person is powerless to affect the decision. "The fate of the thieves, one of whom was saved and the other damned according to the one of the four accounts that everybody believes, becomes as the play progresses a symbol of the condition of man in an unpredictable and arbitrary universe" (Webb, 32).

God, if he exists, contributes to the chaos by his silence. The very fact that God allows such an arbitrary system to continue makes him an accomplice. The French philosopher Pascal noted the arbitrariness of life and that the universe worked on the basis of percentages. He advocated using such arbitrariness to one's advantage, including believing in God because, if he doesn't exist, nobody would care in the end, but if he does, one was on the safe side all along, so one can't lose. It is the same reasoning that Vladimir uses in his remark quoted above, "It's a reasonable percentage." But it is God's silence throughout all this that causes the real hopelessness, and this is what makes "Waiting for Godot" a tragedy amidst all the comical actions of its characters: the silent plea to God for meaning, for answers, which symbolizes the plea of all humanity, and God's silence in response. "The recourse to bookkeeping by the philosopher [Pascal] no less than the clownish tramp shows how helpless we are with respect to God's silence" (Astro, 121). Either God does not exist, or he does not care. Whichever is the case, chance and arbitrariness determine human life in the absence of divine involvement.

The world of "Waiting for Godot" is one without any meaningful pattern, which symbolizes chaos as the dominating force in the world. There is no orderly sequence of events. A tree which was barren one day is covered with leaves the next. The two tramps return to the same place every day to wait for Godot. No one can remember exactly what happened the day before. Night falls instantly, and Godot never comes. The entire setting of the play is meant to demonstrate that time is based on chance, and therefore human life is based on chance.

Time is meaningless as a direct result of chance being the underlying factor of existence. Hence there is a cyclic, albeit indefinite, pattern to events in "Waiting for Godot." Vladimir and Estragon return to the same place each day to wait for Godot and experience the same general events with variations each time. It is not known for how long in the past they have been doing this, or for how long they will continue to do it, but since time is meaningless in this play, it is assumed that past, present, and future mean nothing. Time, essentially is a mess. "One of the seemingly most stable of the patterns that give shape to experience, and one of the most disturbing to see crumble, is that of time" (Webb, 34-35). The ramifications of this on human existence are symbolized by the difference between Pozzo and Lucky in Act I and in Act II. Because time is based on chance and is therefore meaningless, human life is treated arbitrarily and in an almost ruthless manner, and is also meaningless. In Act I Pozzo is travelling to the market to sell Lucky, his slave. Pozzo is healthy as can be, and there seems to be nothing wrong. Lucky used to be such a pleasant slave to have around, but he has become quite annoying, and so Pozzo is going to get rid of him. This is their situation the first time they meet Vladimir and Estragon. The next day, everything has changed. Pozzo is now blind, and Lucky is mute. Pozzo has absolutely no recollection of the previous meeting, and even claims that Lucky has always been mute even though just the day before he gave a long philosophical discourse when commanded to "think." When asked by Vladimir when he became blind, Pozzo responds "I woke up one fine day as blind as Fortune" (Beckett, 55). Vladimir, incredulous, continues asking him for details. Pozzo responds to this (violently), "Don't question me! The blind have no notion of time. The things of time are hidden from them too" (Beckett, 55). Pozzo's situation symbolizes the effects of time on humans. The inherent meaninglessness of a world based on chance degenerates human life into something that is worthless and can be toyed with by Fortune. Beckett uses this change in the situation of Pozzo and Lucky to show that human life is meaningless because time is meaningless. "Although a 'stream of time' doesn't exist any longer, the 'time material' is not petrified yet,...instead of a moving stream, time here has become something like a stagnant mush" (Andres, 143).

Humans try to remain oblivious of their condition. Throughout the play, Vladimir and Estragon remain stupidly cheerful, and seek distraction in pointless activities. In doing so, they act rather comical, which gives the play its humorous element. "The positive attitude of the two tramps thus amounts to a double negation: their inability to recognize the senselessness of their position" (Andres, 143-144). Vladimir and Estragon try to distract themselves from the endless wait by arguing over mundane topics, sleeping, chatting with Pozzo and Lucky (again over mundane topics), and even contemplating suicide. All of this is an attempt to remain oblivious of the fact that they are waiting for a vague figure, partly of their own invention, that will never come. They do not want to realize that their lives are meaningless. This behavior symbolizes humanity's petty distractions. Humans have nothing else to do but try to distract themselves from their situation. "...while, in the case of Vladimir and Estragon, it is just the incessant attempt to make time pass which is so characteristic, and which reflects the specific misery and absurdity of their life" (Andres, 147-148). Vladimir and Estragon's attempts at distraction are attempts to make time pass, to draw them closer to the time when Godot will arrive and solve all their problems. This is pure wishful thinking, but this is all that they have to look forward to, even if the action is meaningless. The only alternative to this is death, which the two contemplate but lack the courage and initiative to carry through. In the end, the only recourse left to humans is to persist in meaningless action or perish. "Pozzo, after his vision of the emptiness and futility of human life, revives his Lucky and cries, 'On!' though they have nowhere to go and nothing to carry but sand" (Webb, 41).

To impose pattern and meaning on their world, humans will rely on nebulous outside forces for relief and distraction from their predicament. This is the only thing that can keep them going. Thus, in the play, Godot is symbolic of such an outside force, which seems to be silent and uncaring. Even so, he is still a pattern, and he infuses the two desperate tramps with a purpose to their absurd lives. By imposing pattern on chaos, Vladimir and Estragon achieve some degree of meaning. In this case, the pattern is waiting. Vladimir, in his philosophical soliloquy while contemplating whether or not to help Pozzo in Act II, declares, "What are we doing here, that is the question. And we are blessed in this, that we happen to know the answer. Yes, in this immense confusion one thing alone is clear. We are waiting for Godot to come-" (Beckett, 51). An illusion of salvation is needed to cope with a meaningless life. Godot is that illusion. Therefore we see that because of all the aforementioned factors, that life is based on chance, that time is meaningless, that human life is meaningless, humans are driven to invent or rely on such "Godots," otherwise they would perish. In essence, "'Waiting for Godot' is the story of two vagabonds who impose on their slovenly wilderness an illusory, but desperately defended, pattern: waiting" (Webb, 26).

It is never clear whether Godot is real or not, which is why he is referred to as an example of a "nebulous force". In both acts, Vladimir and Estragon mistake or suspect Pozzo of being Godot. They have never actually seen Godot, and would not be able to tell him apart from a street passerby. Their only contact with him is his messenger boy that comes at the end of each day to inform them that Godot will again not be coming, but will surely come tomorrow. The boy never remembers one day from the next, another indication of the absence of a meaningful time sequence. At the end of the second act, Vladimir, the more philosophical of the two, gets a glimpse of the truth: that they will forever be waiting for Godot, that he is merely a distraction from their useless lives, and that he can even predict, ironically, when the boy comes again, everything that the boy will say. It is at this point that a great depression overcomes Vladimir at the realisation of the truth. It is the climax of the play and its most tragic part. But Vladimir realizes that he is trapped, that he must persist in the illusion, that he has no choice. This is the definition of "going on" for humanity. There is no point. But it is the only option. "All of these characters go on, but in the old ruts, and only by retreating into patterns of thought that have already been thoroughly discredited. In the universe of this play, 'on' leads nowhere" (Webb, 41).

"Waiting for Godot" is all about how the world is based on chance. A world based on chance can have no orderly time sequence, and thus time has no meaning. The extension, then, is that human life has no meaning. Realizing this, humans will create distractions and diversions, in the form of patterns and reliance on nebulous forces, to provide the purpose and meaning that is inherently lacking in their lives. "Waiting for Godot" is the classical, archetypical presentation of this facet of human existence.

Short Questions with Answers

1.   Vladimir moves with" short, stiff strides, with legs apart" – What does it signify?

Ans: - Vladimir suffers from the enlargement of the prostate gland- a complaint common in old age. His gait reminds us of the king of comedy, Charlie Chaplin.

2.   "Certainly they beat me"- Who is beaten by and by whom?

Ans: - Estragon informs that he had been beaten by some people whom he identifies only as 'they'. What 'they' refers to remain a mystery, much like the malevolent cosmic forces, the tormenters of humanity. 'They' are as mysterious as 'Godot' is to be later.

3.   Who planned to commit suicide by jumping off the Eiffel Tower?

Ans: - Estragon and Vladimir had, during their younger days, together planned to commit suicide by jumping off the Eiffel Tower. But, Vladimir thinks, in their present condition, they would not be allowed to go up the Eiffel Tower and will thus be denied even the most despairing choice (of committing suicide).

4.   What are the nicknames of Estragon and Vladimir?

Ans:- It is interesting to note that only in the list of characters are the tramps named Estragon and Vladimir. Right through the plays the two address each other by their Gogo and Didi.

5.   What is 'mandrakes'? What is its symbolic reference?

Ans:- The two tramps by mentioning 'mandrakes' give an evidence of their love for knowledge. An ancient fertility symbols, mandrake, is believed to grow below the gallows. Notably there, death and birth being two facts of the same coin, Gallows, a symbol of death, is put side by side with mandrakes, fertility symbol.

6.   Where were the Vladimir and Estragon Waiting for Godot?

Ans: - it was a willow tree having scarcely a leave on it or it was a shrub or a bush, under which they were waiting.

7.   Estragon: I'm asking you it we're tied:- How are the two tramps tied and to whom?

Ans:- Here Estragon asks Vladimir whether they are tied. They are tide to waiting for Godot. They can not get away from it was doing so would mean giving up hope, how so ever illusory that hope may be?

8.   "Why doesn't he put down his bags?" – Who is having the bag? Why don't he put down it?

Ans:- There is complementarity in the master- slave relationship in Pazzo- Lucky relationship. While they enter on the stage lucky has a bag on the back. Pazzo's treatment of Lucky as a beast of burden underscores human tragedy. 'Lucky' in order to impress Pazzo, doesn't put down his bags.

9.   Why is lucky given such a name?

Ans:- There might be two suggestions about the source of his name – (i) lucky is 'Lucky' because he gets the bones or (ii) he is 'Lucky' because he has no expectations, hence he will not be disappointed further in his existence . "Blessed are those who do not hope, for they shall not be disappointed."

10.   What does it symbolize by Pazzo's baldness?

Ans:- The intellectual barrenness of Pazzo is symbolized by his baldness, in contrast to Lucky's abundant white hair. Pazzo's baldness fits well in the scheme of things – as then there is all round barrenness.

11.   What is thinking hat? Who wears it and why?

Ans: - it is Lucky who can't think without his hat on. And in order to terminate Lucky's thinking someone has to remove his hat, as if an energizer has been removed from a machine. Thinking, thus, becomes mechanical.

12.   Why which name the boy address Vladimir?

Ans: - The boy address Vladimir as Mr. Albert and Vladimir responds to it.

13.   What is the different do you find the Willow tree in act ii?

Ans:- In act. I we see that the tree, which was leafless in the first act, has four or five leaves.

14.   What the tree stands for in the play?

Ans: - The tree is associated with the central theme of barrenness, nothingness and death. As the two tramps wish to hang themselves on the bough, it reminds us for Christ's crucifixion. Further in act ii when few leaves are seen, it stands for spring, hope and renewals also.

15.   How did the two tramps pass their line of waiting in act- ii?

Ans: - The two tramps as a means of passing time propose different things: to sing, to think or to contradict each other, or ask each other questions.

16.   What was Lucky carrying in his bag? What is the symbolic in it?

Ans:- Lucky in his bag carries sand, a symbol of burden and of time (in hour glass) , in his bag.

17.   What is the profit of Pazzo's blindness?

Ans:- Owning to Pazzo's blindness, he has acquired a new might into the meaning of life. Life is a mere serious of meaningless repetitions activities. Journey from womb to tomb is full of miseries.

18.   What does the song about the dog signify in Waiting for Godot?

Ans:- In the beginning of act ii Vladimir moves about feverishly on the stage and suddenly begins to sing a dog song – an old German Balled. It is a circular song. It is emblematic of the circularity and repetitiveness of the play as a whole.

19.   What does Lucky's 'Dance in a Net' symbolize?

Ans:- Lucky's dance amplifies the agony, strain and entanglement in life to magnify the ultimate suffering of human existence.

5 Marks Questions with Answers

1. Discuss Symbols and imagery in Samuel Beckett's Waiting for Godot

Duality

Waiting for Godot is chock-full of pairs. There's Vladimir and Estragon, the two thieves, the Boy and his brother, Pozzo and Lucky, Cain and Abel, and of course the two acts of the play itself. With these pairs comes the repeated notion of arbitrary, 50/50 chances. One thief is saved and other damned, but for no clear reason. If Vladimir and Estragon try to hang themselves, the bough may or may not break. One man may die, one man may live. Godot may or may not come to save them. In the Bible, Cain's sacrifice was rejected and Abel's accepted for no discernible reason. It's minor, but check out Estragon's line in Act I: "My left lung is very weak [...]. But my right lung is sound as a bell!" More pairs, more arbitrary damnation. Even the tone of Waiting for Godot is filled with duality: two person arguments, back-and-forth questions, disagreement-agreement, questions and (often inadequate) answers.

The tree

The tree is the only distinct piece of the setting, so we're pretty sure it matters. (Also, if you check out the painting that inspired Beckett, you'll see that a big tree features prominently.) Right off the bat you've got the biblical stuff; Jesus was crucified on a cross, but that cross is sometimes referred to as a "tree," as in, "Jesus was nailed to the tree." That Vladimir and Estragon contemplate hanging themselves from the tree is likely a reference to the crucifixion, but it also parodies the religious significance. If Jesus died for the sins of others, Vladimir and Estragon are dying for... nothing. (There's that pesky "nothing" word again. You just can't get rid of it in this play.)

But you can also think of the two men not as Jesus, but rather as the two thieves crucified along with Jesus. This fits quite nicely with gospel's tale as Vladimir tells it; one thief is saved and the other damned, so Didi and Gogo are looking at a fiftyfifty chance. (Duality! Again.) The uncertainty that stems from inconsistency between the four gospels is fitting, too, since Vladimir can't be certain if Godot is coming to save either one of them. (Uncertainty! Again.) (Repetition! Again.)

There's more. Vladimir reports that he was told to wait for Godot by the tree. This should be reassuring – it means the men are in the right place. Right? Wrong. As Estragon points out, they're not sure if this is the right tree. And, come to think of it, they can't even be sure if this is a tree or not. It kind of looks like a shrub.

Now what we find to be completely baffling is the tree's random sprouting of leaves in between Act I and Act II. This is regeneration – it is hopeful, it is growth, it is life! And that doesn't sound anything like Waiting for Godot, especially when you look at how everything else degenerates from Act I to

Act II (we're thinking in particular of Pozzo's going blind and Lucky mute, as well as Gogo and Didi's increasing uncertainty and suffering).

So what gives? Take a look at Vladimir's line early in Act I, when he says, "Hope deferred maketh the something sick, who said that?" As we've mentioned, Vladimir is referring to the biblical proverb that goes a little something like this: "Hope deferred makes the heart sick; but a desire fulfilled is a tree of life."

See that? Tree of life. So the tree's random blooming would suggest that it is something of a tree of life. And, according to the proverb, that means a desire has been fulfilled.

Of course, as far as we can tell, no desires have been fulfilled. At all. This could mean that the proverb is completely without truth and reason, which fits with Godot's general stance on religion. Then again, the tree's sprouting leaves could be an ironic symbol pointing out that, far from fulfilled desires, hopes have been deferred yet another day – much like Vladimir's ironic claim in Act II that "things have changed here since yesterday" when, clearly, nothing at all has. Or it could be something else all together

Nightfall and rising moon

While Vladimir and Estragon wait for Godot, they also wait for nightfall. For some reason (again, arbitrary and uncertain), they don't have to wait for him once the night has fallen. The classic interpretation is that night = dark = death. The falling of night is as much a reprieve from daily suffering as death is from the suffering of a lifetime.

There's also the issue of the moon, as its appearance in the sky is the real signal that night has come and the men can stop waiting for Godot. Estragon, in one of his "wicked smart" moments, comments the moon is "pale for weariness [...] of climbing heaven and gazing on the likes of us." Though the man remembers nothing of yesterday, he does in this moment seem to comprehend the endless repetition of his life. And if the moon is weary just from watching, imagine what that says about the predicament of the men themselves.

The carrot

Carrots and turnips are in one sense just a gag reel for Vladimir and Estragon's comic bits. But we were interested in their disagreement over the vegetable: "Funny," Estragon comments as he munches, "the more you eat, the worse it gets." Vladimir quickly disagrees, adding that, for him, it's "just the opposite." On the one hand, this could be a completely meaningless conversation – the point is simply that Vladimir is in disagreement, playing at opposites, adding to the bickering duality between himself and Gogo.

On the other hand, the carrot could be about the meaning of life. Exclamation point! OK, so the carrot probably isn't about the meaning of life. But it could be a hint as to the differences between the way Vladimir and Estragon live their lives. Vladimir's subsequent comment, an addendum to his carrot claim, is that he "get[s] used to the muck as [he goes] along." He resigns himself to banality. Estragon, on the other hand, wearies as time passes – much like the weary moon he observes in Act II. When Pozzo later dishes about smoking, he claims that a second pipe is "never so sweet [as the first]. But it's sweet just the same." This is a third and distinct answer to the carrot question.

Lucky's Dance

When Lucky is commanded to dance in Act I, Pozzo reveals that he calls his dance "The Net," adding, "He thinks he's entangled in a net." You would think a guy tied up on a rope leash would feel confined enough. Of course, the image of Lucky writhing in an imaginary net is a lasting image for the play as a whole, and especially for the plight of Vladimir and Estragon, who, as we've said before, are confined in a prison – or perhaps a net – of their own imaginations.

The Hats, the Boots and the Vaporizer

There seems to be no shortage of inane props in Waiting for Godot, and these three have one thing in common: they are all absurd objects on which the men have developed irrational dependences. Lucky cannot think without his bowler. Pozzo needs his vaporizer to speak. Estragon seems condemned to forever take his boots on and off, as does Vladimir with his hat. This is another great combination of the tragic and the comic; the situation is hilarious for its absurdity, but dismal at the same time.

Smell

Estragon is repeatedly repelled by smells in Waiting for Godot. Vladimir stinks of garlic, Lucky smells like who knows what, and Pozzo reeks of a fart in Act II. It seems every time Estragon tries to get close to a person, he is repelled by their odor. It looks to us like Smells represent one of the barriers to interpersonal relationships. Estragon isn't just repelled by odors – he's repelled by the visceral humanity of those around him. There's something gritty and base about the odor of a human body, and for Estragon it's too much to handle.

2. Discuss the relationship between Vladimir and Estragon in Samuel Beckett's Waiting for Godot

Before critical analyses of the text of the play "Waiting for Godot", it would be necessary to cast an introductory glance at the play. Samuel Beckett, the most eminent Irish playwright wrote "Waiting for Godot" in French in 1949 and then translated it into English in 1954. This play has been performed as a drama of the absurd with astonishing success in Europe, America and the rest of the world in post second world war era. For this reason, Martin Esslin calls it, "One of the successes of the post-war theatre" (Esslin, Martin, 1980, p.3). In this play, the two tramps, Vladimir and Estragon, who wait expectantly to see Godot near a stunted tree in the middle of nowhere. They do not even know his name, whether he promises to come and visit them, or if, in fact, he actually exists. However, they are still waiting and waiting for him.

The slave-owning Pozzo, his subservient slave, Lucky and the boy, whose name is not mentioned in the play, interrupt their waiting. Godot has nothing significant to do with their lives. They do every possible thing; even intend to commit suicide, just to keep the dreadful silence. The play begins with waiting for Godot and ends with waiting for Godot. Play does not end formally, when the boy, who is as well messenger of Godot, tells the fact to the tramps that Godot is not expected to come this evening.

Vladimir and Estragon are the main protagonists of the play, Waiting for Godot. In hearing the play read, even the most experienced theater person will often confuse one of the characters for the other. Therefore, the similarities are as important as the differences between them.

Vladimir and Estragon are waiting for Godot: some indication that life is meaningful or an escape. Both are tramps dressed in costumes which could be interchanged - big boots which don't necessarily fit, big bowler hats, baggy and ill-fitting suits. Their costumes recall the type found in burlesque or vaudeville houses. The opening scene with Estragon struggling with his boots and Vladimir doffing and donning his hat to inspect it for lice could be a part of a burlesque routine. Such comic episodes continue until the characters — and the audiences — are bored with it.

Vladimir would be the equivalent of the straight man in burlesque comedy. He is also the intellectual who is concerned with a variety of ideas. Of the two, Vladimir makes the decisions and remembers significant aspects of their past. He is the one who constantly reminds Estragon that they must wait for Godot. Vladimir seems to know more about Godot. Vladimir often sees religious or philosophical implications in their discussions of events, and he interprets their actions in religious terms; for example, he is concerned about the religious implications in such stories as the two thieves who were crucified on either side of Jesus. Vladimir correlates some of their actions to the general concerns of mankind. In addition to the larger needs, Vladimir also looks after their physical needs.

In contrast, Estragon is concerned mainly with more mundane matters: He prefers a carrot to a radish or turnip, his feet hurt, and he blames his boots; he constantly wants to leave, and it must be drilled into him that he must wait for Godot. He remembers that he was beaten, but he sees no philosophical significance in the beating. He is willing to beg for money from a stranger (Pozzo), and he eats Pozzo's discarded chicken bones with no shame. Estragon, then, is the more basic of the two. He is not concerned with either religious or philosophical matters. First of all, he has never even heard of the two thieves who were crucified with Christ, and if the Gospels do disagree, then "that's all there is to it," and any further discussion is futile and absurd.

Estragon, however, is dependent upon Vladimir, and essentially he performs what Vladimir tells him to do. For example, Vladimir looks after Estragon's boots, he rations out the carrots, turnips, and radishes, he comforts Estragon's pain, and he reminds Estragon of their need to wait for Godot. Estragon does sometimes suggest that it would be better if they parted, but he never leaves Vladimir for long. Essentially, Estragon is the less intelligent one; he has to have everything explained to him, and he is essentially so bewildered by life that he has to have someone to look after him. Vladimir is more masculine and contemplative and Estragon is more feminine and emotion-driven of the duo.

The relationship of Vladimir and Estragon is contrasted with that of Pozzo and Lucky, who represent the antithesis of friendship. Theirs is also a relationship of intertwinement and dependence, but one of servitude, inequality, and dominance.

Worse than waiting is waiting alone, and loneliness is a form of blindness and invisibility, not seeing or being seen. The play emphasizes the fact that the minimal unit of the human is not the one, but the two, and though the picture is a bleak, unsettling, and painful meditation upon our shared loneliness in the absence of Godot, the fact that we share this loneliness, this eternal waiting, with our friend is what can possibly turn our cries into laughter and our ontological loneliness into love.

3. Discuss Pozzo-Lucky relationship in relation with the theme of Beckett's Waiting for Godot

Or, Even the Relationships In Waiting For Godot Are Absurd.

Do You Agree?

Shaped as they are, by the same culture, the characters in "Waiting for Godot" share a number of common features. Each is split by the same contradiction. On the one hand, he knows himself chiefly as a separate isolated individual, which on the other hand; each is driven to form some kind of relationship with other by need, greed and sometimes by compassion.

A solitary existence is a material impossibility but relationships can be of different kinds. Pozzo and Lucky, master and slave, are joined artificially (because they do not like each other) and by force with their rope, while the partnership of Vladimir and Estragon, though not a voluntary one, seems to be based on genuine natural need and relative equality.

All the relationships between characters are, to different degrees, based on the exploitation and abuse that Beckett observed in a Europe occupied (based on tyranny) by Hitler, an Ireland occupied by Britain and the churches and the similar relationship we find in the Pozzo — Lucky pair where there is no co-operation Lucky is the paid entertainer who does all the work, while Pozzo takes all the credit.

In the play Pozzo appears like a brazen idol—massive, smooth and rigid walking ahead of Lucky, at far end of a long rope, where he is beaten. Although in stark contrast to each other, yet Pozzo and Lucky have one thing in common, they are both driven by a desperate attempt to evade panic, which would grip them if they lose their belief in what Pozzo stands for.

Lucky deserves his name because he has a master who, however, cruelly organizes his life for him. Once we are told, Lucky could by dancing and thinking amuse and inspire Pozzo, but his state of slavery has gradually put an end to all that. His thinking has deteriorated into the endless repletion of meaningless and reminiscent of the "word- salad" of schizophrenic.

The relationship between Pozzo and Lucky is reflected in the physical bond that holds them together — the link of the rope. Pozzo treats Lucky worse than an animal. He invariably refers to him as pig and hog. He attracts his attention by putting the rope violently, which surrounds Lucky's neck. The tramps notice that the rope has eaten a running ulcer into Lucky's flesh. Lucky is made to carry all sorts of baggage. Yet he does not resist or complain. According to Pozzo, Lucky keeps on holding the luggage all the time because he does not want to leave the Pozzo's service, he hopes his zeal might favourably impress his master. However, Pozzo is determined to get rid of the slave. He announces in Act-1, that he is taking Lucky to a fair where he hopes to sell him for a good price. Lucky is vicious to strangers. He kicks Estragon painfully when the latter approaches him, in Act-1, to wipe away his tears. This is the only occasion when Lucky displays human feelings. Pozzo has remarked that creatures like Lucky ought to be exterminated; hearing these words Lucky begins to cry.

Everything about Pozzo resembles our image of the ringmaster of circus and Lucky as a trained or performing animal. Like a ringmaster, Pozzo arrives brandishing a whip, which is the trademark of the professional. In fact, we hear the cracking of Pozzo's whip before we actually see him.

In the Act-II, we see this relationship in an entirely different pose. Pozzo of Act-I is vain and egotistical. He behaves with tramps as well as with Lucky like a lord. While in

Act-II Pozzo is blind and helpless. He needs Lucky to show him the way and is now dependent on him. Little wonder, therefore, that we no longer hear him talk of disposing of his slave. He can no longer command. Rather than driving Lucky as he did earlier, he is now pathetically dragged along by Lucky. From a position of omnipotence and strength and confidence, he has fallen and has become the complete fallen man who maintains that time is irrelevant and that man's existence is meaningless.

In Pozzo, Beckett displays the operation of authority. He shows how power is won and kept, and at the same time, he demonstrates the viciousness and violence of rulers. Pozzo is powerful because he assumes power and because he knows how to wheedle others into his drama, whether by force or flattery. He wants servants and an audience to satisfy his every move, walking standing or sitting to make his figure into the "natural" centre of landscape.

Lucky, the bottom of the packing order in this drama must take much of blame for making the muck- heap on which they all now live. White haired, shaky legged sick, confused of speech in Act-I and dumb in Act-II, his role is to support Pozzo and all that belong to him. His very existence in the drama is a parody of human existence. In Act-II when he arrives completely dumb, it is only a fitting extension of his condition in Act-I, where his speech was virtually incomprehensible. Now he makes no attempt to utter and sound at all. Whatever part of man Lucky represents, we can make the general observation that, he as man is reduced to leading the blind, not by intellect, but by blind instinct.

Thus together they, Pozzo and Lucky, represent the antithesis of each other. Any number of Polarities could be used to apply to them. If Pozzo is the master, then Lucky is the slave. If Pozzo is it circus ringmaster, then Lucky is the performing, trained animal. If Pozzo is the sadist, Lucky is masochist, or Pozzo can be seen as the Ego and Lucky asid.

4. Discuss the importance of parallelism in Samuel Beckett's Waiting for Godo

In "Waiting for Godot", Samuel Becket has portrayed a dismal and shocking condition of man. Becket has used pairing and parallels in establishing the relationships of the characters in such a way as to project the miserable plight of man. There are three pairs of characters: primarily, the attachment between Vladimir and Estragon, intermittently, the association between Pozzo and Lucky, and the relationship between the tramps and the mysterious character, Godot. As a result of these relationships, the playwright is successful in depicting the themes of paralysis, delusion ignorance, loss of memory and uselessness. The characters and relationships create a sheer sense of loss and chaos. The characters are dependent on each other. The relationships are important in associating rays of hope, sympathy and wit as well. Probably, it is due to these relationships that the characters are able to bear the pain and misery. The impact of time reflects the burden of existence for these characters which is contrasted and reflected in their relationships. The two tramps, Estragon and Vladimir, are parallel to each other. They are waiting for Godot, a mysterious and dubious character symbolizing God. Though they are identical and comparable in several aspects, yet they are different personalities having the same sense of loss and painful existence. Vladimir is a strong and shielding friend. He is helpful to Estragon. He seems a bit responsible. Estragon is an emotional fellow always complaining and shouting. Estragon is presented in physical pain while Vladimir is silent and thoughtful. For them time has halted. Estragon echoes "Nothing happens, nobody comes, nobody goes, it's awful...". Everything seems to be changing around them but they can't. Estragon remarks: "They all change, only we can't". Both of them convey the sense of human inability to act. They are lost. They are waiting for rescue. They are waiting for some help from Godot. "Only he can" help them. He can get them out of the trouble. Both of them are waiting for ever and ever. Both of them quit. But both of them wait. The two tramps have symbolic significance and are related to human society in general. They may be seen as paralleled (in relationship) to human society. The human race is as lost as the two tramps. There is loss of identity for both of them. Modern man is directed to a vague path leading nowhere; similarly the two tramps are just making the time pass. They have no purpose. They meet. They intend to go. They intend to commit suicide. They have lack of trust. But they do nothing. They profess "every man to his cross" that everyone has to bear the burden of his existence. Though shown intermittently, yet the relationship between Pozzo and Lucky is of grave importance to the overall theme of the play. Pozzo is the master while Lucky is the slave. We find Pozzo, the haves, dragging Lucky by the rope in his neck. Lucky is wounded on his neck. Pozzo is symbolic of the exploitative society. Lucky represents the oppressed, have-nots, bearing the drudgery and inhuman treatment of Pozzo. This has reduced Lucky to a mere animal. Pozzo feeds Lucky with the bones and leftovers of food. He carries the burden of Pozzo's luggage all the time. He is beaten by Pozzo. Pozzo is so cruel to Lucky that he calls him "pig" and "hog". Pozzo wants to sell Lucky at a fair. But we find him serving Pozzo very faithfully even when Pozzo has gone blind. Lucky appears to be devoid of any human feelings except for a couple of instances. The dead feelings of Pozzo depict the hopelessness of the depressed modern man

The contrast between the two pairs of characters brings out the compulsion of being together. Though the loneliness of the characters can be felt quite vividly, yet none of the characters can remain alone. Estragon threatens to quit the relationship but he cannot. He is even afraid of committing suicide alone. He needs a companion and a protector. Pozzo wants to sell Lucky, he is desirous of getting rid of Lucky. But at the same time he does not do so. Lucky is the most pitiable object in the play but he seems to have gone immune to the pain and misery he has been through. He is comparable to Estragon and Vladimir in his helpless situation. Vladimir and Estragon are desperately waiting for some messiah to rescue them but Lucky has gone "dumb" and utters no word by the end of the play. The blindness of Pozzo is quite significant as well. The characters appear to be stranded in this world. "They give birth astride of a grave, the light gleams an instant, then it's night once more." Pozzo and Lucky represent the dull and drain reality which is very cruel and painful. It reminds us of the burden of existence without hope and any savior while Estragon and Vladimir are the flashing hope which is vague and uncertain. It sinks into darkness every now and then. But firmness in the two tramps illuminates the hope of salvation which is badly needed in human society. The relationship established between Godot and the tramps fulfills the need and presence of God in the overall scheme of the play. Though the wait for the help of God is always on, yet in "Waiting for Godot" the actual support never comes but always imminent and expected. This situation is also highlighted and contrasted by the relationships between the characters of Vladimir and Estragon; they are always quitting but never quit. They are always breaking off the relationship but they don't.

5. Analysis the characters Vladimir and Estragon in Samuel Beckett's Waiting for Godot

Estragon

Since, in "Waiting for Godot", Samuel Becket has portrayed a dismal and shocking condition of man; therefore, it was mandatory for him to create the exact and shocking parallels to his theme. The character of Estragon and Vladimir suits the theme though both of them appal us all with their image of man as well as mankind. Estragon is the real lost one who receives the blows regularly and spends the night in some ditch and begins a new the next day. There seems no change of routines for him throughout the play. He is dependent upon Vladimir for everything including his defence and survival but he still unable to bear the conversation of Vladimir: "Don't touch me! Don't question me! Don't speak to me! Stay with me!" There is no sense of time and place to especially to the character of Estragon. He remembers nothing at all. He doesn't recall of having reached the placed yesterday. He can't even recollect of having left his shoes. He does not even remember Bible. While Vladimir is referring to the incident of two thieves and being saving of the one, Estragon is unable to understand the meaning of what Vladimir says. He asks for details but finding no answer thinks it is about their birth. Vladimir laughs and asks if he ever read Bible and the reply is: "I must have taken a look at it". They discuss about Gospels and Estragon remembers nothing about the book except the map of the holy city. The loss of memory is accompanied by excess of fear for Estragon. He is always afraid and in a sense of pain. Through the mocking episodes of pain and fall of man's glory what we feel for Estragon is the image of human decadence and deteriorating complexities of man's being. Even existence loses meaning in all such circumstances: "We always find something to give us the impression we exist". Well, there is just impression and what about reality! The character of Estragon helps in building the theme of association and society. He cannot survive alone. It is unbearable to be lonely and without society. The role of society, in the form of Vladimir, encourages him to exist and survive though in the words of Vladimir: "To every man his little cross. Till he dies. And is forgotten." So, they are born to die with no purpose and no meaning to their life at all. This is the

Vladimir

In "Waiting for Godot", Samuel Becket's portrayal of Vladimir is to give vent to a dying rim of light, a sort of hope, in contrast with the dismal and shocking condition of man . Vladimir is the sort of character used by Becket to develop the theme by use of pairing and parallels in establishing the relationships of the characters in such a way as to project the miserable plight of man. In comparison to Estragon, Vladimir is quite strong whether it be saving Estragon or it comes to the basic purpose of them being there. It is him that keeps on reminding Estragon that they are waiting for Godot, a mysterious personality supposed to help them out of their terrible condition. Vladimir, though quite different from his parallel Estragon, is not strong of memory either. Though he does remember that they are waiting for Godot but he cannot recall the day Godot is supposed to come. Nor does he remember where he exactly said he would come. Even the time and place is not certain. What he remembers is that Godot would come tomorrow. Therefore, they are waiting for him. He keeps on reminding Estragon that they must wait for Godot though: "He didn ' t say for sure he'd come. " He is similar to Estragon is several aspects including the loss of memory as well the concept of them being lost to the stage where there is very little chance of their survival even if they repent. He proposes Estragon that they should have committed suicide in the days gone by when they had little respect left: "Hand in hand from the top of the Eiffel Tower, among the first. We were respectable in those days. Now it's too late. They wouldn't even let us up." Vladimir is also a ray of hope in the play because he is the only character that remembers something. He is the one that talks of hope and betterment. Only he talks about repentance and redemption though he does admit that chances are little and "It's too much for one man." He too, is unaware of the notion of time. When he comes back to the same place where it was a bare tree "yesterday"; he claims to have separated from Estragon just for one night whereas we can observe the tree has got new leaves and this is not possible in a single night. However, his character is quite strong in comparison to all other characters in the play. He does represent the entire mankind and the little hope with them: "But at this place, at this moment of time, all mankind is us, whether we like it or not. Let us make the most of it, before it is too late!" But unfortunately, he does nothing but to profess that :

6. Discuss the idea of the meaningless of time in Waiting for Godot.

Belonging to the theatre of the absurd, the play, "Waiting for Godot" by Samuel Becket is considered the mirror to the modern man's state of chaotic sense of loss and senselessness in an era of confusion and decadence. The playwright depicts the irrelevance of time where human suffering has reached the climax of it's existence. Two tramps are introduced as miserable creatures repeating the tiresome exercise of waiting for Godot without any change in routine. The characters are, primarily, two tramps that seem to represent human destiny in a vague manner while the two tramps are fatigued of being humans anymore. They are tired and exhausted.

"Waiting for Godot" is a tragic play with two acts depicting the unbearable miserable condition of modern man. There are two tramps; Estragon and Vladimir. They are subject to an apparently endless wait expecting some sort of help from Godot but he does not come except for a vague promise that Godot will come tomorrow. Nothing is certain or clearer in the play

In Waiting for Godot, time is elusive and difficult to pin down. Both Act I and Act II, which have the same beginning and the same ending, occur in the same place at the same time of day. At the end of each act a boy arrives to inform the men that Godot will not arrive but will surely come tomorrow. In this repetitive pattern, everything has happened many times and chances are the pattern will repeat itself, perhaps endlessly, unless Godot ever does in fact arrive and save them. For Vladimir and Estragon, this repetition demonstrates the meaningless of time. Just like the day before, each day has the same purpose—to wait for an unknown someone who never comes. The men cannot tell one day from another: "I don't remember having met anyone yesterday. But tomorrow I won't remember having met anyone today. So don't count on me to enlighten you" (58). When Vladimir questions Estragon, "so, what did we do last night," Estragon replies "yesterday evening we spent blathering about nothing in particular. That's been going on now for half a century" (41).

Thus, because of this remarkable lack of change, time has no meaning, and if yesterday was meaningless, and the days before yesterday were also meaningless, then time itself must indeed be meaningless. The meaningless of time, Beckett would argue, can be applied to the plight of all of humankind.

In Waiting for Godot, what would Samuel Beckett determine is the meaning of human life?

The play begins with the appearance of two tramps on a road with a single tree. Time is evening and the two of them express joy for having met again while none of them shows anything more than mere pretence in words. Estragon remains busy in either taking off his shoe or putting back it on because it hurts him. His shoe does not fit him well. And Vladimir keeps on discussing the chances of survival for human beings are very small. Both of them fight, argue, abuse each other but stay together: "Don't touch me! Don't question me! Don't speak to me! Stay with me!" The playwright literally creates such a scope of nothingness in the life of the characters that: "Nothing happens, nobody comes, nobody goes, it's awful!" The two tramps find themselves lost and their memory is very weak. They commit strange and odd things. They appear very shabby and poor. They seek repentance and want to change their condition but they feel they are unable to do so: "Very likely. They all change. Only we can't" Lucky and Pozzo happen to cross the same road where the two tramps are sitting on a mound. Pozzo, a rich man, treats his servant Lucky no less than an animal. Every act of Lucky is considered as meant for pleasing Pozzo. His labours mean nothing to Pozzo, a symbol of inhuman behaviour attributed to modern man. This visit also exposes the financial weakness of the two tramps that are willing to eat even the bones thrown by rich Pozzo. The fight for bones may also be considered the gloomy failure of human civilization. "The tears of the world are a constant quantity. For each one who begins to weep, somewhere else another stops." The characters seem to have either no memory or a very weak sense of it. Pozzo does not remember to have met the two tramps before: "I don't remember having met anyone yesterday. But tomorrow I won't remember having met anyone today. So don't count on me to enlighten you." The two tramps entertain themselves with conversation, dull, blank, boring as well as sensational words but they do nothing. They even talk about suicide but action is not meant for them. Probably, they mean nothing but to show the burden of existence: "To every man his little cross. Till he dies. And is forgotten." The two tramps keep on waiting for Godot who never comes; however, messenger comes from him giving the message that he would come tomorrow. And the two tramps believe: "We always find something to give us the impression we exist" and they also associate their state of being to the modern man's existence:" But at this place, at this moment of

In Waiting for Godot, Beckett argues that questions regarding the purpose of human life are unanswerable. And, since there is no apparent meaning to life, as humans we are left miserable in an indifferent universe. This dark but absurd existentialist stance forces us then to impose meaning and purpose on our actions and events, not only to soothe our distress and overwhelming sense of helplessness, but also to provide distractions while we await death.

Life, the play insists, is determined by chance. Pozzo responds to Vladimir: "I woke up one fine day as blind as Fortune (56)." Vladimir and Estragon discuss the parable of the two thieves who were crucified next to Jesus: "one of the thieves was saved," he says, "it's a reasonable percentage" (2). The notion that the thief was saved by chance suggests a random universe where life is arbitrary and just a matter of unpredictable chance.

After all is said and done, there is no meaning to Vladimir and Estragon's lives. They live without predictable patterns of time and action. The tree in Act I is "black and bare" and then in Act II it is covered with leaves. How much time has elapsed, days, seasons, years, is anyone's guess (41). Despite Vladimir and Estragon's prayers, pleadings, threats and supplications for Godot to come and save them, an outcome which would give meaning to all that incessant waiting, day after day, Godot fails to show. Indeed, the plot seems to be, like Beckett's idea of life, "without form and void," or if you will, absolutely meaningless.

7. In Act II, Vladimir sings a song about a dog who "stole a crust of bread" (34). Discuss how Beckett utilizes this song to emphasize his idea of repetitiveness in Waiting for Godot.

Vladimir's song at the beginning of Act II underlines the repetitiveness of life. In the song, a dog comes into the kitchen and steals a crust of bed. The cook beats him with a ladle until he is dead. Subsequently other dogs bury their canine friend, with an epitaph warning "for the eyes of dogs to come," after which the ditty begins immediately again in circular fashion. The song can be repeated without change forever.

Although it could be argued that the dog in Vladimir's dog song is analogous to Lucky, who after all "might run amuck any minute," who eats bones and whom Vladimir and Estragon contemplate giving "a good beating," Beckett would have us believe that this song is representative, first, of the repetitive nature of the play and, second, of Vladimir and Estragon's circular lives (51).

Like the dogs in the song, the individual events in the men's lives follow each other endlessly while they wait for Godot who never comes. They are caught in a never ending cycle unable to do anything else or go anywhere else because of this incessant waiting for a man who never appears. The sun will go down, the moon will rise and they will continue, unable to break out of their circular lives.

Lengthy Questions with Answers

1. Do you think Futility, Hopelessness and Meaninglessness are Central Forces leading towards Absurdity in Beckett's Waiting for Godot?

Samuel Beckett, an eminent Irish writer was closely linked with a consciously conceived movement known as "Theatre of the Absurd" that focused on the abandonment of conventional dramatic form to portray the futility of human struggle in a meaningless world. From the beginning, he was fascinated by such innovative formal design employed in the drama. In a seemingly strange play Waiting for Godot, Beckett has depicted the external world as menacing, devouring and unknown. Also he has painted the world that is incoherent, queer and frightening.

Through the play, Beckett has established the idea that if the world is devoid of logic and reason, then man"s inhabitation in such a world becomes purposeless. The fundamental convention on which the play is based is that the spectators are treated as virtually absent in order that they communicate and sustain the illusion that the dramatized world that consisted of characters, situations, problems, physical environment was „real". The purpose was to let the spectators identify themselves uncritically with the dramatized experience and view the play not from within but from outside as advocated by Bertolt Brecht in his concept of „epic" theatre.

The keynote to the play Waiting for Godot appears in the memorable words uttered by Estragon with regard to his own life and that of his friend Vladimir, "Nothing happens, nobody comes, nobody goes, it's awful!" (71) The play presents anxiety, despair and sense of loss at the disappearance of solutions, lack of commitment and dearth of perseverance on the part of human beings who are in turn left bewildered, troubled and threatened by powerful forces prevalent inthe society.

The plot of the play Waiting for Godot revolves around two tramps Estragon (Gogo) and

Vladimir (Didi) waiting for the arrival of unknown Godot. As the play begins, both the tramps are shown sitting on a low mound near a tree on a country road waiting impatiently for Godot.

They try to kill time in several ways. When in spite of waiting for long hours, Godot does not

come, Estragon suggests that they should go away from the spot, but Vladimir objects to it and refuses to go since Godot has not arrived yet. They indulge in nostalgic retreat and compare their past experience with the current state of affairs.

Vladimir is curious to know what Godot has to offer to them because only then, they would be able to understand whether they should accept the offer or refuse it. They are hopeful that this mysterious character Godot will in some way change their lives for the better. But irony is that they neither know the time nor place of their appointment with Godot. Also they do not know how exactly Godot looks like. Estragon and Vladimir believe that Godot will give their lives a purpose and a meaning. Through the characters of two tramps, Beckett suggests the mental state of human beings who continue to live in a cherished dream hoping for its fulfillment at some time in future. But when their dreams are shattered, they concoct another dream and the process continues. The person keeps on waiting for the „right" time which does not come and he is entangled in a web of illusion.

The truth that "The essential doesn't change" (51) and therefore "Nothing to be done"

(51) hovers throughout the play. Vladimir asks Estragon to become alert since he predicts from the sounds of shouting that Godot has come, but to their disappointment, Godot is not seen anywhere. The sound was in fact that of the wind blowing through the reeds. After a while, two other characters Pozzo and Lucky make their appearance at the place. Pozzo drives Lucky by means of a rope tied around his neck. Lucky is carrying a number of articles of his master. Pozzo holds a whip in his hand to control Lucky. He behaves violently with his slave Lucky and jerks the rope so brutally that Lucky falls down with all the baggage in his hands. When Estragon and

Vladimir show their willingness to give a helping hand to Lucky, they are warned by Pozzo that Lucky is wicked in his behavior with strangers. Through Pozzo, Beckett has targeted the elite class of people of society who exploit the lower class people ruthlessly and mercilessly. The excruciating pain through which Lucky undergoes reminds the reader of the callous and sadistic people who derive delight in torturing others by making their lives miserable.

Beckett has revealed the gruesome and frightening aspect of rich people through the character of Pozzo who treats a person not as a human being but as a dumb animal fated to suffer silently.

The bitter aspect of life towards which Beckett has drawn our attention is that a person is valued till he works efficiently and proves his efficacy, but once his energies diminish, he is

abandoned like a scrap. His lifelong dedication and allegiance is soon forgotten as his place is filled by another suitable alternative. When Pozzo and Lucky depart, Vladimir remarks that the visit of these two men had enabled them to pass the time. Estragon says that time would have passed in any case. Vladimir says that time would certainly have passed but not so rapidly. Estragon asks Vladimir what they should do now; Vladimir replies that he does not know. Reacting to the suggestion proffered by Estragon to go away from the spot, Vladimir vehemently objects, "We're waiting for Godot" (78)

A boy now appears on the scene. The boy timorously approaches Vladimir and asks him if he is Mister Albert. Vladimir answers in the affirmative. Estragon asks the boy harshly why he is so late in coming. The boy says that he was afraid of facing the situation. Vladimir tells Estragon that the boy was afraid of "the whip" and "the roars" and "the two big men". Estragon refuses to believe the boy and shaking him by the arm, asks him to come out with the truth. But the boy, trembling with fear, says that what he has said is true. At Vladimir's intervention, Estragon releases the boy and moves away. Vladimir asks the boy if he recognizes him, but the boy refuses. Vladimir asks him if he had come to the same spot yesterday, the boy once again refuses. The boy then says that Mr. Godot had asked him to tell him (Vladimir or Mr. Albert) that Mr. Godot will not come this evening but "surely tomorrow". In reply to other questions, the boy answers that he works for Mr. Godot, looks after his goats, while his brother looks after Mr. Godot's sheep. He also tells that Mr. Godot beats the boy's brother though not the boy.

Moreover Mr. Godot feeds the boy fairly well as against his brother whom he mistreats. When Vladimir asks the boy whether he is happy, the boy replies that he does not know. After a while Vladimir asks the boy to go to Mr. Godot and "Tell him you saw us" (82). The boy leaves the place.

Once again the problem of passing time evolves. Vladimir tells Estragon that they have nothing more to do here. Estragon replies that they have nothing more to do anywhere. Vladimir consoles his friend and advises him not to talk like that because tomorrow things will change and the „situation will become better'. Vladimir reminds Estragon of boy's message that Godot is sure to come tomorrow. As they wait, Vladimir also acquiesces with Estragon that they should go from there. Both decide to go but do not move from the place. The first Act of the play ends here. The incident emphasizes the seamier side of life when human beings become restless; give up hope and throw their arms against the cruel forces of Time. But Time once again intercepts and does not let them act as per their wishes. Hope keeps their lives moving and they again prepare themselves to face the situation.

Estragon asks Vladimir to tell him what he should do. Vladimir replies, "There is nothing to do". (104). Vladimir suggests that they can do certain physical exercises to kill time. Estragon uses the words "movements" and "relaxations" whereas Vladimir uses the terms "elevations" and "elongations" (106) for workouts. As they get tired, they stop their exercises and relax. Pozzo and Lucky now reappear. Pozzo has turned blind while Lucky is carrying the same burden as before. Both the tramps mistake Pozzo and Lucky for Godot.

A strong hope ushers in Vladimir and Estragon that their restless days are over and they will be able to see the bright morning again. But their hope crashes as they find that it is not

Godot but Pozzo and Lucky who left yesterday and have come back again. Since Pozzo has

become blind, he shouts for help, and keeps on shouting at brief intervals whereas Estragon and Vladimir do not pay any heed to him and remain engaged in their conversation. Hearing Pizza's incessant cry for help, Estragon demands a price for the help to be extended. The two tramps help Pozzo to his feet but when they release him, he falls down again. Vladimir remarks that Pozzo used to have good eyesight in the past. To that Pozzo replies that it is true but one fine day when he woke up, he found himself blind as Fortune. Vladimir reminds him that till yesterday, he had good eyesight. Pozzo retorts, "Don't question me! The blind have no notion of time"(116)Pozzo asks Estragon regarding his slave Lucky. Vladimir informs him that he and his slave had slipped and fallen down. When asked by Pozzo about their state of affairs, Estragon answers that they are waiting for Godot. Pozzothen asks Estragon to go and kick his slave Lucky "in the face and the privates" (117) in order to rouse him to action. It shows Pozzo's cruelty even in the event of extremity when he has turned blind and has to depend upon Lucky. When Vladimir asks Pozzo if he remembers having met anybody on the previous day,Pozzo declines and says that he does not remember yesterday's events. A little later Pozzo jerks the rope entwined round Lucky"s neck and orders the dumb slave to move on. Pozzo and Lucky leave the place. After their departure, Vladimir shakes Estragon to wake him up as he had fallen asleep and he (Vladimir) was feeling lonely.

At this time, a messenger boy arrives and addresses Vladimir as Mr. Albert. The boy gives no indication that he recognizes Vladimir. In fact, the boy says that he has come for the first time. The boy informs Vladimir that Godot will not come this evening but that he will come on the following day. On being asked what Godot does, the boy replies, "He does nothing, sir" (121) Vladimir asks if it was the boy"s brother who came yesterday, the boy says that he does not know. On learning that Godot has a beard, a white one, Vladimir emphatically utters, "Christ have mercy on us!" (122) Vladimir asks the boy to tell Godot that he (the boy) had seen him (Vladimir). Seeing Vladimir rushing towards him annoyingly, the boy runs away from there.

Once again the night falls and Estragon suggests that they should go far away from there.

But Vladimir replies that they cannot go away as they have to be at this very place on the

following day in order to wait for Godot. Estragon asks what would happen if they do not waitfor Godot, then Vladimir replies that Godot will in that case punish them. Vladimir now asks Estragon if they should go, Estragon immediately gives his consent. But they do not move and remain there only. The play ends at a note when Estragon and Vladimir are still waiting for Godot who never comes.

Pozzo – Lucky Relationship

Pozzo-Lucky relationship depicted by Beckett is suggestive of incarnate Time's twin qualities of change and changelessness. Pozzo and Lucky are the only characters in the play who undergo a change. Pozzo changes from his „wonderful sight' to complete blindness and Lucky from a teacher of „beautiful things' (63) to an incoherent babbler; from a speaking animal to a dumb automation who cannot even groan. These changes signify Time that moves unceasingly and inexorably towards loss, devitalization and death. The ironic aspect is that life itself is devalued as a brief flash of light that „gleams an instant' between birth and death. On the level of collective existence and experience too, human time is perceived as a devitalizing process in which man continues to „waste and pine'. The changelessness of Time in cyclic fashion is signified by Pozzo and Lucy's perpetual wanderings. Travelling has become a deadening habit with them. They give an impression that they are going somewhere, but actually they are going round and round in a circle. They are in fact ambushed in this circular time of the universe.

Pozzo represents the physical aspect of the human personality and Lucky the spiritual, which in the course of time is desensitized by the harsh treatment he receives by his master Pozzo. Lucky is reduced to inarticulateness; his sudden outburst is observed when his "thinking

hat" is put on his head. Pozzo in the course of time turns blind indicating the transience of

human power and domination. In the play, Beckett also incorporates minor themes such as the inadequacy of human language as a means of communication along with the illusionary concepts of past and future. He has emphasized the fact that the waiting of two tramps is mechanical; in other words, it is a compulsion. They have to wait there even though they resent from doing so and would earnestly like to leave. It is possibly the moral obligation that they are forced to act in a manner contrary to their wish since it involves the possibilities of punishment and reward. If Godot comes, a new chapter would be added into their existence whereas if they leave, they will certainly miss him. Their waiting contains an element of hope, no matter how skeptical they may be about it. They are the champions of the view that life must be meaningful in spite of evidently meaningless situation. The pitiful struggle which the two tramps engage in mirrors our own fate, the fate of multitudes of modern men.

Plight of Modern Worker in Post Modern Era

Through the mechanization of labour, the worker of the postmodern era is deprived of the

opportunity of recognition of his work which has resulted in the reduction of his work to a sheer mock activity. The modern European literature, especially since the First World War, respond to a world that appears to be splitting apart and becoming increasingly meaningless in the wake of the brutal advance of capitalism, rampant individualism and the consequent loss of community, large scale destruction due to the world wars, threat of a nuclear holocaust and the disappearance of the liberal traditions of hope and faith in man"s innate goodness, progress and rationality.

The modern worker has become so exhausted due to the laborious mechanical activity that he now feels a strong urge to restore his equilibrium during his leisure time by engaging himself in substitute activities and hobbies. The modern worker has become deprived of his ability to shape his leisure hours by doing some obsolete forms of production like maintaining terrace garden, preparing some decorative craft or indulging in painting and singing or engaging self in some do-it-yourself carpentering. The situations have so changed that a modern worker Finds great affinity between his working time and leisure time as both occur simultaneously. For instance, in millions of homes and factories, the flow of work and the flow of the radio

transmission are becoming one single stream. In the Postmodern era, the 21st century worker

experiences that the working time and leisure time, activity and indolence, real life and playing have become so closely inter-twined that they have become virtually inseparable. A large number of people increasingly feel that they live in a world in which they do not act but are acted upon. In spite of their inaction and pointlessness of their existence, they do not give up and strive to lead the life with a hope of a better future.

Conclusion

The play Waiting for Godot presents an essential characteristic of the human condition which emphasizes the fact that most often people wait for something which does not materialize just as Godot does not arrive. A man may vainly wait for a job, or promotion or long awaited transfer, or message from a dear friend, or a love letter or a reunion with a divorced wife, and so on. Vladimir and Estragon by their indefinitely waiting without any concrete result symbolize the psyche of millions of human beings who wait for some thing or the other without attaining it. People in the Post Modern era have become victims of the dominance of their superiors who exploit them for gaining personal benefit. This has resulted in depression, frustration and psychological ailments in the modern man. In spite of mechanical and pessimistic life that they are compelled to lead, they move on with a hope that God (Godot) will come to their rescue and transform their lives. The play in this sense gathers universal validity as it touches the chord of every heart of modern man.

2. Discuss Samuel Beckett's Waiting for Godot as an absurd drama

The phrase 'Absurd Drama' or 'The Theatre of Absurd' gained currency after Martin Esslin's book 'The Theatre of Absurd' was published in 1961. Esslin points out that there is no such thing as a regular movement of Absurd dramatists. The term is useful as "A device to make certain fundamental traits which seem to be present in the works of a number of dramatists accessible to discussion by tracing the features they have in common." By 'Absurd', Camus meant a life lived solely for its sake in a universe which no longer made sense because there was no God to resolve the contradictions. In other words, what Camus called 'absurd', Kierkegaard called 'Despair'. And it is on this philosophy that Beckett created his famous play 'Waiting for Godot'. Before the genre of Absurd Drama gained popularity in the hands of Beckett, Adamov, Ionesco and Gennet, plays were characterized by clearly constructed story and subtlety of characterization and motivation. However, the absurd plays were characterized by non specific unrecognizable characters who are presented almost like mechanical puppets. These dramas speak to a deeper level of the audience's mind. It challenges the audience to make sense of non-sense, to face the situation consciously and perceive with laughter the fundamental absurdity.

Samuel Beckett's 'Waiting for Godot' belongs to the tradition of the Theatre of Absurd. It is unconventional in not depicting any dramatic conflicts. In the play, practically nothing happens, no development is to be found, there is no beginning and no end. The entire action boils down in an absurd setting of a country side road with two tramps Vladimir and Estragon who simply idle away their time waiting for Godot, about whom they have only vague ideas. They have nothing substantial to tell each other and yet they must spend the time, for they cannot stop waiting. Two other characters, a cruel master called Pozzo and his half-crazy slave called Lucky appear. Eventually a boy arrives with a message that Godot will arrive the next day. The two tramps decide to go away, but they do not move and the curtain falls, eventually nothing happens. The second act is the replica of the first act, but Pozzo is now blind and Lucky is dumb. The wait of Vladimir and Estragon continues but in despair. This monotony characterized the world after the wars and this condition was captured and depicted in the Theatre of Absurd.

The Absurd theatre delt with a deeper layer of absurdity--- the absurdity of the human condition itself in a world where the decline of religious belief has deprived man of certainties. Like the waiting between birth and death in Gelber's plays, Beckett's 'Waiting for Godot', is also about an absurd wait. According to Martin Esslin, the Theatre of Absurd projected a situation where it was "no longer possible to accept simple and complete systems of values and revelations of divine purpose." Life was projected to face its "ultimate stark reality." What the existential philosopher Kierkegaard believed that "we are thrown into existence here and there", is reflected in the theatre of absurd. And Beckett's 'Waiting for Godot' reveals this stark reality of human existence through the characters of the two tramps.

Beckett's deliberate efforts result in displaying the presence of Vladimir and Estragon on the bare stage stripped of any social position or historical context. The barren stage stands symbolic to the universe where the two tramps are thrown to confront with the basic situations of their existence and undergo through the dilemma of choices and expectations. And this situation ultimately makes Vladimir and Estragon passive and impotent before time. Thus they surrender themselves to the 'absurd waiting' for Godot. Often they grow tedious of the wait and decide to go but they fail as they say :

Estragon:- I'm tired! Let's go.

Vladimir:- We can't Estragon:- why not

Vladimir:- We are waiting for Godot. (Act 1)

The theatre of Absurd is a post world war creation. It is a creation and a search for a way of relief after the two terrible wars. This provided a dignified way for the people to confront the universe deprived of what was once its centre and its living purpose----the God and faith. Beckett also unfolded "Waiting for Godot" with similar view. The title itself is suggestive that the play deals with a prolong wait and the waiting of the two tramps is for Godot. When Beckett was asked who Godot was, he replied, "If I knew, I would have said so in the play." Such a reply forced the critics to offer varied interpretations of the identity of Godot. The very word 'Godot' is suggestive of a weakened or diminutive form of the word 'God'. In fact, the French version of the play "En Attendant Godot", seems to contain an allusion to a book "Attente de Dieu", which further supplies evidence that 'Godot' stands for God.

Beckett very tactfully highlighted some religious references to figure out God as whimsical, partial and capricious. The Biblical story of salvation of one thief and damnation of the other is although narrated as babblings by Vladimir to while away the time, actually raises question on God's partial nature. The messenger who works for Godot, lets Vladimir know that Godot executes physical tortures to his brother, a shepherd, for no reasons. This episode of the play instantaneously draws the readers' attention to the Biblical story of Cane and Able. And pathetic enough one of the brothers receives the Lord's grace without any rational explanation. However, at the same time, Beckett in his play projected the supremacy of Godot and the futile dependence of man on a supreme power. Vladimir and Estragon tell about Godot to Pozzo, whom they took to be Godot :-

Estragon:- . . . we hardly know him

Vladimir:- True . . . we don't know him very well . . . (Act 1)

Godot's identity is in veil to Vladimir and Estragon , and yet they expect their future to be molded on Godot's arrival. Pozzo's utterance gives us an insight tp the minds of the two tramps about Godot.

Pozzo:- . . . Godet . . . Godot . . . Godin . . .

Any how you see who I mean, who has your future in his hand . . . at least your immediate future. (Act 1).

Beckett proves to completely abide by the views of the theatre of Absurd while Constructing his monumental play 'Waiting for Godot'. The dramatists of Absurd theatre were influenced by what Nietzsche said in "Zarathustra" that "God is dead." And at the end, Beckett left a remarkable question mark on the existence of God. However till the end of the play, Godot never turns up, but keeps on procrastinating his visit to which the two tramps eagerly look forward.

The theatre of Absurd is concerned with projecting the author's personal world and so the plays lack objectivity and valid characters. Unlike the communicable social and moral lessons Brecht's narrative epic theatre, Beckett's 'Waiting for Godot' being an Absurd play, does not intend to narrate a story. Rather, 'Waiting for Godot' communicates in a pattern of poetic images. Beckett unfolds the play with a nihilistic approach. Right with the opening dialogue,

Estragon:- Nothing to be done. (Act 1).

The hovering of pessimism in the play comes to the very fore. The tramps suffer a state of vagueness and uncertainty. Although they wait for Godot, they are uncertain of his identity, they are neither sure whether they are waiting in the right place and on the right day, nor do they know what would happen if Godot came. Their ignorance reaches the highest peack as they have no watches , no time-tables and to add to the worse, there is none to fetch them information. There expectation from The hovering of pessimism in the play comes to the very fore. The tramps suffer a state of vagueness and uncertainty. Although they wait for Godot, they are uncertain of his identity, they are neither sure whether they are waiting in the right place and on the right day, nor do they know what would happen if Godot came. Their ignorance reaches the highest peack as they have no watches , no time-tables and to add to the worse, there is none to fetch them information. There expectation from Godot is neither definite:-

Vladimir:- Oh . . . nothing very definite.

Estragon:- A kind of prayer

Vladimir:- Precisely

Estragon:- A vague supplication.

Theatre of Absurd captures the stasis in which the world had fallen after the wars. 'Waiting for Godot' reflects this stasis through the act of endless waiting of the two tramps. The ignorance leads the tramps in a state of impotence. A sense of baffled helplessness is produced as the tramps are forced to remain in a situation which is beyond their control. They indulge in triffles merely as stop-gaps to help pass the time. The waiting is the outcome of ignorance and impotence. And the triffles are the only source to realize and prove their existence as Estragon said, " . . . We always find something , eh Didi, to give us the impression we exist."

The title of the play is of immense significance in reflecting the genre of Absurd theatre.

The play is a superb construction of the dominant action of time and its experience by man. Throughout the play, nothing really happens, and the change is in itself an illusion. Structurally the play is of two acts and the second act is the replica of the first. The play is the dramatization of the themes of habit, boredom and monotony. Out of boredom and monotony 0f waiting in Act 1,

Estragon says :- "Nothing happens ,nobody comes, nobody goes, it's awful."

Habit, boredom, monotony, ignorance and impotence which enveloped the world after the wars and created an absurd existence, is recreated by Beckett in "Waiting for Godot." Beckett captured this situation and depicted it through the deadening condition of the two tramps in a null and void state without any real action. The play has often been interpreted as a parable where Godot stands as God, or for a mythical human being or for the meaning of life, death or something eventful.

3. Write an essay on the existentialism in Samuel Beckett's Waiting for Godot

Samuel Beckett's play Waiting for Godot can be gathered in the category of Existential Drama. All the four characters Estragon , VLADIMIR, Lucky, Pozzo in an absurd way discuss the problems of existence. As is shown they are waiting for an unknown person 'Godot' at an unknown place. They suffer from meaninglessness, isolation, and frustration. As it happens no Godot comes but ironically a messenger comes who informs that Godot will not come .These characters are fed up of waiting. The word 'waiting' is universalized in the play which is an essential feature of any existential drama. Their antics and useless activities lead them nowhere. This is exactly modern man's predicament that is successfully dramatized by the dramatist. The importance of the play as an existential drama lies in the multiplicity of meanings which critics have discovered in it.

If we try to answer the first question, many answers can be given. Existence is a mass of things, objects, ideas. Interestingly, the second question can have the same answer. It is made of things, objects, ideas and actions. If we come to the third question, we see some power or some energy has caused it to exist. It surely has a purpose and this purpose is up to the humanity what they find. The play ' Waiting For Godot' can be and has many interpretations. The question of existence can be noticed in almost all the dialogues of the play. We see two tramps wait beside a tree for a mysterious figure with whom Vladmir asserts and Estragon believes, they have an appointment. This mysterious figure hopefully will change their position for better. The existentialistic element is visible in this dialogue:

Estragon: Didi.

Vladmir: Yes.

Estragon: I can't go on like this.

Vladmir: That's what you think.

Estragon: If we parted? That might be better for us.

Vladmir: We'll hang ourselves tomorrow. Unless Godot comes.

Estragon: And if he comes?

Vladmir: We'll be saved.

We see human beings on earth always expect somebody to save them from all existential problems.

The play does not tell a story, it explores a static situation. "Nothing happens, nobody comes, nobody goes, it's awful", says Estragon. The two heroes of this play neither recognize their own existence as accidental, nor think of transforming it into something positive with which they can identify themselves. What Beckett presents is not nihilism, but the inability of a man to be a nihilist even in a situation of utter hopelessness. Inspite of their inaction and the pointlessness of their existence, these two tramps still want to go on. Millions of people today do not after all give up living even when their life becomes pointless. Even the nihilist wish to go on living. Ruined by their habit of inaction or of acting without their own initiative, they have lost their will power to decide not to go on. Or ultimately, they go on living merely because they happen to exist and because existence does not know of any other alternative but to exist.

Vladmir: I get used to the muck as I go along.

Estragon(after prolonged reflection): Is that the opposite?

Vladmir: Question of temperament.

Estragon: Of character.

Vladmir: Nothing you can do about it.

Estragon: No use struggling.

Vladmir: One is what one is.

Estragon: No use wriggling.

There is another pair in 'Waiting For Godot' which gives it an existential touch. The speech of Pozzo in the following words is remarkable:

Pozzo: Have you not been tormenting me with your accursed time? It's abominable. When? When? One day, is not that enough for you...? They give birth astride of a grave, the light gleams an instant, then its night once more.

Like many existentialists, Beckett is talking about the problem of boredom and problem of living. Pozzo and Vladmir have both entered" the perilous zone when for a moment the boredom of living is replaced by the suffering of being." Neither of them likes what he sees but both know that there is nothing to be done. "On!" cries Pozzo to Lucky as they make their last exit.

"You must go on, I can't go on, I'll go on," says the unnamable. "I can't go on," repeats Vladmir. The basic problem that afflicts mankind is, 'how to get through life?' Beckett's answer is simple and not encouraging: by force of habit, by going on in spite of boredom and pain, by talking, by not listening to the silence, absurdly and without hope. The only consolation man on earth can have to talk about his position or problem but never the solution. Life is to be lived as it is, nothing can be suggested or no change can be brought.

Man's constant search for happiness on this planet has been depicted in the play. In any existence all creatures would seek it. Beckett suggests it in a very effective manner in this conversation of Estragon and Vladmir.

Estragon: I tell you I wasn't doing anything.

Vladmir: Perhaps you weren't. But it's the way of doing it that counts, the way of doing it, if you want to go on living.

Estragon: I wasn't doing anything.

Vladmir: You must be happy, too deep down, if you only knew it.

Estragon: Happy about what?

Vladmir: To be back with me again.

Estragon: Would you say so?

Vladmir: Say you are, even if it's not true.

Estragon: What am I to say?

Vladmir: Say, I am happy.

Estragon: I am happy.

Vladmir: So am I.

Estragon: So am I.

Vladmir: We are happy.

Estragon: We are happy. (silence) What do we do now, now that we are happy?

The problem of everydayness is considered to be a vital issue in existential philosophy. The routine of human beings is such a dull affair that it saps all energy of a man. Man is caught in the web of everyday existence. In the play this problem of everydayness is visible. The second act is almost the repetition of the first act, it is deliberately done.

Vladmir: It's the start that's difficult.

Estragon: You can start from anything.

Vladmir: Yes, but you have to decide.

Estragon: True. Silence

Vladmir: Help me!

Estragon: I'm trying. Silence

Vladmir: When you seek you hear.

Estragon: You do.

Vladmir: That prevents you from finding.

Estragon: It does.

Vladmir: That prevents you from thinking.

Estragon: You think all the same.

So the couple tramp is fed up with the routine life which is too difficult to be handled. This sameness and dullness snatches meaning out of existence.

Another existential trait is visible in the play when Vladmir, Pozzo, Estragon want to leave everything but they cannot, they have to be there.

Estragon: I hear something.

Pozzo: Where?

Vladmir: It's the heart.

Pozzo: Damnation! (disappointed)

Vladmir: Silence!

Estragon: Perhaps it has stopped. They straighten up.

Pozzo: Which of you smells so bad?

Estragon: He has stinking breath and I have stinking feet.

Pozzo: I must go.

Estragon: Then adieu. Pozzo: Adieu.

Vladmir: Adieu. Pozzo: Adieu. Silence. No one moves.

Vladmir: Adieu.

Pozzo: Adieu.

Estragon: Adieu.

Conclusion

We can sum up that 'Waiting For Godot' is an existential drama, as all the four characters are always worried about their lot and try to adjust in the dreary setting of life. They fight with the hopelessness and meaninglessness of life. The uncertainty and unreliability with which Godot surrounds them reveal the existential outlook of the play. At first sight the play does not appear to have any particular relationship with the human predicament. But as we probe through the absurd dialogues we are confronted with the existential element visible in the play. The baffled helplessness of the couple 'Vladimir and Estragon' appeals to us as our own helplessness on earth.

4. Discuss existentialism in Vladimir and Estragon in Samuel Beckett's Waiting for Godot

Vladimir and Estragon are excruciatingly careless in regards to their own condition. They go about repeating their actions each day unaware of the dreariness and imprisonment. They likewise don't enact their brain to address their own particular actions and the thought processes underlying their activities. The "compressed vacuum" in their lives is unvaryingly ignored.

First and foremost mime and tableau, then discourse. Every unit in Act I of the play takes after an expressive superficial action with a conversational trade that first attests something solid about the situation, and after that instantly breaks down that solidity with destructive discourse that comes so rapidly afterward. In the first for example, after the quiet Vladimir spits in nausea at the scent of Estragon's boot, his companion moves to the inside of the stage, ends with his back to the audience, and addresses a remark to the scene: 'charming spot.' Given the stripped scene and the desperation of the characters, each playgoer will smile agreeably at the broad irony here, however what then happens entangles matters impressively. Estragon turns, walks to the front of the stage, faces the audience, and keeps: 'inspiring prospects' – and turning to Vladimir – says 'let's go.'

Vladimir: We can't.

Estragon: Why not?

Vladimir: We're waiting for Godot.

Estragon: (despairingly). Ah! (Pause.) You're sure it was here? (F, 14; G, 10)

On one hand, we are given basic particular informative content: these two seedy men are waiting for somebody named Godot, and Estragon's tone prescribes the plausibility that they have done it before and had been baffled. (In preparations that Beckett coordinated in Berlin and London in 1975 and 1984, the performing artist playing Estragon said 'ah, yes!' rather than simply "Ah!" which affirms the feeling of commonality and disappointed Baziz 17 need.)But the joke pointed at the audience rapidly subverts our certainty that we know the distinction between deception and actuality, a subversion that comes to be progressively more radical as the play goes on. Likewise more intense are ensuing remarks controlled at the observers, who later on are contrasted as agroup with a bog and as and as individuals to corpses and skeletons.

The discussion quickly following the first notice of Godot withdraws any comfort that may have existed in the original statement about waiting. One man says something that he trusts the other will affirm, just to have his companion given occasion to have doubts about whatever thin hope he had basically communicated. The point when Estragon is advised that they should meet Godot close to the tree, he asks what kind of tree it is:

Vladimir: I don't know. A willow.

Estragon: Where are the leaves?

Vladimir: It must be dead.

Estragon: No more weeping.

Vladimir: Or perhaps it's not the season.

Estragon: Looks to me more like a bush.

Vladimir: A shrub. Estragon: A bush.

Vladimir: A—. What are you insinuating? That we've come to the Wrong place? (F, 14; G, 10)

Vladimir's 'i don't know. A willow' is a prototypal occurrence of Beckett's Way of simultaneously attesting and withdrawing significance, and its impact is to describe Vladimir as a genuine skeptic in pursuit of assurance, a man got between obliviousness and a necessity to know. In one appreciation, the willow is just a willow, yet in an additional it capacities as what Antonin Artaud once called 'an enlivened hieroglyphic'. On account of their hanging leaves and frequent area close water, willows are frequently connected with sadness for unrequited love or the loss of a mate. Vladimir's statement that the willow must be dead and Estragon's endeavor to put a closure to sobbing seem a convincing enough enterprise to get past one sort of misfortune; yet the sudden expansion about the probability that this maybe is not the time of year for willows, or that the willow may not indeed be a willow whatsoever, puts the suspicion of mistrust about Godot in yet an alternate and considerably all the more terrifying setting.

Actually, then, space is questioned: this may not be the spot where they are to meet Godot. Then afterward time comes in for its steady cross-examination:

Estragon: And if he doesn't come?

Vladimir: We'll come back tomorrow.

Estragon: And then the day after tomorrow.

Vladimir: Possibly.

Estragon: And so on.

Vladimir: The point is –

Estragon: Until he comes.

Vladimir: You're merciless.

Estragon: We came here yesterday.

Vladimir: Ah no, there you're mistaken.

Estragon: What did we do yesterday?

Vladimir: What did we do yesterday?

Estragon: Yes.

Vladimir: Why . . . (Angrily). Nothing is certain when you're about.

By raising the possibility that Godot may not come, Estragon prompts Vladimir to confirm their relentlessness, yet he needs just to venture the constrained confirmation one day into time to come to uncover its flimsiness and to push his companion into the weaker 'possibly'. Also if tomorrow is questionable, yesterday ends up being more so: not just are they unable to concur that they were here a day prior, yet they can't recall what they did then. With time and the past so unequivocally tossed into inquiry, the main thing that appears to hold its strength is the present. In any case when Vladimir closes 'nothing is sure when you're about', his cleverness word play reminds his companion and us that the present, excessively, rests on a problematic establishment. Toward the conclusion of this normal about the unsteadiness of space and time, the diligent scepticism of Vladimir and Estragon has developed through stylishly executed stichomythic exchange into genuine joke and after that into tumult and alarm, inciting the weary Estragon to call for a truce by inquiring as to whether they may 'stop talking briefly, do you mind?'

In any case to quit talking is to succumb to the silence and the fourth major standard of the first act starts with a mime in which Estragon, having sat down on his mound, floats off into rest, while the frightened Vladimir paces here and there and then here again halting just to gaze off into the cessation of speech as though searching for relief. Unable to endure the end of discourse, he cries out 'gogo! . . . Gogo! . . . Gogo!' to wake his companion up. Estragon, 'restored to the loathsomeness of his situation', needs to escape by portraying a dream he has simply had, however Vladimir in his disturbance won't tune in, a refusal that evokes from Estragon a clearing signal towards the universe and the roaring inquiry: 'this one is sufficient for you?' What takes after is a snappy variety on a by now well-known reaction. Estragon doubts that it may not be better for them to part, and to Vladimir's contemptuous 'you wouldn't go far' he sarcastically replies: 'that might be too awful, truly too terrible . . . At the time you think about the magnificence of the way. Also the goodness of the wayfarers. Wouldn't it, Didi?' Estragon's needling, unexpected utilization of a dialect with scriptural hints presses on to give to the commonplace talk a thunder that serves (as much else does here) to grow the enthusiastic extent and thematic suggestions and to present new pictures and themes that will be rehashed and improved later on.

Right now, a truncated account works in a comparable manner. As their question warms up, Vladimir urges his companion to cool himself; and Estragon energetically gets the word 'calm', strokes it, and inquires as to whether he knows the story of the Englishmen in the brothel. The exchange that accompanies has all the characteristics of an age-old vaudeville schedule. The point when Vladimir concedes he knows the story, Estragon teasingly says 'tell it to me', however when his companion challenges at having been guyed, Estragon unemotionally starts to describe it himself: an inebriated Englishman heads off to a bordello and the madam inquires as to whether he needs 'a reasonable one, a dull one or a red-haired one'. Only then in the depiction, with dazzling timing, Estragon asks his companion to 'go on', yet the bedeviled Vladimir yells 'stop it', and takes off while throwing a mini tantrum.

Right now one can make small a greater amount of the unfinished ribald break, yet the trade about 'do you know the story . . . let it know to me' echoes first experience with the record of the two criminals; and Ruby Cohn reports that in the second demonstration of Beckett's German generation, when Vladimir asks the kid if Mr. Godot's facial hair is reasonable or dark, the German inquiry comes to be 'blonde or . . . (he dithers) dark . . . (he falters) . . . on the other hand red?' (The standard line in English peruses 'fair or . . . (he wavers) . . . on the other hand black?') And Cohn then gives the content of the joke: An Englishman, having tipsy a little more than common, heads off to a massage parlor. The bawd inquires as to whether he needs a reasonable one, a dim one, or a red-haired one. The

Englishman answers that he needs a kid. Stunned, the bawd debilitates to call a policeman, and the Englishman contests: 'oh, no, they're excessively gritty.' along these lines Godot is carried into connection to Gogo's coarse story, comparing – as so regularly in Beckett's play – 'the physical and magical, the foul and ethereal'

As uncovering as this record seems to be, there is no compelling reason to hold up until the close of Act II to perceive how Estragon's bawdy story gives themes for successive unanticipated areas of the play. The fifth significant standard in the early part of Act I starts with a mime in which Estragon signals to hearten the truant Vladimir peeing off stage. Rejoined a couple of minutes after the fact, the two men present their most beloved point – 'what do we do now' – and Estragon recommends that they might as well hang themselves. Vladimir is attracted to the thought in light of the fact that he knows from fables (and maybe from perusing James Joyce's Ulysses) that hanged men of ten get erections.

At the same time hanging in Beckett never works out as conveniently as it may in life or in different books. From companionship and a shockingly refined feeling of noblesse oblige, Vladimir and Estragon cleverly concede to each one in turn and get ensnared in a debate about who is the heavier of the two. After a different trade reminiscent of a scene from a Marx-Brothers film, Estragon strangely gets the better of the contention and prescribes they do nothing, in light of the fact that 'it's safer'.

5. Discuss existentialism in the characters Lucky and Pozzo

Inside the play the significance of the confounding title figure unfolds in distinctive ways. In spite of the fact that the entering Pozzo is sensibly mixed up for Godot (a few qualities make the slip possible and in a few ways tantalizing: the comparable sounding name, the trappings of power, the way that somebody is "tied" to him), he and Lucky import enough importance without anyone else present. From the minute they show up, the howling expert and his shackled slave stand as differentiations to the devastated other couple and appear to exemplify much that is nonattendant in their identities and scenario. Assuming that Vladimir and Estragon are described by their tenuousness – via what they and we don't know of their histories and reason, by the anxious inquiries they ask and the responses denied to them– pozzo and Lucky report themselves quickly as considerable animals of connection and course.

The showy expert radiates power and power; the hampered servant fittingly shows a cowed compliance. 'i present myself: Pozzo . . . Made in God's image!' the whip-wielding figure says and after that gesture with a tyrannical blend of insensitivity and thoughtfulness that seems to reflect a thousand years of inherited run the show. He bluntly tests the two strangers about Godot, is charitable when he studies of their trespassing on his territory, andsettles down pompously to revel in his supper and his funnel. His discourse is stamped by goals, shouts, and influenced apothegms, and he moves here and there and then here again between rave and elocutionary set pieces about the tears of the planet and the foreboding brilliance of the nearby dusk that intrigue in the meantime that they terrify. The slave at the finish of his rope brings and carries on request, practically swoons, however unlike Didi and Gogo never questions his spot.

Vladimir and Estragon are in a flash occupied and abhorrence struck, drawn out of their troubling holding up into the impressive presentation of computed self-presentation. This must be what the planet outside is truly like: all display and surety and altered reason – a sort of considerable theatre. 'i am carrying him to the fair,' says Pozzo of Lucky, 'where I have a specific end goal, which is to get a great cost for him. 'with a dramatic show of such variety and brutality to retain their consideration, Didi and Gogo require not brood about keeping an errand with Godot. At the same time from the begin Pozzo's exhibition is plainly overresolved, and his power is rapidly uncovered to be encroached, factitious not certified. His solution for Estragon's address concerning why Lucky doesn't put down his packs is a drawnout spoof of a legitimate clarification; his mannered upheaval about the slave 'killing him' is more confirmation of the void of his own cases to power. One by one he loses his funnel, his atomizer, and his valuable watch – belonging connected with this feeling of dominance.

Pozzo tries to recuperate his power by assuming the part of producer and offering to do something to divert 'these trustworthy colleagues who are having such a dull, dull time', however his offer to have Lucky move or sing or discuss ends up being the welcome that uncovered his own particular weakness and advances at last to his defeat. (Graver 44-45).

Lucky's shocking tirade is the most realistic of all the customs and routines in a play full of extraordinary set arrangements. In the 1950s, when Godot was initially performed as far and wide as possible, the discourse had a tendency to be perused as an unbalanced, showceasing aria: a mixof drivel, satire, and ominous imagery. Garbage on the grounds that it was generally conveyed at such breakneck speed that it wouldn't be able to be fathomed by a crowd of people (and remained incomprehensible to an onlooker); spoof on the grounds that it was obviously a ridiculing form of a religious verification ('given the being of an individual God . . . subsequently . . .'); and symbolic on the grounds that the implications to Shakespeare's The Tempest, to verses by Verlaine and H"olderlin, to Samuel Johnson (in the early British release) and Bishop Berkeley (in the American) prescribed that the torrent of sections reflected a progressed stage in man's mechanical considering the crumple of Western human advancement. The sum of this is crucial, yet all the more as of late the discourse has been deciphered as a significantly more formal and momentous structure than it had been comprehended to be around then the play initially picked up its acclaim (however neither man nor woman might ever need to defuse its drive as a mindboggling tirade by overemphasizing its cognizance).

The point when Beckett coordinated Godot at the Schiller Theater in 1975, he shockingly advertised to the performing artists on the first day that practices might start with Lucky's discourse, for it was here, he said, that the 'threads and topics' of the play 'are being accumulated together'. He then continued to clarify the development of the piece in a manner that elucidates its shape and noteworthiness. The talk's subject, he told the throws, is 'to shrivel on an outlandish earth under a detached heaven', and it is partitioned into three parts: an emotionless godliness, waning man, and detached nature. Taking after Beckett's lead, one might need likewise to remark in some detail on the texture and the structure of what Lucky says to illustrate further why – incomprehensible and coherent – it is so integral to a gratefulness and comprehension of the play.

From the beginning, one is surprised by Lucky's heartfelt lecture on the grounds that it comes so shockingly out of the hush: not just had he not spoken some time recently, however he appeared a corrupted animal unequipped for any discourse, not to mention the discourse he gives us. Yet then, from the mouth of this creature comes a frenzy driven talk on the way of God and man in the universe that repeats in its extremely development the vital sensational force of everything in the play that has gone before it. Lucky's convulsive endeavor to start by declaring the being of 'a particular God' who 'loves us sincerely with a few exemptions for explanations unknown' parallels the continuous endeavors of Vladimir and Estragon to create a momentous vicinity in their own particular lives;

and the powers of non-sense and cynicism that jumble his attempt are quite a lot such as those that beset theirs.

In any case if their undertaking has been strangely, humorously piercing, his is unnerving not just as a result of the daze in which it is conveyed and yet in light of the fact that he is abruptly demonstrated to convey so much intelligent stuff plus the stuff he really pulls about for Pozzo. Lucky is an unusual resemblance of insightful man at the closure of his tether, beginning to try, through all the education he can gather, to case the biggest reasonability for homo sapiens in the universe. Yet, in spite of the fact that his discourse at the begin takes the manifestation of the old philosophical verification of the being of God, it plunges quickly to an alternate, horrible set of conclusions. The powers on whose work his confirmation rests are a ticket-puncher and a tram-driver (Puncher and Wattmann); the God with the white facial hair (who adores us sincerely for explanations obscure) is portrayed by flexibility from feeling, imperturbability, and the misfortune of the ability to utilize spoken or composed dialect (apathia, athambia, aphasia). The commotion that appears to be automatically to cut Lucky's confirmation ('quaquaquaqua') is identified both to extreme significance and extreme rubbish: "qua" as 'essential being, in the character or limit of . . .' or 'quaquaversal', truly: 'where so ever turned, turned all over the place, inclining descendingfrom the focal point in all bearings' (which Beckett once called an awesome quality). However the staccato "quaquaquaqua" resembles the disparaging clamors made by Ovid's frogs and the skeptic Soliony when he needs to disparage and quiet other individuals in Chekhov's Three Sisters.

As Lucky's distress increments so does the burning disdain guided at foundations and scholastics, all named in coarsely dismissive ways: the Acacacacademy of Anthropopopometry of Essy-in-Possy is both excremental and sterile (esse = 'to be'; group = 'to be able'; i.e. in this setting, 'not to have the capacity to measure man'),andTestew, Cunard, Fartov, and Belcher represent themselves. In any case if the phrasing is rough and convoluted and the way hypercritically prolix, the memo is clear: if God exists, He is truant, inert to us, and in spite of proclaimed strides in sustenance, particular hygiene, drug, and conveyance, mere mortals waste and pine, shrink and decrease.

In spite of the fact that Lucky's destructively humorous, miserable proposition is expressed at practically the definite center of this seventy-two line discourse, the second half is of equivalent imperativeness, for not just does it finish the talk about an uninterested nature supplementing an unresponsive God, yet it presents the key (and from various perspectives startling) Beckett note of safety. Simply at the focus when the contention is generally chillingly prophetically calamitous (the vision of the blurring human skull in the homestead stones), Lucky starts his two end abstains: 'i resume' and 'on on . . .' unstable utterances – rehashed half-twelve times in the second 50% of the discourse, when they were not exhibit whatsoever in the first half. 'to resume': 'to consume or run on with again after interruption' – this is the thing that Lucky does and what Vladimir and Estragon have been doing (and will press on to do) when they reconstitute a burning out planet by some purposive activity or verbal journey.

The interference here, as it regularly is in Beckett's function, is an interruption of some troubling, unwelcome truth, a vital actuality that has beforehand been prohibited by the characters' penchant to live in the grasp of propensity and schedule. 'habit', Vladimir will let us know in his second-enactment talk, is 'a incredible deadener', and Beckett unchangingly copartners it with the human limit for avoidance and self-insurance. Propensity, he composed at twenty-four in his article on Proust, is a tradeoff effected between the single and nature's turf, a 'guarantee of dull inviolability' against the unstable minutes when 'the fatigue of living is traded by the enduring of being'.

Lucky's tirade is one such shattering addition, and when he himself is savagely hushed by Vladimir's pulling off his cap, the movement comes back to the universe of propensity to which we had prior been usual – the carnival universe of indulgent drama with its hinting indications of occasions that are accounted for to have occurred at Calvary (Latin for 'skull') or Golgotha (Hebrew for 'skull'); or, in Lucky's terms: 'on on the skull the skull the skull the skull in Connemara . . .'

After Lucky falls, he is blunderously raised by the two companions in a ridiculous yet troubling farce of the execution. (Pozzo's 'raise him up' emulated by Estragon's (to damnation with him'.)The responses of the others might be taken as a list to the effect of Lucky's 'interruption'. A significant part of the energy of the tirade hails from its having the conclusiveness of a savage fixation: no further examination is conceivable. Not just does it uncover Pozzo's dictator posing, yet it helps Vladimir and Estragon to remember the bleak terms and states of the planet in which they have been holding up to keep their errand with Godot. The abrasive parody of Pozzo's goodbye – the production about the lost watch, the silly cross-cutting trade of 'adieu . . . yes no no' – are compelled enterprises to avoid the implications of lucky's speech , a travesty of habit at the end of its tether. (Graver 47).

After Pozzo and Lucky make their incredible passageway, the zealous movement of the play takes a different imperative turn. We find Vladimir and Estragon in an alternate temperament from that in which we saw them soon after the master/slave exhibition happened. The definitive door of Pozzo and Lucky had eminently expanded the cast offs' feeling of plausibility: the enormous man may be Godot; he could be carrying something to consume; the shenanigans of the voyaging pair might be a yearned for preoccupation. However those illusions are gone the minute Didi and Gogo are separated from everyone else.

Presently they appear considerably a bigger number of cognizant than before of the distress of their scenario and of the dramatic part of their own lives. Throws around the takeoff of what was the main show in town and by an instinct that the crazed Lucky has faultlessly demarcated the states of the planet in which they exist, they begin speaking again about how to hang loose while holding up for Godot. As of right now, on the other hand, there is a discussion that changes both the tone and the suggestions of the movement. Out of the blue, Vladimir comments 'how they've changed!' and the exchange that accompanies uncovers the conceivability that the experience with Pozzo and Lucky may have happened before – a divulgence that abruptly opens the prior activity to another go of elucidations. Assuming that, as now appears conceivable, the two down-and-outers have been acting from the beginning, shrewdly playing stupid for explanations we can just start to conjecture, we may be (as they may be) even further into an universe of riddle and unknowingness than we had acknowledged.

The impacts of the disclosure that much of this may have happened before are complex. To begin with, it further puzzles the gathering of people about the significance and suggestions of the movement. Also, it uplifts the imperativeness of the occasions of the play as theatre, as the knowing mirror image of activities that probably have an actuality somewhere else. Also, at last, it stresses the requirement for the observers and book fans to fix all available attention all the more eagerly on how Vladimir and Estragon react to occasions – the way they perform their parts – as opposed to on the criticalness of the occasions general.

As observers and book fans, we have been mindful from at an opportune time that in Beckett's dreamscape the coherence of circumstances and end results and of ordinary clarification has broken down. Anyway we have accepted, excessively, that for Didi and Gogo what has been occurring on this nation street is this present reality, questionable as they may be if some of it happened before or not. For sure, the unlikely talk, the repetitiveness and unusual goings-on are as vividly true for them as the events and discussion of our day by day lives are liable to be for u us – yet this stuff redundancy may be putting these goings-on in mistrust.(Graver 50).

6. Write an essay on the meaninglessness and nothingness in Beckett's Waiting for Godot

"Nothing to be done"-this very line reminds us the nothingness in Waiting for Godot which is one of the main themes of the play. In this play we find that nothingness pervades everywhere. From the beginning to the ending, the plot, character, setting, theme, language, action, each and everything represent the theme of nothingness. Actually nothingness in the play suggests the absurdity and nothingness of human life in an implied way. So nothingness in Waiting for Godot is an important matter of discussion.

At the very beginning of the play the theme of nothingness is fore grounded through the remark of Estragon: "Nothing to be done". Later on Vladimir also repeat the same remark. It is one of those lines that are repeated throughout the play. The repetition of the line reminds us the nothingness of human life again and again. When the play first opened, it was criticized for lacking meaning, structure, and common sense. These critics, however, failed to see that Beckett chose to have his play, Waiting for Godot, capture the feeling that the world has no apparent meaning. In this misunderstood masterpiece, Beckett asserts numerous existentialist themes one of which is nothingness. So we should consider the theme of nothingness in Waiting for Godot carefully.

Waiting for Godot is a play made up out of nothingness. The spectator or the reader is fascinated by the strangeness of what he witness, hoping for a turn in the situation or a solution, which never comes. The play holds the audience from beginning to end, and the audience remains riveted to the two tramps who do nothing and say practically nothing. The two tramps are incapable of anything more than mere beginnings of impulses, desires, thoughts, moods, memories, and impressions. Everything that arises in them sinks back into forgetfulness before it arrives anywhere. They both live, to a large extent, in a twilight-state and though one of them, Vladimir, is more aware than his companion, complete physical listness prevails throughout. Their incapacity to live or to end life is intimately linked with their love of helplessness and of wish-dreams. They are full of frustrations and resentments, and they cling to each other with a mixture of inter-dependence and affection. They do different types of odd things to pass their time which are totally meaningless.

A critic said that Waiting for Godot was a play in which "nothing happens, twice". We find that he was not far wrong. The keynote to this play is to be found in the memorable words which Estragon utters with regard to his own life of his friend Vladimir. Those words are: "Nothing happens, nobody comes, nobody goes, it's awful!"Because of the strange paucity of action and situation in the play a critic in sheer desperation has remarked that practically nothing happens in it: "There is nothing done in it; no development is to be found; and there is no beginning and no end." Indeed, the entire action boils down to this: On a country road, near a tree, two tramps, Estragon and Vladimir, idle away their time waiting for Godot. One takes off his boots, and the other talks of the Gospels. One eats a carrot which the other offers. They have nothing substantial to say to each other. They address each other by two diminutives Gogo and Didi. They cannot go away, because they are waiting for someone called Godot. Eventually a boy arrives with a message that Godot will not come this evening but surely tomorrow. The two tramps decide to go away and come back again the next day. But they do not move and the curtain falls. Earlier, two other characters, a cruel master called Pozo and his half crazy slave called Lucky, have appeared to create a diversion, and Lucky has delivered an incomprehensible speech made up of disconnected fragments. In Act II the waiting goes on, Pozzo and lucky pass by once more, but the master is now blind and the slave is dumb. The master and the slave stumble and fall and are helped on their way by the tramps. The same boy comes back with the same message, namely that Godot will not come this evening but that he will come on the following day. Everything remains as if it was in the beginning. The two tramps would like to hang themselves, but they have not got a suitable rope. They decide to go away and come back again the next day. But they do not move and the curtain falls. Thus the whole play ends in nothingness without any decisive conclusion.

Nothingness is also suggested by the plot of the play Waiting for Godot. In this play we do not get any logical arrangement of the action or development of plot. There is no plot in the drama; no beginning, no middle, no end. The play starts with waiting and end also with waiting. So there is no plot in this play in the traditional sense of the term. The play ends where it starts. Actually, Waiting for Godot does not tell a story, it explores a static situation. Act II precisely repeats the pattern of Act I. No dramatist had ever taken such an extreme position. Not only have conventions been withheld from the reader. According to the conventional view, a play was to have a certain plot necessitating certain situations and actions, and characters who performed those actions and who were caught up in the tangles of the plot. But the play Waiting for Godot hardly offers a plot. It is as if we were watching a sort of egression beyond nothing. So when Waiting for Godot was first presented on the stage, it offered to theatre-audience an experience unknown before. It was a wholly unconventional dramatic composition. It was unconventional in respect of its plot construction and character portrayal.

The characters also represent the theme of nothingness. The play starts with the waiting for Godot. We do not know what or who the Godot is. At the end of the play it seems to us that Godot is nothing and Estragon and Vladimir are waiting for nothing. Characterization is an important characteristic of a play that is not drawn and seen in Waiting for Godot. Conflict and collision of characters, psychological and inner suffering and developments of characters, turning point of any particular event and fascinating dialogues are the important characteristics of a play which are not found in this play. Instead of it, the play goes through nothingness with false wish. So we can say that in Waiting for Godot nothingness is suggested through the characters and their behavior.

The setting of the play also suggests nothingness. The setting of the play is on a country road, near a tree. The tree is unknown and there are no leaves. The whole setting is like a barren land. We can compare it with the waste land. A kind of hollowness or emptiness pervades everywhere of the setting. Thus the setting of the play also suggests the nothingness.

Nothingness is one of the main themes of the play. The play was a striking success not because of its story or characters, but because of the richness of themes. In the first instance, it seems that the play is about nothing, but this nothingness in itself is very mysterious. In fact, the play is not merely about waiting for a certain Godot, but man's endless wait for Christ or for death. The theme of the purposelessness and meaningless of human life are implied in the play.

The language of the play also expresses the nothingness of the human life. The use of language is very remarkable in the play and it serves Beckett's purpose significantly. The nothingness of life and the impatience mentality of human being are sincerely expressed by Beckett's own language skill. About Lucky's dumbness, Pozzo's answer to Vladimir is very rich in expression: "One day like other day, one day he went dumb, one day I went blind, one day we'll go deaf, one day we were born, one day we shall die, the same day, the same second." Thus throughout the whole play we find the expression of nothingness even through the language also.

Nothingness is also expressed through the actions and behavior of the characters of the play. Both Vladimir and Estragon pass their time by doing some odd things which are meaningless. At the beginning of the play Estragon says "Nothing to be done". From this line it becomes very clear that they have nothing significant to be done because everything is meaningless. Their actions are also illogical. They cannot spend their time in an enjoyable way and they wait for uncertainty. So they spent their time by doing some odd and illogical things which signify nothing. Thus their behaviors make the nothingness of human life more clear to us.

Nothingness pervades everywhere in the play Waiting for Godot because it is a famous absurd drama. All absurdists are concerned with the existence of human being which is meaningless. This is why nothingness is omnipresent in the play. The play is full of nothingness, restless tiredness and childish fun. The for-nothing waiting of the characters and their activities give the play a rich tone of absurdity. Actually Waiting for Godot is a famous absurd play this is why we find nothingness in every layer of the play.

In Waiting for Godot we find another basic existentialist tenet on which Beckett reflects is the meaninglessness of time. Because past, present, and future mean nothing, the play follows a cyclic pattern. Vladimir and Estragon return to the same place each day to wait for Godot and encounter the same basic people each day. Pozzo and Lucky pass by Vladimir and Estragon one day, both in healthy states, and return the next day, one blind and the other mute. Pozzo cannot recollect the previous meeting, and even claims that Lucky has always been mute. In changing Pozzo and Lucky's situation, Beckett shows that time's meaninglessness degrades human life to the point of being equally unpurposed. Likewise, Godot's messenger does not recognize Vladimir and Estragon from day to day. This suggests that the people we meet today are not the same as they were yesterday and will not be the same tomorrow.

In Act II the tree sprouting leaves, Beckett says, is not to show hope or inspiration, but only to record the passage of time. At the time of first production, when Beckett was pressed hard for an answer, he snapped, "If I knew who Godot was, I would have said so in the play." Or "If Godot were God, I would have called him that." We shall not likely find out who Godot is, and shall waste our time trying. On the other hand, nothing can be clearer than what Didi and Gogo are doing. They tell us a dozen times: They are waiting for Godot, and we are to leave it at that.

At the end of the play it seems to us that the Godot will never come. Estragon and Vladimir will remain still waiting for Godot for time infinite. Perhaps we all are wait or waited once or another upon a time. We all have godots of our kind. At the end of the play though Estragon says 'lets go' but they do not move. This immobility gives the play a rich tone of absurdity.

However, in the consideration of the nothingness in Waiting for Godot we should not forget that Samuel Beckett was an absurdist. The absurdist are all time concerned with human existence. This is why he used the existentialist philosophy. The main theme of the existentialist philosophy is nothingness and meaninglessness of human life. Thus nothingness becomes a major theme of the play. Beckett's greatness lies in here that he expressed the great theme of nothingness in the simplest way. This is why there is no plot or character development and there is nothing in this play. Actually Beckett gives us the practical example of nothingness through the play. Simply he expresses nothingness through nothing.

Finally, we can say that Beckett was successful to show the nothingness of human life in Waiting for Godot. This is why it is still considered as one of the most successful absurd drama of the world. We can conclude our discussion by quoting from Shakespeare's Macbeth which also reflects the nothingness of human life like Waiting for Godot- "Life is a tale told by an idiot/Full of sound and fury signifying nothing."

7.Discuss Samuel Beckett's Waiting for Godot as a postmodern text

Or write an essay on postmodernism in Samuel Beckett's Waiting for Godot

Ages, throughout the history, has been identified with the terms. Post modernism is hard to define in one single dimension of any term as still it is a subject of heated debates and discussions for its definition. Hans

Bertens, (critic and author) sums it as, "postmodernism means and has meant different things from humble literary origins in 1950's to level of global conceptualization in 1980's". Generally postmodernism is considered as extension of "poststructural ideas of language". It follows the comprehension of concept that "language is not anchored in reality, that there is infinite uncertainty in the words that we use and that our ideas of what is sane, rational and sensible are just something decided by our particular Discourse which could easily be wrong". Keynotes of post modernist documents and writings are absurdity, ineffectualness, fruitlessness, meaninglessness, aimlessness, feebleness and weariness. In other words post modernist writers tend to play with language and examine interlinks between words and the relation between words and worlds, keeping in view Saussure's idea of arbitrariness of language. It seems like "If words can't be used to tell us truths about the world then we can at least have fun with them." They try to dismantle the traditions of text writing and hopes of audience related to text. Waiting for godot indentifies with "theatre of absurd" and follows up both modernism and post modernism, introducing expressionism and surrealistic techniques in drama. Keeping in view its ambiguous language, paradox, ironical representation of characters, fragmentation, identity and existential problems and subjective approach towards the life makes it more post modernist script than a modernist writing. Theatre of absurd is purely outcome of postmodernism which was greatly influenced by existential philosophy dealing with the nothingness of the world and aimlessness of life which was the result of mass pessimism created by world wars. According to Martin Esslin, a theater critic, this the "one of the successes of the post-war theater"

In the play we see two characters, Vladimir and Estragon, on a country road by the tree waiting for godot who never appears on the scene. Both have nothing significant about their lives they do every possible thing to avoid the silence of universe around them travelling in past present and future unaware of scientific clock. Their lives are interrupted by three characters Pozzo the megalomaniac capitalist, his poor slave lucky and a boy without any name who appears to be messenger of godot. The deserted setting and aimless waiting reflects the psychological bareness and unproductively of modern men after the disastrous world war.

Beginning with a prelude to modernism we believe that modernism to the "lack of central hierarchy" and puts science and technology at backstage, because play starts with waiting for godot and ends with waiting for godot even the title of play signifies the subject matter of play. The play talk about nothingness because here waiting itself is nothing. In post modern world nothing is logical and reality is relative. After world war humanity lost faith in ordered organized and rational universe. Birth, death, every happening is by chance.

The very example of post modernism in waiting for godot is the language game of Vladimir and Estragon. Their absurd fragmented and clueless conversations depict the fruitlessness of human mind and absurd psychological processes of modern man. This fragmentation is the language technique used by post modern writers.

Vladimir: They make a noise like wings

Estragon: Like Leaves

Vladimir: Like Sand

Estragon: Like Leaves [Silence] {(58) act-two}

This fragmented and clueless conversation hints about relative reality and language's arbitrariness. Both have objective reality of their own. This fragmented language and short sentences depict the postmodern writing technique forming a concept about the meaninglessness and nothingness of the world and character's existence. In postmodernism, nonsense makes sense. Both characters depict the meaninglessness of everyday life activities while having fragmented conversations, clueless jokes and nonsense entertainment to kill the time.

Similarly Lucky's mono dialogue shatters the structural existence of language taking it to beyond the reason which is again the trait of postmodern literature that it breaks through the modern reasoning and logic. Topped with grammatical, ungrammatical structure, correlating irrelevant concepts and abrupt order of thoughts expressed in alien words set path for postmodernist writers to make language free from the conventions of absolute reality and make it relative. Waiting for godot shows clear picture of frustrated, megalomaniac and biased society of 21st century through the characters. Pozzo the rich megalomaniac dehumanizing his slave Lucky and Estragon identifies with Marxist set up of modern man creating an illusion civilization which gives equal rights and status to human beings defying their origins, race and color. Through Pozzo's dialogue in act one, "The tears of the world are a constant/quantity. For each one who Begins to weep, somewhere else another stop. The /same is true of the laugh" (line; 837-840) we see the ambiguity related with reality and existence of human being in the nothingness of the world.

Beckett tries to create his own reality through words which seemingly denies the valid nature of truth and reality. Through bleak and ironical language the dramatist tries to illustrate the notion of ultimate reality, its existence and sense of the universe around the characters. But this communication gap proves it a failure and Atheism is the one of pillar of 21st century society, made stronger by existential philosophers which sometimes appear in waiting for godot embedded in frustrated characters. Though we find references of Adam, can able, saints, bible, marry and Christ but still we see secular approach of Vladimir and Estragon considering life a burden. Vladimir's dialogue "I remain in the dark" shows the absence of spiritual realism in 21st century men. In the present society we are suffering from chaotic situations, caused by scientific and technological advancements, which result in frustration, loneliness, alienation and machine like structure of human mind and nervous system. Vladimir and Estragon seem to be effected by chaotic situations as they don't share their dreams, don't trust each other, don't share their views and avoid to help each other sometimes and waiting for godot who never comes and they are uncertain whether his presence will be a beneficial or harmful for them. Even the uncertainty of godot's coming is there in Vladimir and Estragon's dialogues but still they wait for godot.

Vladimir: He said Saturday. (Pause.) I think.

Estragon: You think.

Vladimir: I must have made a note of it. (He fumbles in his pockets, bursting with miscellaneous rubbish.)

Estragon: (very insidious). But what Saturday? And is it Saturday? Is it not rather Sunday? Or Monday? Or Friday?

Vladimir: (looking wildly about him, as though the date was inscribed in the landscape). It's not possible!

Estragon: Or Thursday? (act 1). And the most helplessness is seen when they are not even sure of whether it's the godot they are waiting for someone else.

Estragon: His name is Godot?

Vladimir: I think so.

Apart from everything we don't know who is Godot, when he will come and how he appears and most basic question is why Vladimir and Estragon are waiting for him. The 21st century man has got insecurity and helpless attitude towards life where someone from outside is expected to take lead of lives of suffering souls which are searching for purpose and meaning of life. The only way to feel their existence is the "meaningless and ambiguous conversations/communication" as Estragon mentions it in one his dialogues in act 1: "we always find something, eh Didi, to give us the impression we exist". Uncertainty about life, its purpose and existence in the world are the dilemmas of postmodern society where human beings are unable to set a course of life or unable to understand the order of this world or life. This uncertainty is highlighted by the laziness and inactivity of the character that do nothing to make a change in the reality or life. As in act 1 Estragon says that,

Vladimir: Well? What do we do?

Estragon: Don't let's do anything. It's safer.

Vladimir: Let's wait and see what he says.

Estragon: Who? Vladimir: Godot

Because of this uncertainty both men are afraid of making any movement or change. Even basic notions of life are uncertain including death and birth as Vladimir mentions it as, "Nothing is certain when we are about". Even the forgetfulness of Estragon is the best illustration of chaos and existentialist minds of post modern times for which this world makes no sense and life has no certain purpose. While Vladimir remembers very minute things vaguely.

Vladimir: Wait . . . we embraced . . . we were happy . . . happy . . . what do we do now that we're happy . . . go on waiting . . . waiting . . . let me think . . . it's coming . . . go on waiting . . . now that we're happy . . . let me see . . . ah! The tree! Estragon: The tree?

Vladimir: Do you not remember?

Estragon: I'm tired.

Vladimir: Look at it. They look at the tree.

Estragon: I see nothing.

Vladimir: But yesterday evening it was all black and bare. And now it's covered with leaves.

Estragon: Leaves?

Vladimir: In a single night.

This loss of memory is associated with loss of identity. Postmodernism comes along with globalization. Globalization is the process in which all human beings are unified making one society which eliminates the individual identities and make one culture. Literary trends in association with globalization now deal with subjective issues and ordinary people. The characters of Estragon and Viladimir completely set in frame of globalization. They are ordinary people doing ordinary things (waiting etc.) without any thrilling action like medieval knights and princes. Furthermore setting of the play is not specified nor its time so it can happen at any time anywhere in the world. And it deals with issues of human being, mankind, and whole humanity producing sense of universality. This universality can be seen through the names of characters, Vladimir (Russian name), Estragon (French name), Pozzo (Italian name) and Lucky (English name).their interaction with each other and presence together in one environment indicates that now one culture has dominated the whole global village. Everyone belonging to any identity is sufferings same chaos and problems. In short postmodernism has clutched all the universe in its hands.

Comic element amalgamated with the tragic incidents and environment clutches the human psychology with the recognition of "helpless absurdity" of 21st century man. Vladimir and Estragon talk about nonsense comical things which helps us to understand the mental state of those characters even when Estragon's pants fall he doesn't notice it. Vladimir makes him realize of it.

Estragon: why don't we hang ourselves?

Vladimir: with what?

Estragon: you haven't got a bit of rope?

Vladimir: no Estragon: then we can't

Vladimir: let's go Estragon: oh, wait, there is my belt

Vladimir: it's too short

Estragon: you could hang on to my legs

Vladimir: and who would hang onto mine?

The most amazing part of the play is Lucky's speech which leaves other's mind numb and blank because of alien vocabulary and senselessly linked ideas but from his speech we get certainty of god's existence when he talks about God's presence with human beings and he watches over and suffer with the sufferings of man and loves man. He has white beard. Though we don't see much hope in overall mood of the play but at some instances we see light of hope in deepness of gloom and desperation expressed by the characters in the play. In spite of all the chaos, restlessness and boredom they still remember some of the dreams or hopes from the past when they talk about bible and gospel in act

Vladimir: do you remember the Gospel?

Estragon: I remember the maps of the holy land. Colored they were. Very pretty. The Dead Sea was pale blue .the very look of it made me thirsty. That's where we'll go, I used to say, that's where we'll go for our honeymoon. We'll swim. We'll be happy.

Despite of the fact that their uncertainties and nothingness causes failure and unhappiness but still find hope in each other's existence. Even when they leave each other they come back again and try to make sense of their existence together. In the play Vladimir doesn't let Estragon to sleep and when he asks for a reason, Vladimir says I was feeling lonely. Thus both of them try to exist in relation to each other. Hope for the future is obvious from not their dialogues only but the tree which is dead in act 1 but blossoms up in the second act. We also see fluctuating hope in consistency of Vladimir and Estragon while waiting of godot even a boy brings messages of godot who is always delaying his arrival but both of them talk about leaving while they don't move even and still wait for him.

Post modernism talks about the predetermined norms and traditions which make man suffer in terms of binary opposition. In this sense we can assume that both Estragon and Vladimir are incompatible with each other where Estragon has limited and superficial thinking mostly considering emotions and feeling while Vladimir can be seen a personality with mind who contemplates and has deep understanding as shown in following dialogues in act 1:

Vladimir: One out of four. Of the other three, two don't mention any thieves at all and the third says that both of them abused him.

Estragon: Who?

Vladimir: What?

Estragon: What's all this about? Abused who?

Vladimir: The Savior. Estragon: Why?

Vladimir: Because he wouldn't save them.

Estragon: From hell?

Vladimir: Imbecile! From death.

Estragon: I thought you said hell.

Vladimir: From death.

Postmodernism rejects the traditionalism. Traditionalism says "there are always pre-determined rules, explanations for people and their life and truth is objective". Since there is no objectivism in waiting for godot and we don't see traditional plot in the play, we can say Beckett breaks from traditions of previous stages. We see a circular plot without any proper story and line of action. Literature always has been a source to see reflection of the society in respective ages it's been produced. That's why readers are always able to hint the influence and effect of the times and history in one particularly literary piece of work. Postmodernism supports existentialism that says looking for future and making sense of this world is meaningless as wait of main characters never get accomplisehed and their hopes of being saved by a savior never get fulfilled. Postmodernism states that language is relative and a text can't be assigned one single meaning. Different readers can produce different meanings and language is absurd. It somehow fails to provide the service of communication causing ambiguity and absurdity. As it can be pointed out in throughout the text of waiting for godot which sometimes makes no sense and reader is unable to comprehend it. Waiting for Godot reflects alienation of human being and confused personal realities. It also questions history through discussing different references to previous texts in order to get some organization in their present but vagueness and absurdity of present couldn't let it happen.

8. Discuss Beckett's attitude towards hope in the play. Are there any real signs of hope?

Samuel Beckett's Waiting for Godot is an image of human condition and it is concerned with the theme of survival. The playwright wants to communicate the problematic nature of man's situation in the world. Beckett's plays are not pessimistic even though they deal with the disillusionment and despair of the modern world. What Beckett tries to communicate is not one of despair but of courage and hope to face the human condition as it is , with all its mystery. There is no cause for despondency and despair. Man should face the realities of life and he need not feel disheartened at his suffering and misery. To laugh at our own misery is the only way of coming to terms with it. This paper is an attempt to explain how the theme of exsistence is dealt with by the dramatist in his Waiting for Godot.

It is not fair to see only the negative side of Beckett's thought. As life has proved a disappoint, there is bitterness in his writings. "underlying the Bekettian man's nihilism is a frustrated hunger or the good and the poor. Beckett's writings present to us the sickness of our own times. His way of dealing wit the despair of our times is unorthodox. He has created a black and formless world. He is ruthless in his insistence on the human facts of loneliness and emptiness. Darkness does not eliminate hope. In his dark world we can see a distant point of light and a dim hope.

Frustration is also a promise in Beckett's peculiar art. By abandoning hope and the quest for ultimate meaning, the absurd man realizes the meaning of his condition. If his life is hopeless, he tries to revolt against absurdity. When the absurdity of life is recognized, existence is felt as value in itself. For if lie is hopeless and meaningless, he is at once liberated and put in a position to exercise his freedom in a revolt against absurdity.

Love, pity and hope are possible in the world of Beckett love is one of the most persistence ideals in his writings. Beckett's characters reveal unexpected virtues: charity, compassion and firm resolve to endure. In Waiting for Godot, Pozzo says "Let us not speak ill of our generation, it is not in any way unhappier than its predecessors."

Vladimir sees no leaf in the willow tree and thinks that it must be dead. But Estragon says " No more weeping". His statement shows that there is no use shedding tears over a dead tree. The tree which sprouts some leaves in Actii is a symbol of hope. It represents the possibility of renewal of mankind through God's grace.

The two tramps in Waiting for Godot live in hope and optimism. To them Godot represents hope, peace and rest. They manage to drw themselves back from despair at the end of the play and give up their attempt to commit suicide. They are waiting for Godot with some hope. "As they do not lose hope, are waiting for Godot with some hope, they are neive, incurably optimistic ideologists". Vladimir is an optimist and he is hopeful of Godot's coming. He gives hope to Estragon who doubts Godot's coming. "Ah Gogo, don't go on like that. Tomorrow everything will be better". He hopes that Godot will come and reward them. His answer is an encouraging to Estragon. It represents the enduring hope of mankind. They hope that they are the blessed in their waiting . The tramps waiting resembles the French resistence against the cruelty of the Nazis. The savagery and cruelty of the Nazis were absurd. But te courage nd sacrifice of the group who resisted tem prove man's noble faith and hope in himself. We can believe that godot is god and they boy is god's messenger. It is said that godot is a weakened form of god. As god is invisisble, godot is not seen on the stage. He has sent his messenger. Godot is man's hope. He might be "happiness, eternal life, the unattainable quest of all men."

Godot can be explained as god, love, hope etc. He has several traits in common with the image of God as depicted in the old and new testaments. His white beard reminds us of the image of the old father aspect of God. His irrational preference or one of the two brothers recalls Jehovah's treatment of Cain and Abel. The discrimination between the goatsherd and the shepherd is reminiscent of the son o god as the ultimate Judge as the Saviour for whom men wait. It may be a comment on the second coming of Christ.

The messenger boy comes with the news that Godot will come tomorrow. But Godot inspires less confidence. He has some hold over the tramps which prevents them from cancelling their appointment with him. If he comes, he may bring a change in their present meaningless condition. Godot non-arrival keeps the two tramps waiting for him and their faith in him alive. The godot fails to appear in the play, he is as real a character as other characters in the play. The tramps need godot to give a meaning to their existence. Godot's very absence demonstrated his presence and he dominates the play in which he fails to appear. Their waiting for godot seems to suggest that through the ages mankind has waited or a savior.

Lucky, in his famous speech, points out that inspite of the existence of a loving God is existence of a loving God and progress of various kinds, man is full of decline. His statement shows that God is existing and He is loving and blessing man. Lucky accepts that there are many kinds of progress in the world. Salvation is possible in the world of Beckett. We find "basic metaphysical and theological issues at the heart of all Beckett's work: suffering, death, guilty, judgement and salvstion".

The possibility of salvation is an issue of crucial importance in Beckett's plays. The seed of Waiting for Godot is Luke's account of crucifixion as summarized by St.Augustine: " don't despair: one of the thieves was saved. Do not presume: one o the thieves was damned". The tramps feel guilty like the thieves. Yet one the thieves was saved. The reference to salvation is found in Vladimir's mention of the two th crucified on either side of Christ. So there is a note of hope and optimism. Vladimir says "it's a reasonable percentage".

Vladimir and Estragon represent one man. The connection between the two is a life sustaining relationsip. They are full of frustration but they never leave. There is a profound need which each feels for other. This need transforms their limitation of hatred into tenderness. It is one of genuine friendship. Vladimir as Estragon's protector sings him to sleep. As a teacher to his pupil he teaches many things. He looks after Estragon like a fond parent caring for his child. Their warmth in the middle of despair is the world's.

Pozzo and Lucky are another inseparable pair. Lucky wants to have a good relationship with Pozzo. For this he has sacrificed everything., even his creativeness. He accepts his abject misery and slavery. They represents the two complementary sides of society. They could be as parts of a divided self. They represent one way of getting through with someone else just as Vladimir and Estragon represented another way of doing so. They represented the relationship between body and mind, the relation between material and spiritual sides of man. Without Lucky, Pozzo cannot move forward. Lucky cannot move except Pozzo's orders. In fact Lucky teachers Pozzo all the higer values of life.

So it's clear that Beckett's characters, despite their worries and problems want to enjoy material happiness. They are not ready to lose their hope in life and want to live life fully. They know that their life is full of misery, but they find some kind of happiness in this miserable world. They re courageous enough to face the realities of world and seem to hope that their life is worth living.

So it's clear that Beckett's characters, despite their worries and problems want to enjoy material happiness. They are not ready to lose their hope in life and want to live life fully. They know that their life is full of misery, but they find some kind of happiness in this miserable world. They re courageous enough to face the realities of world and seem to hope that their life is worth living. living means choice. So they exist and find way to survive. Waiting or Godot deals with such a kind of life. The play is about mankind's attempts to fiddle its way through life.

9. Write an essay on the language in Samuel Beckett's Waiting for Godot

Beckett's work is defined by the consciousness that words are incapable of expressing the inner self and by the simultaneous acceptance of the fact that language is intrinsic to the human situation and thus not a removable element. Beckett regards language as constitutive of the identity of the self; it is on this conviction that his despair for the human condition and the power of his writing depend. Despair, because the self can only be approached asymptotically and expressed, words moving in an orbit without ever touching the centre, the essence; power, because he sees in language's struggle to achieve expression the striving of the self to define its own identity. His attitude towards language is, then, the paradoxical acceptance of self-refutation as the condition for any artistic practice; a recognition of the inherent inability of words to correspond to anything other than themselves together with the potentiality of expressing this very inability to express. What Beckett is above all conscious of is the dialectical relationship between the object to be expressed (theme, subject matter) and the mode of expression (form of language, style). Regarding the latter as constitutive of the former, he foregrounds the comic absurdity of their dissociation into two non-interacting elements, whilst maintaining the dialectic through the overall theatrical form. However, because Beckett does not regard language as a self-sufficient system of concepts exoteric to the theme it is bound to express, the imposition of dramatic form is in turn problematized. Only a Naturalistic view of language as having a direct and unambiguous relation to the world can allow for an unproblematic organization of meaning at this level. By radically subverting such a notion of language Beckett sets all elements of his drama into a type of free-play. It is the movement within this free-play, taking in all previously fixed points (self, language, material reality, etc), which I have described as the dialectic in his work. In this context artistic expression can only be formless so long as the world it speaks about is itself formless: '. . . hence the quest for the art form that is capable of accommodating the formless. The only form that can do so is one in which the form itself is at issue'.3 In such a view, form, far from being a servile reflection of an external reality, establishes a much more complicated relationship with it; form is granted a relative autonomy from the substance it expresses and thus actively intervenes in the artistic process by shaping the raw material and by subtly imposing an integral order upon it. The 'formlessness' of any particular form is therefore merely phenomenal, because it actually masks a highly organized and disciplined structure. This-is particularly clear in Beckett's theatre where the almost physical experience of words as a natural and random flow obliterates the audience's elementary awareness that speech on stage is not spontaneous but part of a carefully structured text. Beckett feels that the domain of the writer-playwright is that of a form which creates meaning through its struggle to express meaning. He does not, therefore, resort to the formalistic demand for an art synonymous with form, but rather attempts to solve the problem of their relation by preserving the dialectic. He is on record as saying that the world is a mess; the implication is that, by its very nature, the world is the polar opposite of art, which is form, and thus destructive of the very thing that art holds itself to be. A corollary of this would be that any acceptance of a correspondence between art (form) and the world (substance) would refute the very existence and operation of art. He is naturally very careful, therefore, to make a distinction between the two, to ascribe to each of them a certain autonomy, whilst always seeking to find the 'raison d'être' for the former:

> The form and the chaos remain separate. The latter is not reduced
>
> to the former. That is why the form itself becomes a preoccupation,
>
> because it exists as a problem separate from the material it accom-
>
> modates. To find a form that accomodates the mess, that is the task
>
> of the artist now.4

In his essay on Proust Beckett describes style as pertaining to a particular authorial vision rather than to technique. In the case of the novelist Proust the quality of his language is the predominant factor, the element which incorporates and shapes his vision of the world. In drama, naturally, language cannot play the same absolute role; theatre as a medium provides the playwright with a space to be covered with tangible and visual images, it does not merely serve a context within which the text is animated. Beckett has, of course, fully developed this stage potential in an ascetic dramaturgy organized around verbal constructs of condensed meaning and possessed of a unique ability to articulate visually both silence and absence on stage. Yet Beckett's drama remains primarily one of language, of a language which does not pretend to convey the essence of things, which accepts the existence of the mess and which is aware of its own degradation. His choice of dramatic speech as the fundamental level of action, rather than its subordination to gestures, movements and setting, is therefore far more complicated than at first it seems to be. For whilst such a choice clearly does not entail his abandonment of 'pure' stage elements the power of his purely poetic images threatens to engulf them. And at the same time the choice posits the terms in which, out of its failure to express, language may be re-created. This commits him to an intrinsically self-defeating process. For whilst admitting language to be the primary reality, he is deeply suspicious of the words at his disposal; they are unable either to communicate or to express, and so they can only fail, even though verbal expression may be a compulsive need.5 It is precisely this impulse to speak, this sense of an undefined compulsion to speak, which allows Beckett to attain the apparently impossible, namely the verbal and visual articulation of an unverbalized, undifferentiated self.

In Beckett's plays, for the first time, theatre's potential is extended so as materially to present abstraction and absence, not just as partial components of the main body of speech but as the very subject matter of the drama and as the constitutive elements of dramatic language. 'Self' is seen as a tendency away from any particular spatial and temporal context, away from the concreteness of being and sensation which resides in chaos, mess and rubbish. The only material dimension it is capable of grasping is by virtue of its voice, its capacity to speak even when the whole body is reduced to a head protruding from a dustbin, as in Endgame, or to a pair of lips, as in Not I. Words are the condition. and substance of consciousness and consciousness the only register of existence. For Beckett the self cannot be defined in positivist terms, that is merely temporally and spatially. It strives to exist in an undefined place, outside history, to reach a still point, a world of solitude and peace. The tragedy of the human situation, in his eyes, lies in the fact that language frustrates the very movement which it instigates, by tying us to an inauthentic non-self in the material world. Language only permits the articulation of self in relation to what it is not. Beckett's urge towards stillness and nothingness is in reality an all-pervading desire to transcend the socio-historically determined human condition in order to attain the realm of the real self. The process which runs parallel to this desire in his drama is that whereby theatrical language tries to break logical sequences and associations so as to express the movement and fluidity of consciousness. And for Beckett the only process which corresponds to it is inwards and downwards: 'The only possible spiritual development is in the sense of depth. The artistic tendency is not expansive, but a contraction.

And art is the apotheosis of solitude. There is no communication because there are no vehicles of communication.'6 Beckett's denial of the possibility of communication stems from his awareness that absolute meaning is absent from a world which is in itself the absence of the absolute. Language-as-communication therefore tends to become 'private' because the lack of any absolute external criteria to which it might be compared makes it inherently self-referential. Reality cannot, then, be artistically depicted, even in terms of a sterile description of external characteristics. Beckett's conviction that the subject's perception of a particular object destroys its relation to the object by transforming the object into a mere intellectual pretext, negates the possibility of experiential knowledge and the validity of experiential testimony. His rejection of Naturalism in art stems from a radical repudiation of its very basis, the assumption that the human mind is capable of capturing and accurately registering phenomena exterior to it.7The cause of the absence of absolute meaning is precisely the intellect's inability to establish continuity with the world. The myth of the existence of a unique and totalized world collapses from the very moment that the relationship between reality and mind is disrupted. The two fragments start moving in parallel orbits without ever re-establishing their time-honoured continuity. Beckett's work is a testimony to what kind of human existence is possible within the gap created by the disruption of this previously unquestioned unity.

To a very large extent traditional Western thinking has been based upon attempts to formulate a principle of congruity between Cosmos and Logos. Truth has been identified with WHAT IS, that is with presence testified through the senses; in this tradition WHAT IS NOT cannot be expressed because it is non-recognizable and unexplorable within the paradigm. According to Parmenides 'it is the same thing to think and to be,' and 'that which it is possible to think is identical with that which can be.'8 These statements delineate the nature of the world by ascribing to it a series of characteristics and simultaneously establishing man's relation to it. If visibility and tangibility constitute reality, then absence is non-existence. If to be is synonymous with to think, then the world is intelligible to man, who by using his mind discovers meaning; the path he follows is that of a strict causality already implicit in the initial assumption that equates presence with existence. Man thinks and speaks in harmony with this meaningful causal world of 'objective' phenomena; thus verbal expression, being the extension of reality, reinforces the bipolar unity.

Beckett's refusal of such tenets along with his rejection of Naturalist theatre effectively places him in a very different philosophical tradition; a tradition which makes language its central and crucial concern. It is to this extent that the work of linguist Ferdinand de Saussure can help us in understanding the dynamics of Beckett's work. At the beginning of the present century he defined language as a system of differences, in which a series of binary oppositions sustains the verbal system, with oppositions between presence and absence and positive and negative being the most determinate ones. Within these pairs of antithetical notions the one pole 'is apprehended as positively having a certain feature while the other is apprehended as deprived of the feature in question'.9 In Waiting for Godot Beckett embodies these specific binary oppositions in the very structure of the play. Didi and Gogo stand in opposition to Godot much as presence stands in opposition to absence in the Saussurean system. In line with our expectations Beckett thus deals with the structure and operation of language both at the level of dramatic speech and at the level of dramatic form, using the Saussurean model of presence and absence as a metaphor for his more traditional, sceptical view of perception. Only insofar as they can be seen can Didi and Gogo be sure about their own presence, their own existence. In the first of his 'Three Dialogues witrh Georges Duthuit' Beckett identifies nature as a composite of perceiver and perceived; Waiting for Godot is built upon such a composite. Didi feels lonely when Gogo sleeps because so long as the perceiver (Gogo) does not see, then the perceived (Didi) cannot be sure if he lives. Hence the violence of Didi's outburst to the boy in the second act: 'You're sure you saw me, you won't come and tell me tomorrow that you never saw me!'.10 Presence is always, however, dependent on absence; the latter verifies the existence of the former because it is the very element which constitutes consciousness. Such a relationship, Saussure would argue, is inherent in any language which opposes person (I or thou) to non-person (he or it), the sign of an absence which can never embody itself as presence.11 Didi/ Gogo are in a binary relationship with Godot incapable of dissociation because they are referential one to another. The play is predicated upon this awareness, either by means of direct references to their relation with him (Estragon: 'We're not tied! . . . Vladimir: But to whom. By whom? Estragon: To your man'.)12 or by incorporating the awareness into the texture of their dialogue. In this latter respect words seem to carry them away from the painful knowledge that they depend on Godot. Words enable them to recover from the consciousness of their difference from Godot at the moment of their utterance; but their sense of difference cannot be removed because it is intrinsic to the very language they employ, woven into their very being.

Godot lives outside space in a feedom uncontrolled by temporal restrictions. He is an abstraction existing in the peace of Nothingness. He does nothing. Didi and Gogo are deprived of these specific features. As they move towards the zero point at which they would overlap with the opposite term, they still do something; they wait, think, speak and move. Didi and Gogo are tangible presences; compared with the zero point of Godot they are obviously 'positive'. The repetition of the word 'nothing' ('nothing to be done,' `nothing to show' etc.) does not, then, express their actual situation, so much as their desire to become the nothing. The arrival of Godot would collapse the gulf between desire and actuality because it would render the two poles synonymous: presence would be absence, the positive would be zero. Since Godot does not come, only language remains to articulate their difference from the desired absence-negativity. The circular structure of the play epitomizes the asymptotic and futile movement of the self towards a state of 'authentic being'. This structure challenges the basic assumption of the absolute world that nothingness is equal to non-existence and therefore cannot be experienced. The audience experiences the presence of absence in the lonely gestures of Didi and Gogo, in their tautologous utterances and in the long silences which condense what has, necessarily (given Beckett's views on language), remained unsaid. The recurrence of the phrase 'We are waiting for Godot,' which becomes synonymous with 'We are waiting for nothing,' establishes absence as the very element constitutive of Didi and Gogo's condition of existence. If, as Democritus says in one of Beckett's favourite quotations, 'Nothing is more real than nothing,'13 then it is impossible for man to make any positive statement. When reality is not measured by time and is not limited by spatial boundaries but lies in an infinite time and an abstract space, then words can never be definite about a meaning which must perpetually elude them. The lack of a 'positive' meaning, or rather the existence of a reality difficult or impossible to articulate verbally, compels language to enter a process of self-repudiation. A word like 'unhappy,' for example, a word which inevitably bears an enormous sentimental burden, is too definite to remain unrefuted:

Estragon: I'm unhappy.

Vladimir: Not really! Since when?

Estragon: I'd forgotten.

Vladimir: Extraordinary the tricks that memory plays!14

In this simple exchange each line obliterates the preceding one. Their language is constructed out of an abiding awareness of the nothing, their acceptance of an essential negativity which nullifies any hope of absolute meaning. These innocent, 'clarifying' questions disclose the hollowness of certain words which were basic to a world of 'inner spirit' but which now seem absurd: 'Vladimir:... Two thieves crucified at the same time as our Saviour. One - Estragon: Our what? Vladimir: Our Saviour'.15 The absence of any internal logic in this world or of belief in a supernatural power able to impose a spiritual order upon the mess makes man especially suspicious about those words which have been particularly heavily invested with meaning. At the same time this 'negative' consciousness entails a tormenting recognition on the part of Didi and Gogo of the uncertainty of their particular situation. They attempt to defer this uncertainty by resorting to a series of repetitions which give them the happy illusion of temporary affirmations; yet these very repetitions are soon refuted by the recurrence of the specific word with which they began: 'Vladimir: Say, I am happy. Estragon: I am happy. Vladimir: So am I. Estragon: So am I. Vladimir: We are happy. Estragon: We are happy. (silence)'. . .16 The consolation that the recurrence of the same word appears to offer as something conceptually and audibly familiar is easily transformed into a menace for both speaker and listener; the simplest words become grotesque and forbidding. Repetition, the factor which permits language to establish itself as a code, is used by Beckett as the means whereby it may be repudiated as a system of definite concepts.

In Waiting for Godot, the catalysts of speech are 'Silence' and 'Pause,' the very elements which undermine the emotions to which the characters lay claim and which prevent them occupying any decisive area of commitment. Silence breaks the continuity of words and conveys meaning in its totality. The silences in Beckett's plays effectively 'bracket' the terms an audience might adopt in order to understand them; the meaning is communicated by the intervals between words. In Didi and Gogo's dialogue about the dead voices the silences are evenly distributed, atomizing the exchange into fragments of cross-talk. The empty stage is filled for a moment with the presence of dead people, worn out voices, fragmented whispers, murmurs and rustlings, and this sudden proliferation of the thoughts, speech, and noises of dead people suffocates Didi and Gogo because they themselves are emblematic of that dead humanity. Beckett stages the sounds of silence, the other side of language, and Didi and Gogo, in their yearning for authenticity, aspire to the point of overlap, to the zero, to the point where all difference is obliterated. It is a form of death-wish. The dead voices are heard inside their silences talking of the past, of dreams and hopes; presence is once again commensurate with absence. Their words report what they hear, describe it, even criticise it. But absence is clearly part of their own language and is read out loud by them for the audience. Silence performs the structural function of integrating the dialogue; in this respect it becomes as explicit as speech itself. The causal logic which says that 'what is not' cannot be experienced is here being radically subverted; thought is no longer the servant of material presence and the conclusion is no longer dependent upon the premise. The terminal juxtaposition of 'Let's go' and the stage direction 'They do not move' disrupts the causality between language and gesture. Beckett has the body ignore and annul the language which normally instigates its physical action, once more emphatically relating the discontinuity to that between the basic levels of dramatic form.

Even when utterances appear to have a degree of connection with the stage directions there is a linguistic wit threatening to separate them. The words 'just the same' in the following extract play this role, mocking the attempt being made to establish difference, preference and temporal sequence:

> Pozzo: (having lit his pipe). The second is never so sweet . . . (he
>
> takes the pipe out of his mouth, contemplates it) . . . as the
>
> first, I mean. (He puts the pipe back in his mouth.) But it's
>
> sweet just the same.17

As words gradually acquire more and more independence from their task of inducing causality they are liberated to interact solely with one another. Didi and Gogo play incessantly with words; they treat the same word as its opposite, they find synonyms, they use scientific terms because they sound bombastic, they rhyme. But at the same time they dismantle language into fragments of religious, moral and scientific thought. Biblical quotations ('Hope deferred maketh the something sick') are cited not for their meaning but for the gratification offered by their shape, their musical feeling and their evasive nostalgia. By parodying the pretentious rhetoric and logic of conventional philosophical thinking they demystify Logos by questioning the very elements it is presumed to be endowed with: clarity, intelligibility, rationality, causality. The myth of meaning is demolished. To be replaced with what? The third of the Duthuit dialogues is unequivocal: 'The much to express, the little to express, the ability to express much, the ability to express little, merge in a common anxiety to express as much as possible, or as truly as possible, or as finely as possible, to the best of one's ability.18 It is above all, as commentators on the play have often stated, in Lucky's repetitious, bombastic, pseudo-scientific speech that Beckett congeals the disarticulation of the rational language inaugurated by Didi's playful dealings with quotations. Here unmediated speech is used against the mediated language representative of conventional literary, religious and scientific discourses. Lucky's speech is not, however, merely anti-intellectual, however much it may situate the intellect as the domain responsible for the mind's appropriation of feelings and sensations. For Beckett the problem does not so much reside in the split between the mind and the body which language initiates, but rather in the specific mode of articulation of different discourses with each other for the synthesis of a rational Logos. Lucky systematically disconnects these various discourses from their 'spinal cord,' from their point of convergence: a conception of the world in terms defined by the presence of an absolute. The fragmentation and repetition of his speech reflect the linguisticintellectual chaos which results from the 'absolute absence of the absolute.'19 The 'absolute' organizes human Logos by imposing an internal order; Lucky's speech deconstructs that unity, and with it the congruity of man with the absolute by which it is determined.

The speech starts with a hypothetical statement about the existence of a personal God, outside time, living in divine 'apathia' (non-responsiveness), divine 'aphasia' (speechlessness), and divine 'athambia' (lack of the capacity for amazement). This personal God loves us dearly, with some exceptions, but he does not communicate with us, cannot feel anything for us, and finally condemns us 'for reasons unknown'.20 In this respect he is utterly absent from that humanity which, deprived of the meaning its attachment to any absolute could provide, is scattered in pieces across philosophical, religious and scientific domains. Despite its apparent haphazardness, however, the speech is carefully structured around recurrent phrases and words. The particular phrase 'for reasons unknown' recurs more often than any other; it functions as an effective condensation of Lucky's message to the audience - the impossibility of reasoning when causes are unintelligible. Beckett once said that 'there is an endless verbal germination, maturation, putrefaction, the cyclic dynamism of the intermediate,'21 and Lucky's speech is based precisely upon such a circular movement of language from its initial stage of exemplary articulation (scientific hypothesis) to its final decay (childish gibberish). Human Logos might, we infer, progress towards its perfection insofar as it were able to reflect the internal unity of a world inspired by the absolute, but 'the personal God' (whether absent or present) is neither charitable, intelligent nor in the least bit interested in humanity: Logos as progress is subverted by Logos as regress. Lucky's reduction of speech to a chaotic juxtaposition of irrelevant words expresses the decay of one kind of order, but his 'think' also embodies the germination of another kind; in Andrew Kennedy's words, 'the deteriorating syntax releases, as through fission, isolated word clusters which sound like the lost "true voice" in the speech'.22 In the event, however, even this 'true' voice in its linguistic anarchy fades away; 'There is an end to his thinking' as Pozzo says. In Act II we find out that this has become a permanent condition for the dumb Lucky. Lucky, the slave, has by this time lost the last index of his humanity, the ability to articulate words and thoughts, and definitively regressed to the animal condition which his role as slave implies. But, astonishingly enough, Lucky's deterioration is not accompanied by an concomitant increase in Pozzo's status as master. Pozzo has not only gone blind; he is less articulate than he was in Act I. His loss of articulacy goes hand in hand with his loss of sight; both are emblematic of Pozzo's having himself entered a world in which time and space are meaningless. For to be blind is to be unconscious of whether or not you are perceived by Godot, the timeless/ spaceless witness, whose coming would soothe the anxieties of uncertainty and confirm humanity's existence. Where there is hope for Didi and Gogo, for Pozzo there is only despair. Even if he is perceived by Lucky he can never be reassured that this is the case because Lucky is not in a position to articulate his presence. Furthermore, to be blind is to live in a void, to be unable to perceive either the passage of time or the change of place. The notion of time is even more meaningless than the notion of space because it can in no way be empirically experienced. Time division is arbitrary because it is established in terms of purely subjective criteria; it is the result of a general concensus to accept a certain timing system as the most suitable for given social purposes. Hence Pozzo's outburst to Vladimir:

> Pozzo: (suddenly furious) have you not done tormenting me with your accursed time! It's abominable! When! . . . One day . . .

like any other day, one day he went dumb, one day I went
blind, one day we'll go deaf, one day we were born, one
day we shall die, the same day, the same second, . . .23

For the Pozzo who experiences the flow of time as a raw material there is nothing 'natural' in the names those with sight give to their time divisions. For him words like 'yesterday' and 'today' do not correspond to any physical reality. Time is not for him equal to the hours, days and years which are the mere notation of its passing, its arbitrarily defined time-signs. Here Beckett penetrates to what really undermines the myth of a 'natural' language, the acceptance of the notion of the 'arbitrariness' of the sign.24 Pozzo's experience is of stopped time because in the absence of accredited divisions time cannot be experienced as a movement. He reacts violently to the use of words like 'yesterday' and 'tomorrow' because language as expression has for him ceased to be related to experience in an unproblematically 'natural' manner. If space and time have been dismantled, so too has causality, and with it discourses structured around a coherent internal principle of the validity and efficiency of reasoning. Blind Pozzo, deprived of the experience of those essential notions sustaining rational discourse, is no longer articulate. In the past he derived authority from his eloquence, from his lyricism and from his ability to reason. These three qualities constitute what in Happy days finds its verbal and visual quintessence: the 'old style'.

The Pozzo of Act I seems to be a living embodiment of the 'old style'. He explains (!) the twilight in a lyrical spirit which cannot conceal his fundamentally positivist preconceptions. His speech is larded with phrases which carry a residual poetical feeling ('touch of autumn in the air this evening,' for example) and by witticisms of an ambiguous kind. This vocabulary is enriched with a variety of synonyms noisily put together so as to select the 'right one'. Thus 'impress' is rejected for 'mollify' and this in turn for 'cod' so that he may 'accurately' explain why Lucky 'does not make himself comfortable,' in other words why he suffers. For Pozzo even suffering can be attributed to the free choice of the victim through the distorting effects of reasoning: 'Why he doesn't make himself comfortable? Lets try and get it clear. Has he not the right to? Certainly he has. It follows that he doesn't want to. There's reasoning for you'.25 By disclosing the ground against which 'reasoning' figures, Beckett shatters the illusion that causality is a straightforward and 'objective' mental process and demonstrates the contrary, namely that rational discourse effectively distorts reality because it claims to reflect it. This is the unacceptable face of 'the old style' as reflected in the theatrical language of nineteenth century realism. Pozzo's wit, lyricism and rationality are wiped out by his experience of approaching the zero degree. But even this experience can be dynamic, as Vladimir and Estragon have shown, for it can lead to the attempt to articulate new meanings in new ways. In this respect Waiting for Godot inaugurates the project which underpins all of Beckett's subsequent drama: to present the search for self and meaning in terms of a dramatic language which derives its power from its own self-questioning coupled with its 'obligation to express'. At every level of organization we encounter 'the dynamism of the intermediate'. There are no fixed frames of reference. We are from the start trapped in the realm of human existence, oscillating between the poles of difference, between presence and absence, between self and other, at once longing for and fearing the apotheosis of the zero. It is in accordance with Beckett's views on such matters, as epitomized and dramatized in Waiting for Godot, that value should be seen to reside not so much in any result of the process as in the process itself.

10. Discuss the religious meaning in Samuel Beckett's Waiting for Godot

Waiting for Godot is one of the classic works of theater of the absurd. The play seems absurd but with a deep religious meaning. This text tries to explore the theme in four parts of God and man, breaking the agreement, repentance and imprecation and waiting for salvation. Samuel Beckett is a famous Irish dramatist and novelist and Waiting for Godot is his masterpiece. Since the play was published, it has been suffered different comments. Although it is recognized as the masterpiece of theater of the absurd, it is filled with religious feelings of the writer. "Religious education he received in family and in church when he was in his teens has produced profound influences on his literary creation. Original sin, salvation, second coming of Jesus and other themes in Holy Bible have been ringing in his works."(Sun, 2005, p.296) Beckett's Religious theme has attracted the attention of the researchers. This article will explain Waiting for Godot on basis of the theory of Christian theology in order to help readers to understand the theme of the play more deeply.

God and man

In Waiting for Godot, both Vladimir and Estragon on stage, and Godot, who is away from the vision of the audience, bear a certain symbolic significance. Relationship between them suggests that of God and man.

Needless to say, Godot is similar with God in pronunciation, which is enough to trigger the audience's association with God. Of course, other descriptions of Godot in the play can also make the readers consider him to be God of Christianity. From the description of appearance, Godot has similarities with God. The boy, a messenger, in the play is from Godot's place and he is the only one who has seen Godot. The two tramps once asked him what color Godot's beard is. There is a conversation between them. Vladimir: Has he a beard, Mr. Godot?

Boy: Yes, sir.

Vladimir: Fair or... or black?

Boy: I think it's white, sir.

Vladimir: Christ have mercy on us!

It can be concluded that Godot wears a long white beard, which is in line with what God is like in the Holy Bible. John recorded he had seen the revived Savior in Revelation. He wrote, "he has golden belt in his waist. His hair is as white as snow like wool. His eyes are shining like fire and his feet are glittering as copper. When he speaks, his voice is like flood roaring." (Zeng, 1994, p.696). The beard and hair of God is white as snow, and Godot's beard is exactly the same. This is a description of Godot similar to God in appearance.

There are descriptions about Godot similar in God in spirit. In the play, Godot can save, or punish, or try or take care of man. The tramps in the play think that as long as Godot comes, they will be saved. If they do not waiting for Godot, they would be punished by him. The messenger boy said he and his brother keep sheep for Godot. His brother keeps the sheep and he raise the goats. In the Matthew of the Bible, there are words like this, ""When the Son of Man comes in his glory, and all the angels with him. He will sit on his throne in heavenly glory. All the nations will be gathered before him, and he will separate the people one from another as a shepherd separates the sheep from the goats. He will put the sheep on his right and the goats on his left. (Zeng, 1994, p. 624). He would bless his men and let them live in his glory as long as they remember the contract between God and man.

But what can man do? The modern people have aliened with God for a long time. They have lost the religious heritage and walked on the spiritual wasteland. The two tramps are the representatives of human beings. They are the modern incarnations of the modern people without the concern from the whole religion. There are some words in the play, which can prove this point. They go like this, "in this place, at this moment, all mankind is us, whether we like it or not. Let us make the most of it, before it is too late! Let us represent worthily for once the foul brood to which a cruel fate consigned us!" (Beckett, 2006, p. 351) In the play, the two tramps are in an extremely awkward position. They are waiting for Godot from the very beginning to the end. But Godot does not come, which makes those waiting for him suffer a lot.

Then, why are the lambs of God abandoned? Why do the modern people suffer this?

Breaking the contract

Keeping promise is the theme in Old Testament and New Testament. There are five agreements between God and man and God would gradually complete the plan of salvation for man if man follows the contract. They are agreement of Noah, agreement with Abraham, covenant with Abraham, covenant with Moses, covenant with David and new testament, that is, the covenant of Christ and man. Covenant needs the agreement of both parties. It has constraint force and certain obligations to fulfill. But as for the relationship between God and man, God is the creator, and man is the subject of creation. The covenant between God and man is the gift from God." (Sun, 2006, p. 306). The gift and the blessing from God can ensure man to live a comfortable life. But why man is reduced to waiting for salvation? It seems that the two tramps are waiting for Godot to be saved according to the promise, but Godot does not come. Actually the reason does not lie in Godot for his rudeness but in man, who breaks the promise first. It is just because man broke the promise first and they will receive the punishment of endless waiting from God. It can be seen that the breaking of the covenant by man is vividly demonstrated in the play by Beckett.

Estragon: You are it was this evening?

Vladimir: What?

Estragon: That we were to wait.

Vladimir: He said Saturday. (Pause) I think.

Estragon: You think.

Vladimir: I must have made a note of it.

Estragon: But what Saturday? And is it Saturday? It is not rather Sunday (Pause.) Or Monday? (Pause.) Or Friday?

Vladimir: It is not impossible.

Estragon: Or Thursday?

Vladimir: What'll we do?

According to the Bible, it was on Saturday that God made man. And it was on Saturday that Jesus passed away after he was crucified on Friday. He would revive on Sunday so on Saturday man is waiting his reviving. Such an important day becomes vague in the mind of human beings and the solemn date between God and human beings is abandoned. Man can not remember the date with God or even can not know which day he is alive. How can human beings obey the covenant, obtain the trust and understanding from God? Of course, they would not be saved by God.

Repentance and imprecation

Human beings lose the protection of God and become spiritually homeless. They talk nonsense, do funny movements, but in their bottom of heart, they are longing for the salvation by God. However, it is difficult to repair the relations between the man and God. God will re-test man for he needs man's loyalty. Thus what human beings need to do is to repent and pray.

Estragon: what?

Vladimir: Suppose we repented.

Estragon: repented what?

Vladimir: Oh...We wouldn't have to go into the details.

Estragon: Our being born?

God creates man according to what he is like, showing his love to man. In Genesis of the Holy Bible, God says, "Let us make man in our image, after our likeness: and let them have dominion over the fish of the sea, and over the fowl of the air, and over the cattle, and over all the earth, and over every creeping thing that creepeth upon the earth."(Zeng, 1994, p.22). As a result, men become the most favored creature of God. But eating the Forbidden fruits leads to the breakdown of relations between man and God. Men even declined to be obedient to God and refuse the identity of creature by God. "This is a reversal against creation. The downfall of man discloses that he longs for self-constructed and isolated existence instead of a limited creature. the most basic point in the breakdown in relations between man and God is that human beings want to go beyond the boundaries made by God."

What man had done violated God and was expelled from the Garden of Eden. In the era when Waiting for Godot was performed, men had become homeless on the wilderness. If man wants to return to God, he must confess to gain salvation. And God will display his attitude by the performance of human beings. There are words in the play to show such an idea.

Estragon: What exactly did we ask him for?

Vladimir: Were you not there?

Estragon: I can't have been listening.

Vladimir: Oh... nothing very definite.

Estragon: A kind of prayer.

Vladimir: Precisely.

Estragon: A vague supplication.

Vladimir: Exactly

Estragon: And what did he reply?

Vladimir: That he's seen.

Estragon: That he couldn't promise anything.

Vladimir: That he'd have to think it over.

Whether God accepted the repentance depends on the performance of human beings. Any betrayal is not allowed. Betrayal means the fall of punishment. Man is forced to wait without an end of time. With the development of the plot, Godot delays in his coming and men has reached the brink of collapse. They cried out "Help"

Estragon: We'll soon see. Abel! Abel!

Pozzo: Help! Estragon: Got it in one!

Estragon: Perhaps the other is called Cain! Cain!

Pozzo: Help

Estragon: He is all humanity. (Silence)Look at the little cloud.

In Holy Bible, Abel and Cain are the two sons of Adam and Eve and the ancestors of all human beings. Their voices represent those of the entire human race of looking forward to the coming of the Lord once again to save the humanities suffering heavily.

Waiting for salvation

Waiting is the theme throughout the play. Although Godot breaks his promise, the two tramps have shown perseverance. Despite the heavy blow of painfulness, frustration and disappointment, they still keeps on waiting because that is their only hope for they believe only Godot can save them.

How to get salvation? Drama that the story of two thieves.

Vladimir: Our Savior. Two thieves. One is supposed to have been saved and the other... dammed. Estragon: Saved from what?

Vladimir: Hell.

It is recorded in the Holy Bible that together with Jesus two prisoners were crucified. One of them said, "You're Christ, aren't you? You can save us and yourself!" But the other answered, and rebuking him said, "Do you not even fear God, since you are under the same sentence of condemnation? And we indeed are suffering justly, for we are receiving what we deserve for our deeds; but this man has done nothing wrong." And he was saying, "Jesus, remember me when You come in Your kingdom!" Jesus said to him, "Truly I say to you, today you shall be with Me in Paradise." (Zeng, 1994, P. 646). The thief was saved because of his belief. On the cross, he knew what he had done was wrong and he believed Jesus would come again. So, Jesus told him just in that day he could be with Jesus in paradise. People who believe in God can be saved.

Waiting is a process God added for man's salvation. Suffering means tasting the life. Human beings learn to love'

others in this process. In Act I, the two tramps can be seen to have gaps and Lucky is victimized by Pozzo. Only the boy following Godot lives a life with love. But in Act II, the two tramps sincerely embrace, and Pozzo becomes particularly dependent on Lucky. Furthermore, the tramps' help to Pozzo shows the fraternity among people. Human beings are changing towards what God want them to be.

Although Godot does not come, hope is still there. The withered tree in Act I has a few leaves in Act II. Although there are only a few leaves, after all, they are the embodiment of life. The wilting tree in spring bears some hope for the boring waiting. Human beings' waiting is no longer hopeless. Waiting gives significance to existence.

Waiting for Godot expresses the living condition of the Western people who have been out of contact with God and shows their effort to get rid of the situation. It is an anticipation to rebuild the meaningful system of the universe." (Sun, 2005, P.319). Human beings will be patient to wait on, to wait for the arrival of Godot, and to wait for the realization of salvation. Beckett expresses his sincere thought of human existence in the play, which is seemingly absurd.

12

Waiting For Godot Tragicomedy In 2 Acts By Samuel Beckett

THE CHARACTERS

Estragon

Vladimir

Lucky Pozzo

A Boy

ACT - I

A country road. A tree.

Evening.

He gives up, exhausted, rests, tries again.

As before.

Enter Vladimir.

ESTRAGON:

(giving up again). Nothing to be done.

VLADIMIR:

(advancing with short, stiff strides, legs wide apart). I'm beginning to come round to that opinion. All my life I've tried to put it from me, saying Vladimir, be reasonable, you haven't yet tried everything. And I resumed the struggle. (He broods, musing on the struggle. Turning to ESTRAGON.) So there you are again.

ESTRAGON:

Am I?

VLADIMIR:

I'm glad to see you back. I thought you were gone forever.

ESTRAGON:

Me too.

VLADIMIR:

Together again at last! We'll have to celebrate this. But how? (He reflects.) Get up till I embrace you.

ESTRAGON:

(irritably). Not now, not now.

VLADIMIR:

(hurt, coldly). May one inquire where His Highness spent the night?

ESTRAGON:

In a ditch.

VLADIMIR:

(admiringly). A ditch! Where?

ESTRAGON:

(without gesture). Over there.

VLADIMIR:

And they didn't beat you?

ESTRAGON:

Beat me? Certainly they beat me.

VLADIMIR:

The same lot as usual?

ESTRAGON:

The same? I don't know.

VLADIMIR:

When I think of it. . . all these years . . . but for me . . . where would you be . . . (Decisively.) You'd be nothing more than a little heap of bones at the present minute, no doubt about it.

ESTRAGON:

And what of it?

VLADIMIR:

(gloomily). It's too much for one man. (Pause. Cheerfully.) On the other hand what's the good of losing heart now, that's what I say. We should have thought of it a million years ago, in the nineties.

ESTRAGON:

Ah stop blathering and help me off with this bloody thing.

VLADIMIR:

Hand in hand from the top of the Eiffel Tower, among the first. We were respectable in those days. Now it's too late. They wouldn't even let us up. (ESTRAGON tears at his boot.) What are you doing?

ESTRAGON:

Taking off my boot. Did that never happen to you?

VLADIMIR:

Boots must be taken off every day, I'm tired telling you that. Why don't you listen to me?

ESTRAGON:

(feebly). Help me!

VLADIMIR:

It hurts?

ESTRAGON:

(angrily). Hurts! He wants to know if it hurts!

VLADIMIR:

(angrily). No one ever suffers but you. I don't count. I'd like to hear what you'd say if you had what I have.

ESTRAGON:

It hurts?

VLADIMIR:

(angrily). Hurts! He wants to know if it hurts!

ESTRAGON:

(pointing). You might button it all the same.

VLADIMIR:

(stooping). True. (He buttons his fly.) Never neglect the little things of life.

ESTRAGON:

What do you expect, you always wait till the last moment.

VLADIMIR:

(musingly). The last moment. . . (He meditates.) Hope deferred maketh the something sick, who said that?

ESTRAGON:

Why don't you help me?

VLADIMIR:

Sometimes I feel it coming all the same. Then I go all queer. (He takes off his hat, peers inside it, feels about inside it, shakes it, puts it on again.) How shall I say? Relieved and at the same time . . . (he searches for the word). . . appalled. (With emphasis.) AP-PALLED. (He takes off his hat again, peers inside it.) Funny. (He knocks on the crown as though to dislodge a foreign body, peers into it again, puts it on again.) Nothing to be done. (ESTRAGON with a supreme effort succeeds in pulling off his boot. He peers inside it, feels about inside it, turns it upside down, shakes it, looks on the ground to see if anything has fallen out, finds nothing, feels inside it again, staring sightlessly before him.) Well?

ESTRAGON:

Nothing.

VLADIMIR:

Show me.

ESTRAGON:

There's nothing to show.

VLADIMIR:

Try and put it on again.

ESTRAGON:

(examining his foot). I'll air it for a bit.

VLADIMIR:

There's man all over for you, blaming on his boots the faults of his feet. (He takes off his hat again, peers inside it, feels about inside it, knocks on the crown, blows into it, puts it on again.) This is getting alarming. (Silence. Vladimir deep in thought, ESTRAGON pulling at his toes.) One of the thieves was saved. (Pause.) It's a reasonable percentage. (Pause.) Gogo.

ESTRAGON:

What?

VLADIMIR:

Suppose we repented.

ESTRAGON:

Repented what?

VLADIMIR:

Oh . . . (He reflects.) We wouldn't have to go into the details.

ESTRAGON:

Our being bom?

Vladimir breaks into a hearty laugh which he immediately stifles, his hand pressed to his pubis, his face contorted.

VLADIMIR:

One daren't even laugh any more.

ESTRAGON:

Dreadful privation.

VLADIMIR:

Merely smile. (He smiles suddenly from ear to ear, keeps smiling, ceases as suddenly.) It's not the same thing. Nothing to be done. (Pause.) Gogo.

ESTRAGON:

(irritably). What is it?

VLADIMIR:

Did you ever read the Bible?

ESTRAGON:

The Bible . . . (He reflects.) I must have taken a look at it.

VLADIMIR:

Do you remember the Gospels?

ESTRAGON:

I remember the maps of the Holy Land. Coloured they were. Very pretty. The Dead Sea was pale blue. The very look of it made me thirsty. That's where we'll go, I used to say, that's where we'll go for our honeymoon. We'll swim. We'll be happy.

VLADIMIR:

You should have been a poet.

ESTRAGON:

I was. (Gesture towards his rags.) Isn't that obvious?

Silence.

VLADIMIR:

Where was I. . . How's your foot?

ESTRAGON:

Swelling visibly.

VLADIMIR:

Ah yes, the two thieves. Do you remember the story?

ESTRAGON:

No.

VLADIMIR:

Shall I tell it to you?

ESTRAGON:

No.

VLADIMIR:

It'll pass the time. (Pause.) Two thieves, crucified at the same time as our Saviour. One—

ESTRAGON:

Our what?

VLADIMIR:

Our Saviour. Two thieves. One is supposed to have been saved and the other . . . (he searches for the contrary of saved). . . damned.

ESTRAGON:

Saved from what?

VLADIMIR:

Hell.

ESTRAGON:

I'm going.

He does not move.

VLADIMIR:

And yet. . . (pause). . . how is it -this is not boring you I hope- how is it that of the four Evangelists only one speaks of a thief being saved. The four of them were there -or thereabouts- and only one speaks of a thief being saved. (Pause.) Come on, Gogo, return the ball, can't you, once in a way?

ESTRAGON:

(with exaggerated enthusiasm). I find this really most extraordinarily interesting.

VLADIMIR:

One out of four. Of the other three, two don't mention any thieves at all and the third says that both of them abused him.

ESTRAGON:

Who?

VLADIMIR:

What?

ESTRAGON:

What's all this about? Abused who?

VLADIMIR:

The Saviour.

ESTRAGON:

Why?

VLADIMIR:

Because he wouldn't save them.

ESTRAGON:

From hell?

VLADIMIR:

Imbecile! From death.

ESTRAGON:

I thought you said hell.

VLADIMIR:

From death, from death.

ESTRAGON:

Well what of it?

VLADIMIR:

Then the two of them must have been damned.

ESTRAGON:

And why not?

VLADIMIR:

But one of the four says that one of the two was saved.

ESTRAGON:

Well? They don't agree and that's all there is to it.

VLADIMIR:

But all four were there. And only one speaks of a thief being saved. Why believe him rather than the others?

ESTRAGON:

Who believes him?

VLADIMIR:

Everybody. It's the only version they know.

ESTRAGON:

People are bloody ignorant apes.

He rises painfully, goes limping to extreme left, halts, gazes into distance off with his hand screening his eyes, turns, goes to extreme right, gazes into distance. Vladimir watches him, then goes and picks up the boot, peers into it, drops it hastily.

VLADIMIR:

Pah!

He spits. ESTRAGON moves to center, halts with his back to auditorium.

ESTRAGON:

Charming spot. (He turns, advances to front, halts facing auditorium.) Inspiring prospects. (He turns to Vladimir.) Let's go.

VLADIMIR:

We can't.

ESTRAGON:

Why not?

VLADIMIR:

We're waiting for Godot.

ESTRAGON:

(despairingly). Ah! (Pause.) You're sure it was here?

VLADIMIR:

What?

ESTRAGON:

That we were to wait.

VLADIMIR:

He said by the tree. (They look at the tree.) Do you see any others?

ESTRAGON:

What is it?

VLADIMIR:

I don't know. A willow.

ESTRAGON:

Where are the leaves?

ESTRAGON:

No more weeping.

VLADIMIR:

Or perhaps it's not the season.

ESTRAGON:

Looks to me more like a bush.

VLADIMIR:

A shrub.

ESTRAGON:

A bush.

VLADIMIR:

A—. What are you insinuating? That we've come to the wrong place?

ESTRAGON:

He should be here.

VLADIMIR:

He didn't say for sure he'd come.

ESTRAGON:

And if he doesn't come?

VLADIMIR:

We'll come back tomorrow.

ESTRAGON:

And then the day after tomorrow.

VLADIMIR:

Possibly.

ESTRAGON:

And so on.

VLADIMIR:

The point is—

ESTRAGON:

Until he comes.

VLADIMIR:

You're merciless.

ESTRAGON:

We came here yesterday.

VLADIMIR:

Ah no, there you're mistaken.

ESTRAGON:

What did we do yesterday?

VLADIMIR:

What did we do yesterday?

ESTRAGON:

Yes.

VLADIMIR:

Why . . . (Angrily.) Nothing is certain when you're about.

ESTRAGON:

In my opinion we were here.

VLADIMIR:

(looking round). You recognize the place?

ESTRAGON:

I didn't say that.

VLADIMIR:

Well?

ESTRAGON:

That makes no difference.

VLADIMIR:

All the same . . . that tree . . . (turning towards auditorium) that bog .

ESTRAGON:

You're sure it was this evening?

VLADIMIR:

What?

ESTRAGON:

That we were to wait.

VLADIMIR:

He said Saturday. (Pause.) I think.

ESTRAGON:

You think.

VLADIMIR:

I must have made a note of it. (He fumbles in his pockets, bursting with miscellaneous rubbish.)

ESTRAGON:

(very insidious). But what Saturday? And is it Saturday? Is it not rather Sunday? (Pause.) Or Monday? (Pause.) Or Friday?

VLADIMIR:

(looking wildly about him, as though the date was inscribed in the landscape). It's not possible!

ESTRAGON:

Or Thursday?

VLADIMIR:

What'll we do?

ESTRAGON:

If he came yesterday and we weren't here you may be sure he won't come again today.

VLADIMIR:

But you say we were here yesterday.

ESTRAGON:

I may be mistaken. (Pause.) Let's stop talking for a minute, do you mind?

VLADIMIR:

(feebly). All right. (ESTRAGON sits down on the mound. Vladimir paces agitatedly to and fro, halting from time to time to gaze into distance off. ESTRAGON falls asleep. Vladimir halts finally before ESTRAGON.) Gogo! . . . Gogo! . . . GOGO! ESTRAGON wakes with a start.

ESTRAGON:

(restored to the horror of his situation). I was asleep! (Despairingly.) Why will you never let me sleep?

VLADIMIR:

I felt lonely.

ESTRAGON:

I had a dream.

VLADIMIR:

Don't tell me!

ESTRAGON:

I dreamt that—

VLADIMIR:

DON'T TELL ME!

ESTRAGON:

(gesture toward the universe). This one is enough for you? (Silence.) It's not nice of you, Didi. Who am I to tell my private nightmares to if I can't tell them to you?

VLADIMIR:

Let them remain private. You know I can't bear that.

ESTRAGON:

(coldly.) There are times when I wonder if it wouldn't be better for us to part.

VLADIMIR:

You wouldn't go far.

ESTRAGON:

That would be too bad, really too bad. (Pause.) Wouldn't it, Didi, be really too bad? (Pause.) When you think of the beauty of the way. (Pause.) And the goodness of the wayfarers. (Pause. Wheedling.) Wouldn't it, Didi?

VLADIMIR:

Calm yourself.

ESTRAGON:

(voluptuously.) Calm . . . calm . . . The English say cawm. (Pause.) You know the story of the Englishman in the brothel?

VLADIMIR:

Yes.

ESTRAGON:

Tell it to me.

VLADIMIR:

Ah stop it!

ESTRAGON:

An Englishman having drunk a little more than usual proceeds to a brothel. The bawd asks him if he wants a fair one, a dark one or a red-haired one. Go on.

VLADIMIR:

STOP IT!

Exit Vladimir hurriedly. ESTRAGON gets up and follows him as far as the limit of the stage. Gestures of ESTRAGON like those of a spectator encouraging a pugilist. Enter Vladimir. He brushes past ESTRAGON, crosses the stage with bowed head. ESTRAGON takes a step towards him, halts.

ESTRAGON:

(gently.) You wanted to speak to me? (Silence. ESTRAGON takes a step forward.) You had something to say to me? (Silence. Another step forward.) Didi. . .

VLADIMIR:

(without turning). I've nothing to say to you.

ESTRAGON:

(step forward). You're angry? (Silence. Step forward). Forgive me. (Silence. Step forward. ESTRAGON lays his hand on Vladimir's shoulder.) Come, Didi. (Silence.) Give me your hand. (Vladimir half turns.) Embrace me! (Vladimir stiffens.) Don't be stubborn! (Vladimir softens. They embrace. ESTRAGON recoils.) You stink of garlic!

VLADIMIR:

It's for the kidneys. (Silence. ESTRAGON looks attentively at the tree.) What do we do now?

ESTRAGON:

Wait.

VLADIMIR:

Yes, but while waiting.

ESTRAGON:

What about hanging ourselves?

VLADIMIR:

Hmm. It'd give us an erection.

ESTRAGON:

(highly excited). An erection!

VLADIMIR:

With all that follows. Where it falls mandrakes grow. That's why they shriek when you pull them up. Did you not know that?

ESTRAGON:

Let's hang ourselves immediately!

VLADIMIR:

From a bough? (They go towards the tree.) I wouldn't trust it.

ESTRAGON:

We can always try.

VLADIMIR:

Go ahead.

ESTRAGON:

After you.

VLADIMIR:

No no, you first.

ESTRAGON:

Why me?

VLADIMIR:

You're lighter than I am.

ESTRAGON:

Just so!

VLADIMIR:

I don't understand.

ESTRAGON:

Use your intelligence, can't you?

Vladimir uses his intelligence.

VLADIMIR:

(finally). I remain in the dark.

ESTRAGON:

This is how it is. (He reflects.) The bough . . . the bough . . . (Angrily.) Use your head, can't you?

VLADIMIR:

You're my only hope.

ESTRAGON:

(with effort). Gogo light—bough not break—Gogo dead. Didi heavy—bough break—Didi alone. Whereas—

VLADIMIR:

I hadn't thought of that.

ESTRAGON:

If it hangs you it'll hang anything.

VLADIMIR:

But am I heavier than you?

ESTRAGON:

So you tell me. I don't know. There's an even chance. Or nearly.

VLADIMIR:

Well? What do we do?

ESTRAGON:

Don't let's do anything. It's safer.

VLADIMIR:

Let's wait and see what he says.

ESTRAGON:

Who?

VLADIMIR:

Godot.

ESTRAGON:

Good idea.

VLADIMIR:

Let's wait till we know exactly how we stand.

ESTRAGON:

On the other hand it might be better to strike the iron before it freezes.

VLADIMIR:

I'm curious to hear what he has to offer. Then we'll take it or leave it.

ESTRAGON:

What exactly did we ask him for?

VLADIMIR:

Were you not there?

ESTRAGON:

I can't have been listening.

VLADIMIR:

Oh . . . Nothing very definite.

ESTRAGON:

A kind of prayer.

VLADIMIR:

Precisely.

ESTRAGON:

A vague supplication.

VLADIMIR:

Exactly.

ESTRAGON:

And what did he reply?

VLADIMIR:

That he'd see.

ESTRAGON:

That he couldn't promise anything.

VLADIMIR:

That he'd have to think it over.

ESTRAGON:

In the quiet of his home.

VLADIMIR:

Consult his family.

ESTRAGON:

His friends.

VLADIMIR:

His agents.

ESTRAGON:

His correspondents.

VLADIMIR:

His books.

ESTRAGON:

His bank account.

VLADIMIR:

Before taking a decision.

ESTRAGON:

It's the normal thing.

VLADIMIR:

Is it not?

ESTRAGON:

I think it is.

VLADIMIR:

I think so too.

Silence.

ESTRAGON:

(anxious). And we?

VLADIMIR:

I beg your pardon?

ESTRAGON:

I said, And we?

VLADIMIR:

I don't understand.

ESTRAGON:

Where do we come in?

VLADIMIR:

Come in?

ESTRAGON:

Take your time.

VLADIMIR:

Come in? On our hands and knees.

ESTRAGON:

As bad as that?

VLADIMIR:

Your Worship wishes to assert his prerogatives?

ESTRAGON:

We've no rights any more?

Laugh of Vladimir, stifled as before, less the smile.

VLADIMIR:

You'd make me laugh if it wasn't prohibited.

ESTRAGON:

We've lost our rights?

VLADIMIR:

(distinctly). We got rid of them.

Silence. They remain motionless, arms dangling, heads sunk, sagging at knees.

ESTRAGON:

(feebly). We're not tied? (Pause.) We're not—

VLADIMIR:

Listen!

They listen, grotesquely rigid.

ESTRAGON:

I hear nothing.

VLADIMIR:

Hsst! (They listen. ESTRAGON loses his balance, almost falls. He clutches the arm of Vladimir, who totters. They listen, huddled together.) Nor I.

Sighs of relief. They relax and separate.

ESTRAGON:

You gave me a fright.

VLADIMIR:

I thought it was he.

ESTRAGON:

Who?

VLADIMIR:

Godot.

ESTRAGON:

Pah! The wind in the reeds.

VLADIMIR:

I could have sworn I heard shouts.

ESTRAGON:

And why would he shout?

VLADIMIR:

At his horse.

Silence.

ESTRAGON:

(violently). I'm hungry!

VLADIMIR:

Do you want a carrot?

ESTRAGON:

Is that all there is?

VLADIMIR:

I might have some turnips.

ESTRAGON:

Give me a carrot. (Vladimir rummages in his pockets, takes out a turnip and gives it to ESTRAGON who takes a bite out of it. Angrily.) It's a turnip!

VLADIMIR:

Oh pardon! I could have sworn it was a carrot. (He rummages again in his pockets, finds nothing but turnips.) All that's turnips. (He rummages.) You must have eaten the last. (He rummages.) Wait, I have it. (He brings out a carrot and gives it to ESTRAGON.) There, dear fellow.

(ESTRAGON wipes the carrot on his sleeve and begins to eat it.) Make it last, that's the end of them.

ESTRAGON:

(chewing). I asked you a question.

VLADIMIR:

Ah.

ESTRAGON:

Did you reply?

VLADIMIR:

How's the carrot?

ESTRAGON:

It's a carrot.

VLADIMIR:

So much the better, so much the better. (Pause.) What was it you wanted to know?

ESTRAGON:

I've forgotten. (Chews.) That's what annoys me. (He looks at the carrot appreciatively, dangles it between finger and thumb.) I'll never forget this carrot. (He sucks the end of it meditatively.) Ah yes, now I remember.

VLADIMIR:

Well?

ESTRAGON:

(his mouth full, vacuously). We're not tied?

VLADIMIR:

I don't hear a word you're saying.

ESTRAGON:

(chews, swallows). I'm asking you if we're tied.

VLADIMIR:

Tied?

ESTRAGON:

Ti-ed.

VLADIMIR:

How do you mean tied?

ESTRAGON:

Down.

VLADIMIR:

But to whom? By whom?

ESTRAGON:

To your man.

VLADIMIR:

To Godot? Tied to Godot! What an idea! No question of it. (Pause.) For the moment.

ESTRAGON:

His name is Godot?

VLADIMIR:

I think so.

ESTRAGON:

Fancy that. (He raises what remains of the carrot by the stub of leaf, twirls it before his eyes.) Funny, the more you eat the worse it gets.

VLADIMIR:

With me it's just the opposite.

ESTRAGON:

In other words?

VLADIMIR:

I get used to the muck as I go along.

ESTRAGON:

(after prolonged reflection). Is that the opposite?

VLADIMIR:

Question of temperament.

ESTRAGON:

Of character.

VLADIMIR:

Nothing you can do about it.

ESTRAGON:

No use struggling.

VLADIMIR:

One is what one is.

ESTRAGON:

No use wriggling.

VLADIMIR:

The essential doesn't change.

ESTRAGON:

Nothing to be done. (He proffers the remains of the carrot to Vladimir.) Like to finish it?

A terrible cry, close at hand. ESTRAGON drops the carrot. They remain motionless, then together make a sudden rush towards the wings. ESTRAGON stops halfway, runs back, picks up the carrot, stuffs it in his pocket, runs to rejoin Vladimir who is waiting for him, stops again, runs back, picks up his boot, runs to rejoin Vladimir. Huddled together, shoulders hunched, cringing away from the menace, they wait.

Enter Pozzo and Lucky. Pozzo drives Lucky by means of a rope passed round his neck, so that Lucky is the first to enter, followed by the rope which is long enough to let him reach the middle of the stage before Pozzo appears. Lucky carries a heavy bag, a folding stool, a picnic basket and a greatcoat, Pozzo a whip.

POZZO:

(off). On! (Crack of whip. Pozzo appears. They cross the stage. Lucky passes before Vladimir and ESTRAGON and exit. Pozzo at the sight of Vladimir and ESTRAGON stops short. The rope tautens. Pozzo jerks at it violently.) Back!

Noise of Lucky falling with all his baggage. Vladimir and ESTRAGON turn towards him, half washing halffearing to go to his assistance. Vladimir takes a step towards Lucky, ESTRAGON holds him back by the sleeve.

VLADIMIR:

Let me go!

ESTRAGON:

Stay where you are!

POZZO:

Be careful! He's wicked. (Vladimir and ESTRAGON turn towards Pozzo.) With strangers.

ESTRAGON:

(undertone). Is that him?

VLADIMIR:

Who?

ESTRAGON:

(trying to remember the name). Er . . .

VLADIMIR:

Godot?

ESTRAGON:

Yes.

POZZO:

I present myself: Pozzo.

VLADIMIR:

(to ESTRAGON). Not at all!

ESTRAGON:

He said Godot.

VLADIMIR:

Not at all!

ESTRAGON:

(timidly, to Pozzo). You're not Mr. Godot, Sir?

POZZO:

(terrifying voice). I am Pozzo! (Silence.) Pozzo! (Silence.) Does that name mean nothing to you? (Silence.) I say does that name mean nothing to you?

Vladimir and ESTRAGON look at each other questioningly.

ESTRAGON:

(pretending to search). Bozzo . . . Bozzo . . .

VLADIMIR:

(ditto). Pozzo . . . Pozzo . . .

POZZO:

PPPOZZZO!

ESTRAGON:

Ah! Pozzo ... let me see . . . Pozzo . . .

VLADIMIR:

Is it Pozzo or Bozzo?

ESTRAGON:

Pozzo . . . no . . . I'm afraid I... no ... I don't seem to . . .

Pozzo advances threateningly.

VLADIMIR:

(conciliating). I once knew a family called Gozzo. The mother had the clap.

ESTRAGON:

(hastily). We're not from these parts, Sir.

POZZO:

(halting). You are human beings none the less. (He puts on his glasses.) As far as one can see. (He takes off his glasses.) Of the same species as myself. (He bursts into an enormous laugh.) Of the same species as Pozzo! Made in God's image!

VLADIMIR:

Well you see—

POZZO:

(peremptory). Who is Godot?

ESTRAGON:

Godot?

POZZO:

You took me for Godot.

VLADIMIR:

Oh no, Sir, not for an instant, Sir.

POZZO:

Who is he?

VLADIMIR:

Oh he's a . . . he's a kind of acquaintance.

ESTRAGON:

Nothing of the kind, we hardly know him

VLADIMIR:

True ... we don't know him very well . . . but all the same . . .

ESTRAGON:

Personally, I wouldn't even know him if I saw him.

POZZO:

You took me for him

ESTRAGON:

(,recoiling before Pozzo). That's to say . . . you understand . . . the dusk . .
. the strain . . . waiting ... I confess ... I imagined ... for a second . . .

POZZO:

Waiting? So you were waiting for him?

VLADIMIR:

Well you see—

POZZO:

Here? On my land?

VLADIMIR:

We didn't intend any harm.

ESTRAGON:

We meant well.

POZZO:

The road is free to all.

VLADIMIR:

That's how we looked at it.

POZZO:

It's a disgrace. But there you are.

ESTRAGON:

Nothing we can do about it.

POZZO:

(with magnanimous gesture). Let's say no more about it. (He jerks the rope.) Up pig! (Pause.) Every time he drops he falls asleep. (Jerks the rope.) Up hog! (Noise of Lucky getting up and picking up his baggage. Pozzo jerks the rope.) Back! (Enter Lucky backwards.) Stop! (Lucky stops.) Turn! (Lucky turns. To

Vladimir and ESTRAGON, affably.) Gentlemen, I am happy to have met you.

(Before their incredulous expression.) Yes yes, sincerely happy. (He jerks the rope.) Closer! (Lucky advances.) Stop! (Lucky stops.) Yes, the road seems long when one journeys all alone for . . . (he consults his watch). . . yes . . . (he calculates) . . . yes, six hours, that's right, six hours on end, and never a soul in sight. (To Lucky.) Coat! (Luckyputs down the bag, advances, gives the coat, goes back to his place, takes up the bag.) Hold that! (Pozzo holds out the whip. Lucky advances and, both his hands being occupied, takes the whip in his mouth, then goes back to his place. Pozzo begins to put on his coat, stops.)

Coat! (Lucky puts down the bag, basket and stool, helps Pozzo on with his coat, goes back to his place and takes up bag, basket and stool.) Touch of autumn in the air this evening. (Pozzo finishes buttoning up his coat, stoops, inspects himself, straightens up.) Whip! (Lucky advances, stoops, Pozzo snatches the whip from his mouth, Lucky goes back to his place.) Yes, gentlemen, I cannot go for long without the society of my likes (he puts on his glasses and looks at the two likes) even when the likeness is an imperfect one. (He takes off his glasses.) Stool! (Lucky puts down bag and basket, advances, opens stool, puts it down, goes back to his place, takes up bag and basket.) Closer! (Lucky puts down bag and basket, advances, moves stool, goes back to his place, takes up bag and basket. Pozzo sits down, places the butt of his whip against Lucky's chest and pushes.) Back! (Lucky takes a step back.) Further! (Lucky takes another step back.) Stop! (Lucky stops. To Vladimir and ESTRAGON.) That is why, with your permission, I propose to dally with you a moment, before I venture any further. Basket! (Lucky advances, gives the basket, goes back to his place.) The fresh air stimulates the jaded appetite. (He opens the basket, takes out a piece of chicken and a bottle of vine.) Basket! (Lucky advances, picks up the basket and goes back to his place.) Further! (Lucky takes a step back.) He stinks. Happy days!

He drinks from the bottle, puts it down and begins to eat. Silence.

Vladimir and ESTRAGON, cautiously at first, then more boldly, begin to circle about Lucky, inspecting him up and down. Pozzo eats his chicken voraciously, throwing away the bones after having sucked them. Lucky sags slowly, until bag and basket touch the ground, then straightens up with a start and begins to sag again. Rhythm of one sleeping on his feet.

ESTRAGON:

What ails him?

VLADIMIR:

He looks tired.

ESTRAGON:

Why doesn't he put down his bags?

VLADIMIR:

How do I know? (They close in on him.) Careful!

ESTRAGON:

Say something to him.

VLADIMIR:

Look!

ESTRAGON:

What?

VLADIMIR:

(pointing). His neck!

ESTRAGON:

(looking at the neck). I see nothing.

VLADIMIR:

Here.

ESTRAGON goes over beside Vladimir.

ESTRAGON:

Oh I say!

VLADIMIR:

A running sore!

ESTRAGON:

It's the rope.

VLADIMIR:

It's the rubbing.

ESTRAGON:

It's inevitable.

VLADIMIR:

It's the knot.

ESTRAGON:

It's the chafing.

They resume their inspection, dwell on the face.

VLADIMIR:

(grudgingly). He's not bad looking.

ESTRAGON:

(shrugging his shoulders, wry face.) Would you say so?

VLADIMIR:

A trifle effeminate.

ESTRAGON:

Look at the slobber.

VLADIMIR:

It's inevitable.

ESTRAGON:

Look at the slaver.

VLADIMIR:

Perhaps he's a halfwit.

ESTRAGON:

A cretin.

VLADIMIR:

(,looking closer). Looks like a goiter.

ESTRAGON:

(ditto). It's not certain.

VLADIMIR:

He's panting.

ESTRAGON:

It's inevitable.

VLADIMIR:

And his eyes!

ESTRAGON:

What about them?

VLADIMIR:

Goggling out of his head.

ESTRAGON:

Looks like his last gasp to me.

VLADIMIR:

It's not certain. (Pause.) Ask him a question.

ESTRAGON:

Would that be a good thing?

VLADIMIR:

What do we risk?

ESTRAGON:

(timidly). Mister . . .

VLADIMIR:

Louder.

ESTRAGON:

(louder). Mister . . .

POZZO:

Leave him in peace! (They turn toward Pozzo who, having finished eating, wipes his mouth with the back of his hand.) Can't you see he wants to rest? Basket! (He strikes a match and begins to light his pipe. ESTRAGON sees the chicken bones on the ground and stares at them greedily. As Lucky does not move Pozzo throws the match angrily away andjerks the rope.) Basket! (Lucky starts, almost falls, recovers his senses, advances, puts the bottle in the basket and goes back to his place. ESTRAGON stares at the bones. Pozzo strikes another match and lights his pipe.) What can you expect, it's not his job. (Eke pulls at his pipe, stretches out his legs.) Ah! That's better.

ESTRAGON:

(timidly). Please Sir . . .

POZZO:

What is it, my good man?

ESTRAGON:

Er . . . you've finished with the . . . er . . . you don't need the . . . er . . . bones,

Sir?

VLADIMIR:

(scandalized). You couldn't have waited?

POZZO:

No no, he does well to ask. Do I need the bones? (He turns them over with the end of his whip.) No, personally I do not need them any more. (ESTRAGON takes a step towards the bones.) But. . . (ESTRAGON stops short). . . but in theory the bones go to the carrier. He is therefore the one to ask. (ESTRAGON turns towards Lucky, hesitates.) Go on, go on, don't be afraid, ask him, he'll tell you.

ESTRAGON goes towards Lucky, stops before him.

ESTRAGON:

Mister . . . excuse me, Mister . . .

POZZO:

You're being spoken to, pig! Reply! (To ESTRAGON.) Try him again.
ESTRAGON:

Excuse me, Mister, the bones, you won't be wanting the bones?

Lucky looks long at ESTRAGON.

POZZO:

(in raptures). Mister! (Lucky bows his head.) Reply! Do you want them or don't you? (Silence of Lucky. To ESTRAGON.) They're yours. (ESTRAGON makes a dart at the bones, picks them up and begins to gnaw them.) I don't like it. I've never known him to refuse a bone before. (He looks anxiously at Lucky.) Nice business it'd be if he fell sick on me!

He puffs at his pipe.

VLADIMIR:

(exploding). It's a scandal!

Silence. Flabbergasted, ESTRAGON stops gnawing, looks at Pozzo and Vladimir in turn. Pozzo outwardly calm. Vladimir embarrassed.

POZZO:

(To Vladimir). Are you alluding to anything in particular?

VLADIMIR:

(stutteringly resolute). To treat a man . . . (gesture towards Lucky). . . like that.

. . I think that... no ... a human being ... no ... if s a scandal!

ESTRAGON:

(not to be outdone). A disgrace!

He resumes his gnawing.

POZZO:

You are severe. (To Vladimir.) What age are you, if it's not a rude question? (Silence.) Sixty? Seventy? (To ESTRAGON.) What age would you say he was?

ESTRAGON:

Eleven.

POZZO:

I am impertinent. (He knocks out his pipe against the whip, gets up.) I must be getting on. Thank you for your society. (He reflects.) Unless I smoke another pipe before I go. What do you say? (They say nothing.) Oh I'm only a small smoker, a very small smoker, I'm not in the habit of smoking two pipes one on top of the other, it makes (hand to heart, sighing) my heart go pit-a-pat. (Silence.) It's the nicotine, one absorbs it in spite of one's precautions. (Sighs.) You know how it is. (Silence.) But perhaps you don't smoke? Yes? No? It's of no importance. (Silence.) But how am I to sit down now, without affectation, now that I have risen? Without appearing to -how shall I say-without appearing to falter. (To Vladimir.) I beg your pardon? (Silence.) Perhaps you didn't speak? (Silence.) It's of no importance. Let me see . . .

He reflects.

ESTRAGON:

Ah! That's better.

He puts the bones in his pocket.

VLADIMIR:

Let's go.

ESTRAGON:

So soon?

POZZO:

One moment! (He jerks the rope.) Stool! (Hepoints with his whip. Lucky moves the stool.) More! There! (He sits down. Lucky goes back to his place.) Done it! He fdls his pipe.

VLADIMIR:

(vehemently). Let's go!

POZZO:

I hope I'm not driving you away. Wait a little longer, you'll never regret it.

ESTRAGON:

(scenting charity). We're in no hurry.

POZZO:

(having lit his pipe). The second is never so sweet. . . (he takes the pipe out of his mouth, contemplates it)... as the first I mean. (He puts the pipe back in his mouth.) But it's sweet just the same.

VLADIMIR:

I'm going.

POZZO:

He can no longer endure my presence. I am perhaps not particularly human, but who cares? (To Vladimir.) Think twice before you do anything rash. Suppose you go now while it is still day, for there is no denying it is still day. (They all look up at the sky.) Good. (They stop looking at the sky.) What happens in that case- (he takes the pipe out of his mouth, examines it) -I'm out- (he relights his pipe) -in that case- (puff) -in that case- (puff) -what happens in that case to your appointment with this . . . Godet. . . Godot. . . Godin . . . anyhow you see who I mean, who has your future in his hands . . . (pause) ... at least your immediate future?

VLADIMIR:

Who told you?

POZZO:

He speaks to me again! If this goes on much longer we'll soon be old friends.

ESTRAGON:

Why doesn't he put down his bags?

POZZO:

I too would be happy to meet him. The more people I meet the happier I become. From the meanest creature one departs wiser, richer, more conscious of one's blessings. Even you . . . (he looks at them ostentatiously in turn to make it clear they are both meant). . . even you, who knows, will have added to my store.

ESTRAGON:

Why doesn't he put down his bags?

POZZO:

But that would surprise me.

VLADIMIR:

You're being asked a question.

POZZO:

(delighted). A question! Who? What? A moment ago you were calling me Sir, in fear and trembling. Now you're asking me questions. No good will come of this!

VLADIMIR:

(to ESTRAGON). I think he's listening.

ESTRAGON:

(circling about Lucky). What?

VLADIMIR:

You can ask him now. He's on the alert.

ESTRAGON:

Ask him what?

VLADIMIR:

Why he doesn't put down his bags.

ESTRAGON:

I wonder.

VLADIMIR:

Ask him, can't you?

POZZO:

(who has followed these exchanges with anxious attention, fearing lest the question get lost). You want to know why he doesn't put down his bags, as you call them.

VLADIMIR:

That's it.

POZZO:

(to ESTRAGON). You are sure you agree with that?

ESTRAGON:

He's puffing like a grampus.

POZZO:

The answer is this. (To ESTRAGON). But stay still, I beg of you, you're making me nervous!

VLADIMIR:

Here.

ESTRAGON:

What is it?

VLADIMIR:

He's about to speak.

ESTRAGON goes over beside Vladimir. Motionless, side by side, they wait.

POZZO:

Good. Is everybody ready? Is everybody looking at me? (He looks at Lucky, jerks the rope. Lucky raises his head.) Will you look at me, pig! (Lucky looks at him.) Good. (He puts the pipe in his pocket, takes out a little vaporizer and sprays his throat, puts back the vaporizer in his pocket, clears his throat, spits, takes out the vaporizer again, sprays his throat again, puts back the vaporizer in his pocket.) I am ready. Is everybody listening? Is everybody ready? (He looks at them all in turn, jerks the rope.) Hog! (Lucky raises his head.) I don't like talking in a vacuum. Good. Let me see.

He reflects.

ESTRAGON:

I'm going.

POZZO:

What was it exactly you wanted to know?

VLADIMIR:

Why he—

POZZO:

(angrily). Don't interrupt me! (Pause. Calmer.) If we all speak at once we'll never get anywhere. (Pause.) What was I saying? (Pause. Louder.) What was I saying?

Vladimir mimics one carrying a heavy burden. Pozzo looks at him, puzzled.

ESTRAGON:

(forcibly). Bags. (Hepoints at Lucky.) Why? Always hold. (He sags, panting.) Never put down. (He opens his hands, straightens up with relief.) Why?

POZZO:

Ah! Why couldn't you say so before? Why he doesn't make himself comfortable? Let's try and get this clear. Has he not the right to? Certainly he has. It follows that he doesn't want to. There's reasoning for you. And why doesn't he want to? (Pause.) Gentlemen, the reason is this.

VLADIMIR:

(to ESTRAGON). Make a note of this.

POZZO:

He wants to impress me, so that I'll keep him.

ESTRAGON:

What?

POZZO:

Perhaps I haven't got it quite right. He wants to mollify me, so that I'll give up the idea of parting with him. No, that's not exactly it either.

VLADIMIR:

You want to get rid of him?

POZZO:

He wants to cod me, but he won't.

VLADIMIR:

You want to get rid of him?

POZZO:

He imagines that when I see how well he carries I'll be tempted to keep him on in that capacity.

ESTRAGON:

You've had enough of him?

POZZO:

In reality he carries like a pig. It's not his job.

VLADIMIR:

You want to get rid of him?

POZZO:

He imagines that when I see him indefatigable I'll regret my decision. Such is his miserable scheme. As though I were short of slaves! (All three look at Lucky.) Atlas, son of Jupiter! (Silence.) Well, that's that, I think. Anything else? Vaporizer.

VLADIMIR:

You want to get rid of him?

POZZO:

Remark that I might just as well have been in his shoes and he in mine. If chance had not willed otherwise. To each one his due.

VLADIMIR:

Y ou waagerrim?

POZZO:

I beg your pardon?

VLADIMIR:

You want to get rid of him?

POZZO:

I do. But instead of driving him away as I might have done, I mean instead of simply kicking him out on his arse, in the goodness of my heart I am bringing him to the fair, where I hope to get a good price for him. The truth is you can't drive such creatures away. The best thing would be to kill them.

Lucky weeps.

ESTRAGON:

He's crying!

POZZO:

Old dogs have more dignity. (He proffers his handkerchief to ESTRAGON.) Comfort him, since you pity him. (ESTRAGON hesitates.) Come on. (ESTRAGON takes the handkerchief.) Wipe away his tears, he'll feel less forsaken.

ESTRAGON hesitates.

VLADIMIR:

Here, give it to me, I'll do it.

ESTRAGON refuses to give the handkerchief.

Childish gestures.

POZZO:

Make haste, before he stops. (ESTRAGON approaches Lucky and makes to wipe his eyes. Lucky kicks him violently in the shins. ESTRAGON drops the handkerchief recoils, staggers about the stage howling with pain.) Hanky!

Lucky puts down bag and basket, picks up handkerchief and gives it to Pozzo, goes back to his place, picks up bag and basket.

ESTRAGON:

Oh the swine! (He pulls up the leg of his trousers.) He's crippled me!

POZZO:

I told you he didn't like strangers.

VLADIMIR:

(;to ESTRAGON). Show me. (ESTRAGON shows his leg. To Pozzo, angrily.) He's bleeding!

POZZO:

It's a good sign.

ESTRAGON:

(on one leg). I'll never walk again!

VLADIMIR:

(tenderly). I'll carry you. (Pause.) If necessary.

POZZO:

He's stopped crying. (To ESTRAGON.) You have replaced him as it were. (Lyrically.) The tears of the world are a constant quantity. For each one who begins to weep, somewhere else another stops. The same is true of the laugh.

(He laughs.) Let us not then speak ill of our generation, it is not any unhappier than its predecessors. (Pause.) Let us not speak well of it either. (Pause.) Let us not speak of it at all. (Pause. Judiciously.) It is true the population has increased.

VLADIMIR:

Try and walk.

ESTRAGON takes a few limping steps, stops before Lucky and spits on him, then goes and sits down on the mound.

POZZO:

Guess who taught me all these beautiful things. (Pause. Pointing to Lucky.) My Lucky!

VLADIMIR:

(looking at the sky.) Will night never come?

POZZO:

But for him all my thoughts, all my feelings, would have been of common things. (Pause. With extraordinary vehemence.) Professional worries! (Calmer.) Beauty, grace, truth of the first water, I knew they were all beyond me. So I took a knook.

VLADIMIR:

(startled from his inspection of the sky). A knook?

POZZO:

That was nearly sixty years ago . . . (he consults his watch). . . yes, nearly sixty. (Drawing himself up proudly.) You wouldn't think it to look at me, would you? Compared to him I look like a young man, no? (Pause.) Hat! (Lucky puts down the basket and takes off his hat. His long white hair falls about his face. He puts his hat under his arm and picks up the basket.) Now look. (Pozzo takes off his hat. [All four wear bowlers.] He is completely bald. He puts on his hat again.) Did you see?

VLADIMIR:

And now you turn him away? Such an old and faithful servant!

ESTRAGON:

Swine!

Pozzo more and more agitated.

VLADIMIR:

After having sucked all the good out of him you chuck him away like a . . . like a banana skin. Really . . .

POZZO:

(groaning, clutching his head). I can't bear it. . . any longer . . . the way he goes on . . . you've no idea . . .it's terrible ... he must go . . . (he waves his arms). . .

I'm going mad . . . (he collapses, his head in his hands) ... I can't bear it. . . any longer . . .

Silence. All look at Pozzo.

VLADIMIR:

He can't bear it.

ESTRAGON:

Any longer.

VLADIMIR:

He's going mad.

ESTRAGON:

It's terrible.

VLADIMIR:

(to Lucky). How dare you! It's abominable! Such a good master! Crucify him like that! After so many years! Really!

POZZO:

(sobbing). He used to be so kind ... so helpful. . . and entertaining . . . my good angel. . . and now ... he's killing me.

ESTRAGON:

(to Vladimir). Does he want to replace him?

VLADIMIR:

What?

ESTRAGON:

Does he want someone to take his place or not?

VLADIMIR:

I don't think so.

ESTRAGON:

What?

VLADIMIR:

I don't know.

ESTRAGON:

Ask him

POZZO:

(calmer). Gentlemen, I don't know what came over me. Forgive me. Forget all I said. (More and more his old self.) I don't remember exactly what it was, but you may be sure there wasn't a word of truth in it. (Drawing himself up, striking his chest.) Do I look like a man that can be made to suffer? Frankly? (He rummages in his pockets.) What have I done with my pipe?

VLADIMIR:

Charming evening we're having.

ESTRAGON:

Unforgettable.

VLADIMIR:

And it's not over.

ESTRAGON:

Apparently not.

VLADIMIR:

It's only beginning.

ESTRAGON:

It's awful.

VLADIMIR:

Worse than the pantomime.

ESTRAGON:

The circus.

VLADIMIR:

The music-hall.

ESTRAGON:

The circus.

POZZO:

What can I have done with that briar?

ESTRAGON:

He's a scream. He's lost his dudeen.

Laughs noisily.

VLADIMIR:

I'll be back.

He hastens towards the wings.

ESTRAGON:

End of the corridor, on the left.

VLADIMIR:

Keep my seat.

Exit Vladimir.

POZZO:

(on the point of tears). I've lost my Kapp and Peterson!

ESTRAGON:

(convulsed with merriment). He'll be the death of me!

POZZO:

You didn't see by any chance- (He misses Vladimir.) Oh! He's gone! Without saying goodbye! How could he! He might have waited!

ESTRAGON:

He would have burst.

POZZO:

Oh! (Pause.) Oh well then of course in that case . . .

ESTRAGON:

Come here.

POZZO:

What for?

ESTRAGON:

You'll see.

POZZO:

You want me to get up?

ESTRAGON:

Quick! (Pozzo gets up and goes over beside ESTRAGON. ESTRAGON points off.) Look!

POZZO:

(havingput on his glasses). Oh I say!

ESTRAGON:

It's all over.

Enter Vladimir, somber. He shoulders Lucky out of his way, kicks over the stool, comes and goes agitatedly.

POZZO:

He's not pleased.

ESTRAGON:

(;to Vladimir). You missed a treat. Pity.

Vladimir halts, straightens the stool, comes and goes, calmer.

POZZO:

He subsides. (Looking round.) Indeed all subsides. A great calm descends. (Raising his hand.) Listen! Pan sleeps.

VLADIMIR:

Will night never come?

All three look at the sky.

POZZO:

You don't feel like going until it does?

ESTRAGON:

Well you see—

POZZO:

Why it's very natural, very natural. I myself in your situation, if I had an appointment with a Godin . . . Godet. . . Godot. . . anyhow, you see who I mean, I'd wait till it was black night before I gave up. (He looks at the stool.) I'd very much like to sit down, but I don't quite know how to go about it.

ESTRAGON:

Could I be of any help?

POZZO:

If you asked me perhaps.

ESTRAGON:

What?

POZZO:

If you asked me to sit down.

ESTRAGON:

Would that be a help?

POZZO:

I fancy so.

ESTRAGON:

Here we go. Be seated, Sir, I beg of you.

POZZO:

No no, I wouldn't think of it! (Pause. Aside.) Ask me again.

ESTRAGON:

Come come, take a seat I beseech you, you'll get pneumonia.

POZZO:

You really think so?

ESTRAGON:

Why it's absolutely certain.

POZZO:

No doubt you are right. (He sits down.) Done it again! (Pause.) Thank you, dear fellow. (He consults his watch.) But I must really be getting along, if I am to observe my schedule.

VLADIMIR:

Time has stopped.

POZZO:

(cuddling his watch to his ear). Don't you believe it, Sir, don't you believe it.

(He puts his watch back in his pocket.) Whatever you like, but not that.

ESTRAGON:

(;to Pozzo). Everything seems black to him today.

POZZO:

Except the firmament. (He laughs, pleased with this witticism.) But I see what it is, you are not from these parts, you don't know what our twilights can do. Shall I tell you? (Silence. ESTRAGON is fiddling with his boot again, Vladimir with his hat.) I can't refuse you. (Vaporizer.) A little attention, if you please. (Vladimir and ESTRAGON continue their fiddling, Lucky is half asleep. Pozzo cracks his whip feebly.) What's the matter with this whip? (He gets up and cracks it more vigorously, finally with success. Lucky jumps. Vladimir's hat, ESTRAGON's boot, Lucky's hat, fall to the ground. Pozzo throws down the whip.) Worn out, this whip. (He looks at Vladimir and ESTRAGON.) What was I saying?

VLADIMIR:

Let's go.

ESTRAGON:

But take the weight off your feet, I implore you, you'll catch your death.

POZZO:

True. (He sits down. To ESTRAGON.) What is your name?

ESTRAGON:

Adam.

POZZO:

(who hasn't listened). Ah yes! The night. (He raises his head.) But be a little more attentive, for pity's sake, otherwise we'll never get anywhere. (He looks at the sky.) Look! (All look at the sky except Lucky who is dozing off again. Pozzo jerks the rope.) Will you look at the sky, pig! (Lucky looks at the sky.) Good, that's enough. (They stop looking at the sky.) What is there so extraordinary about it? Qua sky. It is pale and luminous like any sky at this hour of the day. (Pause.) In these latitudes. (Pause.) When the weather is fine. (Lyrical.) An hour ago (he looks at his watch, prosaic) roughly (lyrical) after having poured forth even since (he hesitates, prosaic) say ten o'clock in the morning (lyrical) tirelessly torrents of red and white light it begins to lose its effulgence, to grow pale (gesture of the two hands lapsing by stages) pale, ever a little paler, a little paler until (dramatic pause, ample gesture of the two hands flung wide apart) pppfff! finished! it comes to rest. But- (hand raised in admonition)- but behind this veil of gentleness and peace, night is charging (vibrantly) and will burst upon us (snaps his fingers) pop! like that! (his inspiration leaves him) just when we least expect it. (Silence. Gloomily.) That's how it is on this bitch of an earth. Long silence.

ESTRAGON:

So long as one knows.

VLADIMIR:

One can bide one's time.

ESTRAGON:

One knows what to expect.

VLADIMIR:

No further need to worry.

ESTRAGON:

Simply wait.

VLADIMIR:

We're used to it.

He picks up his hat, peers inside it, shakes it, puts it on.

POZZO:

How did you find me? (Vladimir and ESTRAGON look at him blankly.) Good?

Fair? Middling? Poor? Positively bad?

VLADIMIR:

(first to understand). Oh very good, very very good.

POZZO:

(to **ESTRAGON**). And you, Sir?

ESTRAGON:

Oh tray bong, tray tray tray bong.

POZZO:

(fervently). Bless you, gentlemen, bless you! (Pause.) I have such need of encouragement! (Pause.) I weakened a little towards the end, you didn't notice?

VLADIMIR:

Oh perhaps just a teeny weeny little bit.

ESTRAGON:

I thought it was intentional.

POZZO:

You see my memory is defective.

Silence.

ESTRAGON:

In the meantime, nothing happens.

POZZO:

You find it tedious?

ESTRAGON:

Somewhat.

POZZO:

(to Vladimir). And you, Sir?

VLADIMIR:

I've been better entertained.

Silence. Pozzo struggles inwardly.

POZZO:

Gentlemen, you have been . . . civil to me.

ESTRAGON:

Not at all!

VLADIMIR:

What an idea!

POZZO:

Yes yes, you have been correct. So that I ask myself is there anything I can do in my turn for these honest fellows who are having such a dull, dull time.

ESTRAGON:

Even ten francs would be a help.

VLADIMIR:

We are not beggars!

POZZO:

Is there anything I can do, that's what I ask myself, to cheer them up? I have given them bones, I have talked to them about this and that, I have explained the twilight, admittedly. But is it enough, that's what tortures me, is it enough?

ESTRAGON:

Even five.

VLADIMIR:

(;to ESTRAGON, indignantly). That's enough!

ESTRAGON:

I couldn't accept less.

POZZO:

Is is enough? No doubt. But I am liberal. It's my nature. This evening. So much the worse for me. (He jerks the rope. Lucky looks at him.) For I shall suffer, no doubt about that. (He picks up the whip.) What do you prefer? Shall we have him dance, or sing, or recite, or think, or—

ESTRAGON:

Who?

POZZO:

Who! You know how to think, you two?

VLADIMIR:

He thinks?

POZZO:

Certainly. Aloud. He even used to think very prettily once, I could listen to him for hours. Now . . . (he shudders). So much the worse for me. Well, would you like him to think something for us?

ESTRAGON:

I'd rather he dance, it'd be more fun.

POZZO:

Not necessarily.

ESTRAGON:

Wouldn't it, Didi, be more fun?

VLADIMIR:

I'd like well to hear him think.

ESTRAGON:

Perhaps he could dance first and think afterwards, if it isn't too much to ask him.

VLADIMIR:

(to Pozzo). Would that be possible?

POZZO:

By all means, nothing simpler. It's the natural order.

He laughs briefly.

VLADIMIR:

Then let him dance.

Silence.

POZZO:

Do you hear, hog?

ESTRAGON:

He never refuses?

POZZO:

He refused once. (Silence.) Dance, misery!

Lucky puts down bag and basket, advances towards front, turns to Pozzo. Lucky dances. He stops.

ESTRAGON:

Is that all?

POZZO:

Encore!

Lucky executes the same movements, stops.

ESTRAGON:

Pooh! I'd do as well myself. (He imitates Lucky, almost falls.) With a little practice.

POZZO:

He used to dance the farandole, the fling, the brawl, the jig, the fandango and even the hornpipe. He capered. For joy. Now that's the best he can do. Do you know what he calls it?

ESTRAGON:

The Scapegoat's Agony.

VLADIMIR:

The Hard Stool.

POZZO:

The Net. He thinks he's entangled in a net.

VLADIMIR:

(squirming like an aesthete). There's something about it. . .

Lucky makes to return to his burdens.

POZZO:

Woaa!

Lucky stiffens.

ESTRAGON:

Tell us about the time he refused.

POZZO:

With pleasure, with pleasure. (He fumbles in his pockets.) Wait. (He fumbles.) What have I done with my spray? (He fumbles.) Well now isn't that. . . (He looks up, consternation on his features. Faintly.) I can't find my pulverizer!

ESTRAGON:

(faintly). My left lung is very weak! (He coughs feebly. In ringing tones.) But my right lung is as sound as a bell!

POZZO:

(normal voice). No matter! What was I saying. (Heponders.) Wait. (Ponders.) Well now isn't that. . . (He raises his head.) Help me!

ESTRAGON:

Wait!

VLADIMIR:

Wait!

POZZO:

Wait!

All three take off their hats simultaneously, press their hands to their foreheads, concentrate.

ESTRAGON:

(triumphantly). Ah!

VLADIMIR:

He has it.

POZZO:

(impatient). Well?

ESTRAGON:

Why doesn't he put down his bags?

VLADIMIR:

Rubbish!

POZZO:

Are you sure?

VLADIMIR:

Damn it haven't you already told us?

POZZO:

I've already told you?

ESTRAGON:

He's already told us?

VLADIMIR:

Anyway he has put them down.

ESTRAGON:

(,glance at Lucky). So he has. And what of it?

VLADIMIR:

Since he has put down his bags it is impossible we should have asked why he does not do so.

POZZO:

Stoutly reasoned!

ESTRAGON:

And why has he put them down?

POZZO:

Answer us that.

VLADIMIR:

In order to dance.

ESTRAGON:

True!

POZZO:

True!

Silence. They put on their hats.

ESTRAGON:

Nothing happens, nobody comes, nobody goes, it's awful!

VLADIMIR:

(to Pozzo). Tell him to think.

POZZO:

Give him his hat.

VLADIMIR:

His hat?

POZZO:

He can't think without his hat.

VLADIMIR:

(to ESTRAGON). Give him his hat.

ESTRAGON:

Me! After what he did to me! Never!

VLADIMIR:

I'll give it to him He does not move.

ESTRAGON:

(to Pozzo). Tell him to go and fetch it.

POZZO:

It's better to give it to him.

VLADIMIR:

I'll give it to him

He picks up the hat and tenders it at arm's length to Lucky, who does not move.

POZZO:

You must put it on his head.

ESTRAGON:

(to Pozzo). Tell him to take it.

POZZO:

It's better to put it on his head.

VLADIMIR:

I'll put it on his head.

He goes round behind Lucky, approaches him cautiously, puts the hat on his head and recoils smartly. Lucky does not move. Silence.

ESTRAGON:

What's he waiting for?

POZZO:

Stand back! (Vladimir and ESTRAGON move away from Lucky. Pozzo jerks the rope. Lucky looks at Pozzo.) Think, pig! (Pause. Lucky begins to dance.) Stop! (Lucky stops.) Forward! (Lucky advances.) Stop! (Lucky stops.) Think!

Silence.

LUCKY:

On the other hand with regard to—

POZZO:

Stop! (Lucky stops.) Back! (Lucky moves back.) Stop! (Lucky stops.) Turn! (Lucky turns towards auditorium.) Think!

During Lucky's tirade the others react as follows.

1)   Vladimir and ESTRAGON all attention, Pozzo dejected and disgusted.

2)   Vladimir and ESTRAGON begin to protest, Pozzo's sufferings increase.

3)   Vladimir and ESTRAGON attentive again, Pozzo more and more agitated and groaning.

4)   Vladimir and ESTRAGON protest violently. Pozzo jumps up, pulls on the rope. General outcry. Lucky pulls on the rope, staggers, shouts his text. All three throw themselves on Lucky who struggles and shouts his text.

LUCKY:

Given the existence as uttered forth in the public works of Puncher and Wattmann of a personal God quaquaquaqua with white beard quaquaquaqua outside time without extension who from the heights of divine apathia divine athambia divine aphasia loves us dearly with some exceptions for reasons unknown but time will tell and suffers like the divine Miranda with those who for reasons unknown but time will tell are plunged in torment plunged in fire whose fire flames if that continues and who can doubt it will fire the firmament that is to say blast hell to heaven so blue still and calm so calm with a calm which even though intermittent is better than nothing but not so fast and considering what is more that as a result of the labors left unfinished crowned by the Acacacacademy of Anthropopopometry of Essy-in-Possy of Testew and Cunard it is established beyond all doubt all other doubt than that which clings to the labors of men that as a result of the labors unfinished of Testew and Cunnard it is established as hereinafter but not so fast for reasons unknown that as a result of the public works of Puncher and Wattmann it is established beyond all doubt that in view of the labors of Fartov and Belcher left unfinished for reasons unknown of Testew and Cunard left unfinished it is established what many deny that man in Possy of Testew and Cunard that man in Essy that man in short that man in brief in spite of the strides of alimentation and defecation wastes and pines wastes and pines and concurrently simultaneously what is more for reasons unknown in spite of the strides of physical culture the practice of sports such as tennis football running cycling swimming flying floating riding gliding conating camogie skating tennis of all kinds dying flying sports of all sorts autumn summer winter winter tennis of all kinds hockey of all sorts penicillin and succedanea in a word I resume flying gliding golf over nine and eighteen holes tennis of all sorts in a word for reasons unknown in Feckham Peckham Fulham Clapham namely concurrently simultaneously what is more for reasons unknown but time will tell fades away I resume Fulham Clapham in a word the dead loss per head since the death of Bishop Berkeley being to the tune of one inch four ounce per head approximately by and large more or less to the nearest decimal good measure round figures stark naked in the stockinged feet in Connemara in a word for reasons unknown no matter what matter the facts are there and considering what is more much more grave that in the light of the labors lost of Steinweg and Peterman it appears what is more much more grave that in the light the light the light of the labors lost of Steinweg and Peterman that in the plains in the mountains by the seas by the rivers running water running fire the air is the same and then the earth namely the air and then the earth in the great cold the great dark the air and the earth abode of stones in the great cold alas alas in the year of their Ford six hundred and something the air the earth the sea the earth abode of stones in the great deeps the great cold on sea on land and in the air I resume for reasons unknown in spite of the tennis the facts are there but time will tell I resume alas alas on on in short in fine on on abode of stones who can doubt it I resume but not so fast I resume the skull fading fading fading and concurrently simultaneously what is more for reasons unknown in spite of the tennis on on the beard the flames the tears the stones so blue so calm alas alas on on the skull the skull the skull the skull in Connemara in spite of the tennis the labors abandoned left unfinished graver still abode of stones in a word I resume alas alas abandoned unfinished the skull the skull in Connemara in spite of the tennis the skull alas the stones Cunard (melee, final vociferations)

. . . tennis . . . the stones ... so calm . . . Cunard . . . unfinished . . .

POZZO:

His hat!

Vladimir seizes Lucky's hat. Silence of Lucky. He falls. Silence. Panting of the victors.

ESTRAGON:

Avenged!

Vladimir examines the hat, peers inside it.

POZZO:

Give me that! (He snatches the hat from Vladimir, throws it on the ground, tramples on it.) There's an end to his thinking!

VLADIMIR:

But will he be able to walk?

POZZO:

Walk or crawl! (He kicks Lucky.) Up pig!

ESTRAGON:

Perhaps he's dead.

VLADIMIR:

You'll kill him

POZZO:

Up scum! (He ierks the rope.) Help me!

VLADIMIR:

How?

POZZO:

Raise him up!

Vladimir and ESTRAGON hoist Lucky to his feet, support him an instant, then let him go. He falls.

ESTRAGON:

He's doing it on purpose!

POZZO:

You must hold him (Pause.) Come on, come on, raise him up.

ESTRAGON:

To hell with him!

VLADIMIR:

Come on, once more.

ESTRAGON:

What does he take us for?

They raise Lucky, hold him up.

POZZO:

Don't let him go! (Vladimir andESTRAGON totter.) Don't move! (Pozzo fetches bag and basket and brings them towards Lucky.) Hold him tight! (Heputs the bag in Lucky's hand. Lucky drops it immediately.) Don't let him go! (Heputs back the bag in Lucky's hand. Gradually, at the feel of the bag, Lucky recovers his senses and his fingers finally close round the handle.) Hold him tight! (As before with basket.)

Now! You can let him go. (Vladimir and ESTRAGON move away from Lucky who totters, reels, sags, but succeeds in remaining on his feet, bag and basket in his hands. Pozzo steps back, cracks his whip.) Forward! (Lucky totters forward.) Back! (Lucky totters back.) Turn! (Lucky turns.) Done it! He can walk. (Turning to Vladimir and ESTRAGON.) Thank you, gentlemen, and let me . . . (he fumbles in his pockets)... let me wish you . . . (fumbles). . . wish you . . . (fumbles). . . what have I done with my watch? (Fumbles.) A genuine half-hunter, gentlemen, with deadbeat escapement! (Sobbing.) Twas my granpa gave it to me! (He searches on the ground, Vladimir and ESTRAGON likewise. Pozzo turns over with his foot the remains of Lucky's hat.) Well now isn't that just—

VLADIMIR:

Perhaps it's in your fob.

POZZO:

Wait! (He doubles up in an attempt to apply his ear to his stomach, listens. Silence.) I hear nothing. (He beckons them to approach, Vladimir and ESTRAGON go over to him, bend over his stomach.) Surely one should hear the tick-tick.

VLADIMIR:

Silence!

All listen, bent double.

ESTRAGON:

I hear something.

POZZO:

Where?

VLADIMIR:

It's the heart.

POZZO:

(idisappointed). Damnation!

VLADIMIR:

Silence!

ESTRAGON:

Perhaps it has stopped.

They straighten up.

POZZO:

Which of you smells so bad?

ESTRAGON:

He has stinking breath and I have stinking feet.

POZZO:

I must go.

ESTRAGON:

And your half-hunter?

POZZO:

I must have left it at the manor.

Silence.

ESTRAGON:

Then adieu.

POZZO:

Adieu.

VLADIMIR:

Adieu.

POZZO:

Adieu.

Silence. No one moves.

VLADIMIR:

Adieu.

POZZO:

Adieu.

ESTRAGON:

Adieu.

Silence.

POZZO:

And thank you.

VLADIMIR:

Thank you.

POZZO:

Not at all.

ESTRAGON:

Yes yes.

POZZO:

No no.

VLADIMIR:

Yes yes.

ESTRAGON:

No no.

Silence.

POZZO:

I don't seem to be able . . . (long hesitation)... to depart.

ESTRAGON:

Such is life.

Pozzo turns, moves away from Lucky towards the wings, paying out the rope as he goes.

VLADIMIR:

You're going the wrong way.

POZZO:

I need a running start. (Having come to the end of the rope, i. e., off stage, he stops, turns and cries.) Stand back! (Vladimir andESTRAGON stand back, look towards Pozzo. Crack of whip.) On! On!

ESTRAGON:

On!

VLADIMIR:

On!

Lucky moves off.

POZZO:

Faster! (He appears, crosses the stage preceded by Lucky. Vladimir and ESTRAGON wave their hats. Exit Lucky.) On! On! (On the point of disappearing in his turn he stops and turns. The rope tautens. Noise of Lucky falling off.) Stool! (Vladimir fetches stool and gives it to Pozzo who throws it to Lucky.) Adieu!

VLADIMIR and ESTRAGON:

(waving). Adieu! Adieu!

POZZO:

Up! Pig! (Noise of Lucky getting up.) On! (Exit Pozzo.) Faster! On! Adieu! Pig! Yip! Adieu!

Long silence.

VLADIMIR:

That passed the time.

ESTRAGON:

It would have passed in any case.

VLADIMIR:

Yes, but not so rapidly.

Pause.

ESTRAGON:

What do we do now?

VLADIMIR:

I don't know.

ESTRAGON:

Let's go.

VLADIMIR:

We can't.

ESTRAGON:

Why not?

VLADIMIR:

We're waiting for Godot.

ESTRAGON:

(idespairingly). Ah!

Pause.

VLADIMIR:

How they've changed!

ESTRAGON:

Who?

VLADIMIR:

Those two.

ESTRAGON:

That's the idea, let's make a little conversation.

VLADIMIR:

Haven't they?

ESTRAGON:

What?

VLADIMIR:

Changed.

ESTRAGON:

Very likely. They all change. Only we can't.

VLADIMIR:

Likely! It's certain. Didn't you see them?

ESTRAGON:

I suppose I did. But I don't know them.

VLADIMIR:

Yes you do know them.

ESTRAGON:

No I don't know them.

VLADIMIR:

We know them, I tell you. You forget everything. (Pause. To himself.) Unless they're not the same . . .

ESTRAGON:

Why didn't they recognize us then?

VLADIMIR:

That means nothing. I too pretended not to recognize them. And then nobody ever recognizes us.

ESTRAGON:

Forget it. What we need- Ow! (Vladimir does not react.) Ow!

VLADIMIR:

(to himself). Unless they're not the same . . .

ESTRAGON:

Didi! It's the other foot!

He goes hobbling towards the mound.

VLADIMIR:

Unless they're not the same . . .

BOY:

(off). Mister!

ESTRAGON halts. Both look towards the voice.

ESTRAGON:

Off we go again.

VLADIMIR:

Approach, my child.

Enter Boy, timidly. He halts.

BOY:

Mister Albert. . . ?

VLADIMIR:

Yes.

ESTRAGON:

What do you want?

VLADIMIR:

Approach!

The Boy does not move.

ESTRAGON:

(forcibly). Approach when you're told, can't you?

The Boy advances timidly, halts.

VLADIMIR:

What is it?

BOY:

Mr. Godot. . .

VLADIMIR:

Obviously . . . (Pause.) Approach.

ESTRAGON:

(violently). Will you approach! (The Boy advances timidly.) What kept you so late?

VLADIMIR:

You have a message from Mr. Godot?

BOY:

Yes Sir.

VLADIMIR:

Well, what is it?

ESTRAGON:

What kept you so late?

The Boy looks at them in turn, not knowing to which he should reply.

VLADIMIR:

(to ESTRAGON). Let him alone.

ESTRAGON:

(violently). You let me alone. (Advancing, to the Boy.) Do you know what time it is?

BOY:

(recoiling). It's not my fault, Sir.

ESTRAGON:

And whose is it? Mine?

BOY:

I was afraid, Sir.

ESTRAGON:

Afraid of what? Of us? (Pause.) Answer me!

VLADIMIR:

I know what it is, he was afraid of the others.

ESTRAGON:

How long have you been here?

A good while, Sir.

VLADIMIR:

You were afraid of the whip?

BOY:

Yes Sir.

VLADIMIR:

The roars?

BOY:

Yes Sir.

VLADIMIR:

The two big men.

BOY:

Yes Sir.

VLADIMIR:

Do you know them?

BOY:

No Sir.

VLADIMIR:

Are you a native of these parts? (Silence.) Do you belong to these parts?

BOY:

Yes Sir.

ESTRAGON:

That's all a pack of lies. (Shaking the Boy by the arm.) Tell us the truth!

BOY:

(trembling). But it is the truth, Sir!

VLADIMIR:

Will you let him alone! What's the matter with you?

(ESTRAGON releases the Boy, moves away, covering his face with his hands. Vladimir and the Boy observe him. ESTRAGON drops his hands. His face is convulsed.) What's the matter with you?

ESTRAGON:

I'm unhappy.

VLADIMIR:

Not really! Since when?

ESTRAGON:

I'd forgotten.

VLADIMIR:

Extraordinary the tricks that memory plays! (ESTRAGON tries to speak, renounces, limps to his place, sits down and begins to take off his boots. To Boy.) Well9

BOY:

Mr. Godot—

VLADIMIR:

I've seen you before, haven't I?

BOY:

I don't know, Sir.

VLADIMIR:

You don't know me?

BOY:

No Sir.

VLADIMIR:

It wasn't you came yesterday?

BOY:

No Sir.

VLADIMIR:

This is your first time?

BOY:

Yes Sir.

Silence.

VLADIMIR:

Words words. (Pause.) Speak.

BOY:

(in a rush). Mr. Godot told me to tell you he won't come this evening but surely tomorrow.

Silence.

VLADIMIR:

Is that all?

BOY:

Yes Sir.
Silence.

VLADIMIR:

You work for Mr. Godot?

BOY:

Yes Sir.

VLADIMIR:

What do you do?

BOY:

I mind the goats, Sir.

VLADIMIR:

Is he good to you?

BOY:

Yes Sir.

VLADIMIR:

He doesn't beat you?

No Sir, not me.

VLADIMIR:

Whom does he beat?

BOY:

He beats my brother, Sir.

VLADIMIR:

Ah, you have a brother?

BOY:

Yes Sir.

VLADIMIR:

What does he do?

BOY:

He minds the sheep, Sir.

VLADIMIR:

And why doesn't he beat you?

BOY:

I don't know, Sir.

VLADIMIR:

He must be fond of you.

BOY:

I don't know, Sir.

Silence.

VLADIMIR:

Does he give you enough to eat? (The Boy hesitates.) Does he feed you well?

BOY:

Fairly well, Sir.

VLADIMIR:

You're not unhappy? (The Boy hesitates.) Do you hear me?

BOY:

Yes Sir.

VLADIMIR:

Well?

BOY:

I don't know, Sir.

VLADIMIR:

You don't know if you're unhappy or not?

BOY:

No Sir.

VLADIMIR:

You're as bad as myself. (Silence.) Where do you sleep?

BOY:

In the loft, Sir.

VLADIMIR:

With your brother?

BOY:

Yes Sir.

VLADIMIR:

In the hay?

Yes Sir.

Silence.

VLADIMIR:

All right, you may go.

BOY:

What am I to tell Mr. Godot, Sir?

VLADIMIR:

Tell him . . . (he hesitates). . . tell him you saw us. (Pause.) You did see us, didn't you?

BOY:

Yes Sir.

He steps back, hesitates, turns and exit running. The light suddenly fails. In a moment it is night. The moon rises at back, mounts in the sky, stands still, shedding a pale light on the scene.

VLADIMIR:

At last! (ESTRAGON gets up and goes towards Vladimir, a boot in each hand. He puts them down at edge of stage, straightens and contemplates the moon.)

What are you doing?

ESTRAGON:

Pale for weariness.

VLADIMIR:

Eh?

ESTRAGON:

Of climbing heaven and gazing on the likes of us.

VLADIMIR:

Your boots, what are you doing with your boots?

ESTRAGON:

(;turning to look at the boots). I'm leaving them there. (Pause.) Another will come, just as ... as ... as me, but with smaller feet, and they'll make him happy.

VLADIMIR:

But you can't go barefoot!

ESTRAGON:

Christ did.

VLADIMIR:

Christ! What has Christ got to do with it. You're not going to compare yourself to Christ!

ESTRAGON:

All my life I've compared myself to him

VLADIMIR:

But where he lived it was warm, it was dry!

ESTRAGON:

Yes. And they crucified quick.

Silence.

VLADIMIR:

We've nothing more to do here.

ESTRAGON:

Nor anywhere else.

VLADIMIR:

Ah Gogo, don't go on like that. Tomorrow everything will be better.

ESTRAGON:

How do you make that out?

VLADIMIR:

Did you not hear what the child said?

ESTRAGON:

No.

VLADIMIR:

He said that Godot was sure to come tomorrow. (Pause.) What do you say to that?

ESTRAGON:

Then all we have to do is to wait on here.

VLADIMIR:

Are you mad? We must take cover. (He takes ESTRAGON by the arm.) Come on. He draws ESTRAGON after him. ESTRAGON yields, then resists. They halt.

ESTRAGON:

(looking at the tree). Pity we haven't got a bit of rope.

VLADIMIR:

Come on. It's cold.

He draws ESTRAGON after him. As before.

ESTRAGON:

Remind me to bring a bit of rope tomorrow.

VLADIMIR:

Yes. Come on.

He draws him after him. As before.

ESTRAGON:

How long have we been together all the time now?

VLADIMIR:

I don't know. Fifty years maybe.

ESTRAGON:

Do you remember the day I threw myself into the Rhone?

VLADIMIR:

We were grape harvesting.

ESTRAGON:

You fished me out.

VLADIMIR:

That's all dead and buried.

ESTRAGON:

My clothes dried in the sun.

VLADIMIR:

There's no good harking back on that. Come on.

He draws him after him. As before.

ESTRAGON:

Wait!

VLADIMIR:

I'm cold!

ESTRAGON:

Wait! (He moves away from Vladimir.) I sometimes wonder if we wouldn't have been better off alone, each one for himself. (He crosses the stage and sits down on the mound.) We weren't made for the same road.

VLADIMIR:

(without anger). It's not certain.

ESTRAGON:

No, nothing is certain.

Vladimir slowly crosses the stage and sits down beside ESTRAGON.

VLADIMIR:

We can still part, if you think it would be better.

ESTRAGON:

It's not worthwhile now.

Silence.

VLADIMIR:

No, it's not worthwhile now.

Silence.

ESTRAGON:

Well, shall we go?

Silence.

VLADIMIR:

No, it's not worthwhile now.

Silence.

ESTRAGON:

Well, shall we go?

VLADIMIR:

Yes, let's go.

They do not move.

ACT - II

Next day. Same time.

Same place.

Estragon's boots front center, heels together, toes splayed.

Lucky's hat at same place.

The tree has four or five leaves.

Enter Vladimir agitatedly. He halts and looks long at the tree, then suddenly begins to move feverishly about the stage. He halts before the boots, picks one up, examines it, sniffs it, manifests disgust, puts it back carefully. Comes and goes. Halts extreme right and gazes into distance off, shading his eyes with his hand. Comes and goes.

Halts extreme left, as before. Comes and goes. Halts suddenly and begins to sing loudly.

VLADIMIR:

A dog came in-

Having begun too high he stops, clears his throat, resumes:

A dog came in the kitchen And stole a crust of bread.

Then cook up with a ladle And beat him till he was dead.

Then all the dogs came running And dug the dog a tomb-

He stops, broods, resumes:

Then all the dogs came running And dug the dog a tomb

And wrote upon the tombstone For the eyes of dogs to come:

A dog came in the kitchen And stole a crust of bread.

Then cook up with a ladle And beat him till he was dead.

Then all the dogs came running And dug the dog a tomb-

He stops, broods, resumes:

Then all the dogs came running And dug the dog a tomb-

He stops, broods. Softly.

And dug the dog a tomb . . .

He remains a moment silent and motionless, then begins to move feverishly about the stage. He halts before the tree, comes and goes, before the boots, comes and goes, halts extreme right, gazes into distance, extreme left, gazes into distance. Enter Estragon right, barefoot, head bowed. He slowly crosses the stage. Vladimir turns and sees him.

VLADIMIR:

You again! (Estragon halts but does not raise his head. Vladimir goes towards him.) Come here till I embrace you.

ESTRAGON:

Don't touch me!

Vladimir holds back, pained.

VLADIMIR:

Do you want me to go away? (Pause.) Gogo! (Pause. Vladimir observes him attentively.) Did they beat you? (Pause.) Gogo! (Estragon remains silent, head bowed.) Where did you spend the night?

ESTRAGON:

Don't touch me! Don't question me! Don't speak to me! Stay with me!

VLADIMIR:

Did I ever leave you?

ESTRAGON:

You let me go.

VLADIMIR:

Look at me. (Estragon does not raise his head. Violently.) Will you look at me! Estragon raises his head. They look long at each other, then suddenly embrace, clapping each other on the back. End of the embrace. Estragon, no longer supported, almost falls.

ESTRAGON:

What a day!

VLADIMIR:

Who beat you? Tell me.

ESTRAGON:

Another day done with.

VLADIMIR:

Not yet.

ESTRAGON:

For me it's over and done with, no matter what happens. (Silence.) I heard you singing.

VLADIMIR:

That's right, I remember.

ESTRAGON:

That finished me. I said to myself, He's all alone, he thinks I'm gone for ever, and he sings.

VLADIMIR:

One is not master of one's moods. All day I've felt in great form. (Pause.) I didn't get up in the night, not once!

ESTRAGON:

(sadly). You see, you piss better when I'm not there.

VLADIMIR:

I missed you . . . and at the same time I was happy. Isn't that a strange thing?

ESTRAGON:

(shocked). Happy?

VLADIMIR:

Perhaps it's not quite the right word.

ESTRAGON:

And now?

VLADIMIR:

Now? . . . (Joyous.) There you are again . . . (Indifferent.) There we are again. . . (Gloomy.) There I am again.

ESTRAGON:

You see, you feel worse when I'm with you. I feel better alone too.

VLADIMIR:

(vexed). Then why do you always come crawling back?

ESTRAGON:

I don't know.

VLADIMIR:

No, but I do. It's because you don't know how to defend yourself. I wouldn't have let them beat you.

ESTRAGON:

You couldn't have stopped them.

VLADIMIR:

Why not?

ESTRAGON:

There was ten of them.

VLADIMIR:

No, I mean before they beat you. I would have stopped you from doing whatever it was you were doing.

ESTRAGON:

I wasn't doing anything.

VLADIMIR:

Then why did they beat you?

ESTRAGON:

I don't know.

VLADIMIR:

Ah no, Gogo, the truth is there are things that escape you that don't escape me, you must feel it yourself.

ESTRAGON:

I tell you I wasn't doing anything.

VLADIMIR:

Perhaps you weren't. But it's the way of doing it that counts, the way of doing it, if you want to go on living.

ESTRAGON:

I wasn't doing anything.

VLADIMIR:

You must be happy too, deep down, if you only knew it.

ESTRAGON:

Happy about what?

VLADIMIR:

To be back with me again.

ESTRAGON:

Would you say so?

VLADIMIR:

Say you are, even if it's not true.

ESTRAGON:

What am I to say?

VLADIMIR:

Say, I am happy.

ESTRAGON:

I am happy.

VLADIMIR:

So am I.

ESTRAGON:

So am I.

VLADIMIR:

We are happy.

ESTRAGON:

We are happy. (Silence.) What do we do now, now that we are happy?

VLADIMIR:

Wait for Godot. (Estragon groans. Silence.) Things have changed here since yesterday.

ESTRAGON:

And if he doesn't come?

VLADIMIR:

(after a moment of bewilderment). We'll see when the time comes. (Pause.) I was saying that things have changed here since yesterday.

ESTRAGON:

Everything oozes.

VLADIMIR:

Look at the tree.

ESTRAGON:

It's never the same pus from one second to the next.

VLADIMIR:

The tree, look at the tree.

Estragon looks at the tree.

ESTRAGON:

Was it not there yesterday?

VLADIMIR:

Yes of course it was there. Do you not remember? We nearly hanged ourselves from it. But you wouldn't. Do you not remember?

ESTRAGON:

You dreamt it.

VLADIMIR:

Is it possible you've forgotten already?

ESTRAGON:

That's the way I am. Either I forget immediately or I never forget.

VLADIMIR:

And Pozzo and Lucky, have you forgotten them too?

ESTRAGON:

Pozzo and Lucky?

VLADIMIR:

He's forgotten everything!

ESTRAGON:

I remember a lunatic who kicked the shins off me. Then he played the fool.

VLADIMIR:

That was Lucky.

ESTRAGON:

I remember that. But when was it?

VLADIMIR:

And his keeper, do you not remember him?

ESTRAGON:

He gave me a bone.

VLADIMIR:

That was Pozzo.

ESTRAGON:

And all that was yesterday, you say?

VLADIMIR:

Yes of course it was yesterday.

ESTRAGON:

And here where we are now?

VLADIMIR:

Where else do you think? Do you not recognize the place?

ESTRAGON:

(suddenly furious). Recognize! What is there to recognize? All my lousy life I've

crawled about in the mud! And you talk to me about scenery! (Looking wildly about him.) Look at this muckheap! I've never stirred from it!

VLADIMIR:

Calm yourself, calm yourself.

ESTRAGON:

You and your landscapes! Tell me about the worms!

VLADIMIR:

All the same, you can't tell me that this (gesture) bears any resemblance to . . . (he hesitates)... to the Macon country for example. You can't deny there's a big difference.

ESTRAGON:

The Macon country! Who's talking to you about the Macon country?

VLADIMIR:

But you were there yourself, in the Macon country.

ESTRAGON:

No I was never in the Macon country! I've puked my puke of a life away here, I tell you! Here! In the Cackon country!

VLADIMIR:

But we were there together, I could swear to it! Picking grapes for a man called . . (he snaps his fingers). . . can't think of the name of the man, at a place called . . . (snaps his fingers). . . can't think of the name of the place, do you not remember?

ESTRAGON:

(a little calmer). It's possible. I didn't notice anything.

VLADIMIR:

But down there everything is red!

ESTRAGON:

(exasperated). I didn't notice anything, I tell you!

Silence. Vladimir sighs deeply.

VLADIMIR:

You're a hard man to get on with, Gogo.

ESTRAGON:

It'd be better if we parted.

VLADIMIR:

You always say that and you always come crawling back.

ESTRAGON:

The best thing would be to kill me, like the other.

VLADIMIR:

What other? (Pause.) What other?

ESTRAGON:

Like billions of others.

VLADIMIR:

(sententious). To every man his little cross. (He sighs.) Till he dies. (Afterthought.) And is forgotten.

ESTRAGON:

In the meantime let us try and converse calmly, since we are incapable of keeping silent.

VLADIMIR:

You're right, we're inexhaustible.

ESTRAGON:

It's so we won't think.

VLADIMIR:

We have that excuse.

ESTRAGON:

It's so we won't hear.

VLADIMIR:

We have our reasons.

ESTRAGON:

All the dead voices.

VLADIMIR:

They make a noise like wings.

ESTRAGON:

Like leaves.

VLADIMIR:

Like sand.

ESTRAGON:

Like leaves.

Silence.

VLADIMIR:

They all speak at once.

ESTRAGON:

Each one to itself.

Silence.

VLADIMIR:

Rather they whisper.

ESTRAGON:

They rustle.

VLADIMIR:

They murmur.

ESTRAGON:

They rustle.

Silence.

VLADIMIR:

What do they say?

ESTRAGON:

They talk about their lives.

VLADIMIR:

To have lived is not enough for them.

ESTRAGON:

They have to talk about it.

VLADIMIR:

To be dead is not enough for them.

ESTRAGON:

It is not sufficient.

Silence.

VLADIMIR:

They make a noise like feathers.

ESTRAGON:

Like leaves.

VLADIMIR:

Likes ashes.

ESTRAGON:

Like leaves.

Long silence.

VLADIMIR:

Say something!

ESTRAGON:

I'm trying.

Long silence.

VLADIMIR:

(in anguish). Say anything at all!

ESTRAGON:

What do we do now?

VLADIMIR:

Wait for Godot.

ESTRAGON:

Ah!

Silence.

VLADIMIR:

This is awful!

ESTRAGON:

Sing something.

VLADIMIR:

No no! (He reflects.) We could start all over again perhaps.

ESTRAGON:

That should be easy.

VLADIMIR:

It's the start that's difficult.

ESTRAGON:

You can start from anything.

VLADIMIR:

Yes, but you have to decide.

ESTRAGON:

True.

Silence.

VLADIMIR:

Help me!

ESTRAGON:

I'm trying.

Silence.

VLADIMIR:

When you seek you hear.

ESTRAGON:

You do.

VLADIMIR:

That prevents you from finding.

ESTRAGON:

It does.

VLADIMIR:

That prevents you from thinking.

ESTRAGON:

You think all the same.

VLADIMIR:

No no, it's impossible.

ESTRAGON:

That's the idea, let's contradict each another.

VLADIMIR:

Impossible.

ESTRAGON:

You think so?

VLADIMIR:

We're in no danger of ever thinking any more.

ESTRAGON:

Then what are we complaining about?

VLADIMIR:

Thinking is not the worst.

ESTRAGON:

Perhaps not. But at least there's that.

VLADIMIR:

That what?

ESTRAGON:

That's the idea, let's ask each other questions.

VLADIMIR:

What do you mean, at least there's that?

ESTRAGON:

That much less misery.

VLADIMIR:

True.

ESTRAGON:

Well? If we gave thanks for our mercies?

VLADIMIR:

What is terrible is to have thought.

ESTRAGON:

But did that ever happen to us?

VLADIMIR:

Where are all these corpses from?

ESTRAGON:

These skeletons.

VLADIMIR:

Tell me that.

ESTRAGON:

True.

VLADIMIR:

We must have thought a little.

ESTRAGON:

At the very beginning.

VLADIMIR:

A charnel-house! A charnel-house!

ESTRAGON:

You don't have to look.

VLADIMIR:

You can't help looking.

ESTRAGON:

True.

VLADIMIR:

Try as one may.

ESTRAGON:

I beg your pardon?

VLADIMIR:

Try as one may.

ESTRAGON:

We should turn resolutely towards Nature.

VLADIMIR:

We've tried that.

ESTRAGON:

True.

VLADIMIR:

Oh it's not the worst, I know.

ESTRAGON:

What?

VLADIMIR:

To have thought.

ESTRAGON:

Obviously.

VLADIMIR:

But we could have done without it.

ESTRAGON:

Que voulez-vous?

VLADIMIR:

I beg your pardon?

ESTRAGON:

Que voulez-vouz.

VLADIMIR:

Ah! que voulez-vous. Exactly.

Silence.

ESTRAGON:

That wasn't such a bad little canter.

VLADIMIR:

Yes, but now we'll have to find something else.

ESTRAGON:

Let me see.

He takes off his hat, concentrates.

VLADIMIR:

Let me see. (He takes off his hat, concentrates. Long silence.) Ah!

They put on their hats, relax.

ESTRAGON:

Well?

VLADIMIR:

What was I saying, we could go on from there.

ESTRAGON:

What were you saying when?

VLADIMIR:

At the very beginning.

ESTRAGON:

The very beginning of WHAT?

VLADIMIR:

This evening ... I was saying ... I was saying . . .

ESTRAGON:

I'm not a historian.

VLADIMIR:

Wait... we embraced ... we were happy . . . happy . . . what do we do now that we're happy ... go on waiting . . . waiting . . . let me think . . . it's coming ... go on waiting . . . now that we're happy ... let me see ... ah! The tree!

ESTRAGON:

The tree?

VLADIMIR:

Do you not remember?

ESTRAGON:

I'm tired.

VLADIMIR:

Look at it.

They look at the tree.

ESTRAGON:

I see nothing.

VLADIMIR:

But yesterday evening it was all black and bare. And now it's covered with leaves.

ESTRAGON:

Leaves?

VLADIMIR:

In a single night.

ESTRAGON:

It must be the Spring.

VLADIMIR:

But in a single night!

ESTRAGON:

I tell you we weren't here yesterday. Another of your nightmares.

VLADIMIR:

And where were we yesterday evening according to you?

ESTRAGON:

How would I know? In another compartment. There's no lack of void.

VLADIMIR:

(sure of himself). Good. We weren't here yesterday evening. Now what did we do yesterday evening?

ESTRAGON:

Do?

VLADIMIR:

Try and remember.

ESTRAGON:

Do ... I suppose we blathered.

VLADIMIR:

(controlling himself). About what?

ESTRAGON:

Oh . . . this and that I suppose, nothing in particular. (With assurance.) Yes, now I remember, yesterday evening we spent blathering about nothing in particular. That' been going on now for half a century.

VLADIMIR:

You don't remember any fact, any circumstance?

ESTRAGON:

(weary). Don't torment me, Didi.

VLADIMIR:

The sun. The moon. Do you not remember?

ESTRAGON:

They must have been there, as usual.

VLADIMIR:

You didn't notice anything out of the ordinary?

ESTRAGON:

Alas!

VLADIMIR:

And Pozzo? And Lucky?

ESTRAGON:

Pozzo?

VLADIMIR:

The bones.

ESTRAGON:

They were like fishbones.

VLADIMIR:

It was Pozzo gave them to you.

ESTRAGON:

I don't know.

VLADIMIR:

And the kick.

ESTRAGON:

That's right, someone gave me a kick.

VLADIMIR:

It was Lucky gave it to you.

ESTRAGON:

And all that was yesterday?

VLADIMIR:

Show me your leg.

ESTRAGON:

Which?

VLADIMIR:

Both. Pull up your trousers. (Estragon gives a leg to Vladimir, staggers. Vladimir takes the leg. They stagger.) Pull up your trousers.

ESTRAGON:

I can't.

Vladimir pulls up the trousers, looks at the leg, lets it go. Estragon almost falls.

VLADIMIR:

The other. (Estragon gives the same leg.) The other, pig! (Estragon gives the other leg. Triumphantly.) There's the wound! Beginning to fester!

ESTRAGON:

And what about it?

VLADIMIR:

{letting go the leg). Where are your boots?

ESTRAGON:

I must have thrown them away.

VLADIMIR:

When?

ESTRAGON:

I don't know.

VLADIMIR:

Why?

ESTRAGON:

(exasperated). I don't know why I don't know!

VLADIMIR:

No, I mean why did you throw them away?

ESTRAGON:

(exasperated). Because they were hurting me!

VLADIMIR:

(triumphantly, pointing to the boots). There they are! (Estragon looks at the boots.) At the very spot where you left them yesterday!

Estragon goes towards the boots, inspects them closely.

ESTRAGON:

They're not mine.

VLADIMIR:

(stupefied). Not yours!

ESTRAGON:

Mine were black. These are brown.

VLADIMIR:

You're sure yours were black?

ESTRAGON:

Well they were a kind of gray.

VLADIMIR:

And these are brown. Show me.

ESTRAGON:

(picking up a boot). Well they're a kind of green.

VLADIMIR:

Show me. (Estragon hands him the boot. Vladimir inspects it, throws it down angrily.) Well of all the—

ESTRAGON:

You see, all that's a lot of bloody—

VLADIMIR:

Ah! I see what it is. Yes, I see what's happened.

ESTRAGON:

All that's a lot of bloody—

VLADIMIR:

It's elementary. Someone came and took yours and left you his.

ESTRAGON:

Why?

VLADIMIR:

His were too tight for him, so he took yours.

ESTRAGON:

But mine were too tight.

VLADIMIR:

For you. Not for him.

ESTRAGON:

(having tried in vain to work it out). I'm tired! (Pause.) Let's go.

VLADIMIR:

We can't.

ESTRAGON:

Why not?

VLADIMIR:

We're waiting for Godot.

ESTRAGON:

Ah! (Pause. Despairing.) What'll we do, what'll we do!

VLADIMIR:

There's nothing we can do.

ESTRAGON:

But I can't go on like this!

VLADIMIR:

Would you like a radish?

ESTRAGON:

Is that all there is?

VLADIMIR:

There are radishes and turnips.

ESTRAGON:

Are there no carrots?

VLADIMIR:

No. Anyway you overdo it with your carrots.

ESTRAGON:

Then give me a radish. (Vladimir fumbles in his pockets, finds nothing but turnips, finally brings out a radish and hands it to Estragon who examines it, sniffs it.) It's black!

VLADIMIR:

It's a radish.

ESTRAGON:

I only like the pink ones, you know that!

VLADIMIR:

Then you don't want it?

ESTRAGON:

I only like the pink ones!

VLADIMIR:

Then give it back to me.

Estragon gives it back.

ESTRAGON:

I'll go and get a carrot.

He does not move.

VLADIMIR:

This is becoming really insignificant.

ESTRAGON:

Not enough.

Silence.

VLADIMIR:

What about trying them.

ESTRAGON:

I've tried everything.

VLADIMIR:

No, I mean the boots.

ESTRAGON:

Would that be a good thing?

VLADIMIR:

It'd pass the time. (Estragon hesitates.) I assure you, it'd be an occupation.

ESTRAGON:

A relaxation.

VLADIMIR:

A recreation.

ESTRAGON:

A relaxation.

VLADIMIR:

Try.

ESTRAGON:

You'll help me?

VLADIMIR:

I will of course.

ESTRAGON:

We don't manage too badly, eh Didi, between the two of us?

VLADIMIR:

Yes yes. Come on, we'll try the left first.

ESTRAGON:

We always find something, eh Didi, to give us the impression we exist?

VLADIMIR:

(impatiently). Yes yes, we're magicians. But let us persevere in what we have resolved, before we forget. (Hepicks up a boot.) Come on, give me your foot. (Estragon raises his foot.) The other, hog! (Estragon raises the other foot.) Higher!

(Wreathed together they stagger about the stage. Vladimir succeeds finally in getting on the boot.) Try and walk. (Estragon walks.) Well?

ESTRAGON:

It fits.

VLADIMIR:

(taking string from his pocket). We'll try and lace it.

ESTRAGON:

(vehemently). No no, no laces, no laces!

VLADIMIR:

You'll be sorry. Let's try the other. (As before.) Well?

ESTRAGON:

(grudgingly). It fits too.

VLADIMIR:

They don't hurt you?

ESTRAGON:

Not yet.

VLADIMIR:

Then you can keep them.

ESTRAGON:

They're too big.

VLADIMIR:

Perhaps you'll have socks some day.

ESTRAGON:

True.

VLADIMIR:

Then you'll keep them?

ESTRAGON:

That's enough about these boots.

VLADIMIR:

Yes, but—

ESTRAGON:

(violently). Enough! (Silence.) I suppose I might as well sit down.

He looks for a place to sit down, then goes and sits down on the mound.

VLADIMIR:

That's where you were sitting yesterday evening.

ESTRAGON:

If I could only sleep.

VLADIMIR:

Yesterday you slept.

ESTRAGON:

I'll try.

He resumes his foetal posture, his head between his knees.

VLADIMIR:

Wait. (He goes over and sits down beside Estragon and begins to sing in a loud voice.)

Bye bye bye bye Bye bye-

ESTRAGON:

(looking up angrily). Not so loud!

VLADIMIR:

(softly).

Bye bye bye bye Bye bye bye bye Bye bye bye bye

Bye bye . . .

Estragon sleeps. Vladimir gets up softly, takes off his coat and lays it across Estragon's shoulders, then starts walking up and down, swinging his arms to keep himself warm. Estragon wakes with a start, jumps up, casts about wildly. Vladimir runs to him, puts his arms around him.) There . . . there . . . Didi is here . . . don't be afraid . . .

ESTRAGON:

Ah!

VLADIMIR:

There . . . there ... it's all over.

ESTRAGON:

I was falling—

VLADIMIR:

It's all over, it's all over.

ESTRAGON:

I was on top of a—

VLADIMIR:

Don't tell me! Come, we'll walk it off.

He takes Estragon by the arm and walks him up and down until Estragon refuses to go any further.

ESTRAGON:

That's enough. I'm tired.

VLADIMIR:

You'd rather be stuck there doing nothing?

ESTRAGON:

Yes.

VLADIMIR:

Please yourself.

He releases Estragon, picks up his coat and puts it on.

ESTRAGON:

Let's go.

VLADIMIR:

We can't.

ESTRAGON:

Why not?

VLADIMIR:

We're waiting for Godot.

ESTRAGON:

Ah! (Vladimir walks up and down.) Can you not stay still?

VLADIMIR:

I'm cold.

ESTRAGON:

We came too soon.

VLADIMIR:

It's always at nightfall.

ESTRAGON:

But night doesn't fall.

VLADIMIR:

It'll fall all of a sudden, like yesterday.

ESTRAGON:

Then it'll be night.

VLADIMIR:

And we can go.

ESTRAGON:

Then it'll be day again. (Pause. Despairing.) What'll we do, what'll we do!

VLADIMIR:

(halting, violently). Will you stop whining! I've had about my bellyful of your lamentations!

ESTRAGON:

I'm going.

VLADIMIR:

(seeingLucky's hat). Well!

ESTRAGON:

Farewell.

VLADIMIR:

Lucky's hat. (He goes towards it.) I've been here an hour and never saw it. (Very pleased.) Fine!

ESTRAGON:

You'll never see me again.

VLADIMIR:

I knew it was the right place. Now our troubles are over. (He picks up the hat, contemplates it, straightens it.) Must have been a very fine hat. (He puts it on in place of his own which he hands to Estragon.) Here.

ESTRAGON:

What?

VLADIMIR:

Hold that.

Estragon takes Vladimir's hat. Vladimir adjusts Lucky's hat on his head. Estragon puts on Vladimir's hat in place of his own which he hands to Vladimir. Vladimir takes Estragon's hat. Estragon adjusts Vladimir's hat on his head. Vladimir puts on Estragon's hat in place of Lucky's which he hands to Estragon. Estragon takes Lucky's hat. Vladimir adjusts Estragon's hat on his head. Estragon puts on Lucky's hat in place of Vladimir's which he hands to Vladimir. Vladimir takes his hat, Estragon adjusts Lucky's hat on his head. Vladimir puts on his hat in place of Estragon's which he hands to Estragon. Estragon takes his hat. Vladimir adjusts his hat on his head. Estragon puts on his hat in place of Lucky's which he hands to Vladimir. Vladimir takes Lucky's hat. Estragon adjusts his hat on his head. Vladimir puts on Lucky's hat in place of his own which he hands to Estragon. Estragon takes Vladimir's hat. Vladimir adjusts Lucky's hat on his head. Estragon hands Vladimir's hat back to Vladimir who takes it and hands it back to Estragon who takes it and hands it back to Vladimir who takes it and throws it down.

How does it fit me?

ESTRAGON:

How would I know?

VLADIMIR:

No, but how do I look in it?

He turns his head coquettishly to andfro, minces like a mannequin.

ESTRAGON:

Hideous.

VLADIMIR:

Yes, but not more so than usual?

ESTRAGON:

Neither more nor less.

VLADIMIR:

Then I can keep it. Mine irked me. (Pause.) How shall I say? (Pause.) It itched me.

He takes off Lucky's hat, peers into it, shakes it, knocks on the crown, puts it on again.

ESTRAGON:

I'm going.

Silence.

VLADIMIR:

Will you not play?

ESTRAGON:

Play at what?

VLADIMIR:

We could play at Pozzo and Lucky.

ESTRAGON:

Never heard of it.

VLADIMIR:

I'll do Lucky, you do Pozzo. (He imitates Lucky sagging under the weight of his baggage. Estragon looks at him with stupefaction.) Go on.

ESTRAGON:

What am I to do?

VLADIMIR:

Curse me!

ESTRAGON:

(after reflection). Naughty!

VLADIMIR:

Stronger!

ESTRAGON:

Gonococcus! Spirochete!

Vladimir sways back andforth, doubled in two.

VLADIMIR:

Tell me to think.

ESTRAGON:

What?

VLADIMIR:

Say, Think, pig!

ESTRAGON:

Think, pig!

Silence.

VLADIMIR:

I can't.

ESTRAGON:

That's enough of that.

VLADIMIR:

Tell me to dance.

ESTRAGON:

I'm going.

VLADIMIR:

Dance, hog! (He writhes. Exit Estragon left, precipitately.) I can't! (He looks up, misses Estragon.) Gogo! (He moves wildly about the stage. Enter Estragon left, panting. He hastens towards Vladimir, falls into his arms.) There you are again at last!

ESTRAGON:

I'm accursed!

VLADIMIR:

Where were you? I thought you were gone for ever.

ESTRAGON:

They're coming!

VLADIMIR:

Who?

ESTRAGON:

I don't know.

VLADIMIR:

How many?

ESTRAGON:

I don't know.

VLADIMIR:

(triumphantly). It's Godot! At last! Gogo! It's Godot! We're saved! Let's go and meet him! (He drags Estragon towards the wings. Estragon resists, pulls himself free, exit right.) Gogo! Come back! (Vladimir runs to extreme left, scans the horizon. Enter Estragon right, he hastens towards Vladimir, falls into his arms.) There you are again again!

ESTRAGON:

I'm in hell!

VLADIMIR:

Where were you?

ESTRAGON:

They're coming there too!

VLADIMIR:

We're surrounded! (Estragon makes a rush towards back.) Imbecile! There's no way out there. (He takes Estragon by the arm and drags him towards front. Gesture towards front.) There! Not a soul in sight! Off you go! Quick! (He pushes Estragon towards auditorium. Estragon recoils in horror.) You won't? (He contemplates auditorium.) Well I can understand that. Wait till I see. (He reflects.) Your only hope left is to disappear.

ESTRAGON:

Where?

VLADIMIR:

Behind the tree. (Estragon hesitates.) Quick! Behind the tree. (Estragon goes and crouches behind the tree, realizes he is not hidden, comes out from behind the tree.) Decidedly this tree will not have been the slightest use to us.

ESTRAGON:

(calmer). I lost my head. Forgive me. It won't happen again. Tell me what to do.

VLADIMIR:

There's nothing to do.

ESTRAGON:

You go and stand there. (He draws Vladimir to extreme right and places him with his back to the stage.) There, don't move, and watch out. (Vladimir scans horizon, screening his eyes with his hand. Estragon runs and takes up same position extreme left. They turn their heads and look at each other.) Back to back like in the good old days. (They continue to look at each other for a moment, then resume their watch. Long silence.) Do you see anything coming?

VLADIMIR:

(turning his head). What?

ESTRAGON:

(louder). Do you see anything coming?

VLADIMIR:

No.

ESTRAGON:

Nor I.

They resume their watch. Silence.

VLADIMIR:

You must have had a vision.

ESTRAGON:

(turning his head). What?

VLADIMIR:

(louder). You must have had a vision.

ESTRAGON:

No need to shout!

They resume their watch. Silence.

VLADIMIR and ESTRAGON:

(turning simultaneously). Do you—

VLADIMIR:

Oh pardon!

ESTRAGON:

Carry on.

VLADIMIR:

No no, after you.

ESTRAGON:

No no, you first.

VLADIMIR:

I interrupted you.

ESTRAGON:

On the contrary.

They glare at each other angrily.

VLADIMIR:

Ceremonious ape!

ESTRAGON:

Punctilious pig!

VLADIMIR:

Finish your phrase, I tell you!

ESTRAGON:

Finish your own!

Silence. They draw closer, halt.

VLADIMIR:

Moron!

ESTRAGON:

That's the idea, let's abuse each other.

They turn, move apart, turn again and face each other.

VLADIMIR:

Moron!

ESTRAGON:

Vermin!

VLADIMIR:

Abortion!

ESTRAGON:

Morpion!

VLADIMIR:

Sewer-rat!

ESTRAGON:

Curate!

VLADIMIR:

Cretin!

ESTRAGON:

(with finality). Crritic!

VLADIMIR:

Oh!

He wilts, vanquished, and turns away.

ESTRAGON:

Now let's make it up.

VLADIMIR:

Gogo!

ESTRAGON:

Didi!

VLADIMIR:

Your hand!

ESTRAGON:

Take it!

VLADIMIR:

Come to my arms!

ESTRAGON:

Yours arms?

VLADIMIR:

My breast!

ESTRAGON:

Off we go!

They embrace.

They separate. Silence.

VLADIMIR:

How time flies when one has fun! Silence.

ESTRAGON:

What do we do now?

VLADIMIR:

While waiting.

ESTRAGON:

While waiting.

Silence.

VLADIMIR:

We could do our exercises.

ESTRAGON:

Our movements.

VLADIMIR:

Our elevations.

ESTRAGON:

Our relaxations.

VLADIMIR:

Our elongations.

ESTRAGON:

Our relaxations.

VLADIMIR:

To warm us up.

ESTRAGON:

To calm us down.

VLADIMIR:

Off we go.

Vladimir hops from one foot to the other. Estragon imitates him.

ESTRAGON:

(stopping). That's enough. I'm tired.

VLADIMIR:

(stopping). We're not in form. What about a little deep breathing?

ESTRAGON:

I'm tired breathing.

VLADIMIR:

You're right. (Pause.) Let's just do the tree, for the balance.

ESTRAGON:

The tree?

Vladimir does the tree, staggering about on one leg.

VLADIMIR:

(stopping). Your turn.

Estragon does the tree, staggers.

ESTRAGON:

Do you think God sees me?

VLADIMIR:

You must close your eyes.

Estragon closes his eyes, staggers worse.

ESTRAGON:

(stopping, brandishing his fists, at the top of his voice.) God have pity on me!

VLADIMIR:

(vexed). And me?

ESTRAGON:

On me! On me! Pity! On me!

Enter Pozzo and Lucky. Pozzo is blind. Lucky burdened as before. Rope as before, but much shorter, so that Pozzo may follow more easily. Lucky wearing a different hat. At the sight of Vladimir and Estragon he stops short. Pozzo, continuing on his way, bumps into him.

VLADIMIR:

Gogo!

POZZO:

(clutching onto Lucky who staggers). What is it? Who is it?

Lucky falls, drops everything and brings down Pozzo with him. They lie helpless among the scattered baggage.

ESTRAGON:

Is it Godot?

VLADIMIR:

At last! (He goes towards the heap.) Reinforcements at last!

POZZO:

Help!

ESTRAGON:

Is it Godot?

VLADIMIR:

We were beginning to weaken. Now we're sure to see the evening out.

POZZO:

Help!

ESTRAGON:

Do you hear him?

VLADIMIR:

We are no longer alone, waiting for the night, waiting for Godot, waiting for . . . waiting. All evening we have struggled, unassisted. Now it's over. It's already tomorrow.

POZZO:

Help!

VLADIMIR:

Time flows again already. The sun will set, the moon rise, and we away . . . from here.

POZZO:

Pity!

VLADIMIR:

Poor Pozzo!

ESTRAGON:

I knew it was him.

VLADIMIR:

Who?

ESTRAGON:

Godot.

VLADIMIR:

But it's not Godot.

ESTRAGON:

It's not Godot?

VLADIMIR:

It's not Godot.

ESTRAGON:

Then who is it?

VLADIMIR:

It's Pozzo.

POZZO:

Here! Here! Help me up!

VLADIMIR:

He can't get up.

ESTRAGON:

Let's go.

VLADIMIR:

We can't.

ESTRAGON:

Why not?

VLADIMIR:

We're waiting for Godot.

ESTRAGON:

Ah!

VLADIMIR:

Perhaps he has another bone for you.

ESTRAGON:

Bone?

VLADIMIR:

Chicken. Do you not remember?

ESTRAGON:

It was him?

VLADIMIR:

Yes.

ESTRAGON:

Ask him.

VLADIMIR:

Perhaps we should help him first.

ESTRAGON:

To do what?

VLADIMIR:

To get up.

ESTRAGON:

He can't get up?

VLADIMIR:

He wants to get up.

ESTRAGON:

Then let him get up.

VLADIMIR:

He can't.

ESTRAGON:

Why not?

VLADIMIR:

I don't know.

Pozzo writhes, groans, beats the ground with his fists.

ESTRAGON:

We should ask him for the bone first. Then if he refuses we'll leave him there.

VLADIMIR:

You mean we have him at our mercy?

ESTRAGON:

Yes.

VLADIMIR:

And that we should subordinate our good offices to certain conditions?

ESTRAGON:

What?

VLADIMIR:

That seems intelligent all right. But there's one thing I'm afraid of.

POZZO:

Help!

ESTRAGON:

What?

VLADIMIR:

That Lucky might get going all of a sudden. Then we'd be ballocksed.

ESTRAGON:

Lucky?

VLADIMIR:

The one that went for you yesterday.

ESTRAGON:

I tell you there was ten of them.

VLADIMIR:

No, before that, the one that kicked you.

ESTRAGON:

Is he there?

VLADIMIR:

As large as life. (Gesture towards Lucky.) For the moment he is inert. But he might run amuck any minute.

POZZO:

Help!

ESTRAGON:

And suppose we gave him a good beating, the two of us.

VLADIMIR:

You mean if we fell on him in his sleep?

ESTRAGON:

Yes.

VLADIMIR:

That seems a good idea all right. But could we do it? Is he really asleep? (Pause.) No, the best would be to take advantage of Pozzo's calling for help—

POZZO:

Help!

VLADIMIR:

To help him—

ESTRAGON:

We help him?

VLADIMIR:

In anticipation of some tangible return.

ESTRAGON:

And suppose he—

VLADIMIR:

Let us not waste our time in idle discourse! (Pause. Vehemently.) Let us do something, while we have the chance! It is not every day that we are needed. Not indeed that we personally are needed. Others would meet the case equally well, if not better. To all mankind they were addressed, those cries for help still ringing in our ears! But at this place, at this moment of time, all mankind is us, whether we like it or not. Let us make the most of it, before it is too late! Let us represent worthily for once the foul brood to which a cruel fate consigned us! What do you say? (Estragon says nothing.) It is true that when with folded arms we weigh the pros and cons we are no less a credit to our species. The tiger bounds to the help of his congeners without the least reflection, or else he slinks away into the depths of the thickets. But that is not the question. What are we doing here, that is the question. And we are blessed in this, that we happen to know the answer. Yes, in this immense confusion one thing alone is clear. We are waiting for Godot to come—

ESTRAGON:

Ah!

POZZO:

Help!

VLADIMIR:

Or for night to fall. (Pause.) We have kept our appointment and that's an end to that. We are not saints, but we have kept our appointment. How many people can boast as much?

ESTRAGON:

Billions.

VLADIMIR:

You think so?

ESTRAGON:

I don't know.

VLADIMIR:

You may be right.

POZZO:

Help!

VLADIMIR:

All I know is that the hours are long, under these conditions, and constrain us to beguile them with proceedings which -how shall I say- which may at first sight seem reasonable, until they become a habit. You may say it is to prevent our reason from foundering. No doubt. But has it not long been straying in the night without end of the abyssal depths? That's what I sometimes wonder. You follow my reasoning?

ESTRAGON:

(iaphoristic for once). We are all born mad. Some remain so.

POZZO:

Help! I'll pay you!

ESTRAGON:

How much?

POZZO:

One hundred francs!

ESTRAGON:

It's not enough.

VLADIMIR:

I wouldn't go so far as that.

ESTRAGON:

You think it's enough?

VLADIMIR:

No, I mean so far as to assert that I was weak in the head when I came into the world. But that is not the question.

POZZO:

Two hundred!

VLADIMIR:

We wait. We are bored. {He throws up his hand.) No, don't protest, we are bored to death, there's no denying it. Good. A diversion comes along and what do we do? We

let it go to waste. Come, let's get to work! (He advances towards the heap, stops in his stride.) In an instant all will vanish and we'll be alone once more, in the midst of nothingness!

He broods.

POZZO:

Two hundred!

VLADIMIR:

We're coming!

He tries to pull Pozzo to his feet, fails, tries again, stumbles, falls, tries to get up, fails.

ESTRAGON:

What's the matter with you all?

VLADIMIR:

Help!

ESTRAGON:

I'm going.

VLADIMIR:

Don't leave me! They'll kill me!

POZZO:

Where am I?

VLADIMIR:

Gogo!

POZZO:

Help!

VLADIMIR:

Help!

ESTRAGON:

I'm going.

VLADIMIR:

Help me up first, then we'll go together.

ESTRAGON:

You promise?

VLADIMIR:

I swear it!

ESTRAGON:

And we'll never come back?

VLADIMIR:

Never!

ESTRAGON:

We'll go to the Pyrenees.

VLADIMIR:

Wherever you like.

ESTRAGON:

I've always wanted to wander in the Pyrenees.

VLADIMIR:

You'll wander in them.

ESTRAGON:

(recoiling). Who farted?

VLADIMIR:

Pozzo.

POZZO:

Here! Here! Pity!

ESTRAGON:

It's revolting!

VLADIMIR:

Quick! Give me your hand!

ESTRAGON:

I'm going. (Pause. Louder.) I'm going.

VLADIMIR:

Well I suppose in the end I'll get up by myself. (He tries, fails.) In the fullness of time.

ESTRAGON:

What's the matter with you?

VLADIMIR:

Go to hell.

ESTRAGON:

Are you staying there?

VLADIMIR:

For the time being.

ESTRAGON:

Come on, get up, you'll catch a chill.

VLADIMIR:

Don't worry about me.

ESTRAGON:

Come on, Didi, don't be pig-headed!

He stretches out his hand which Vladimir makes haste to seize.

VLADIMIR:

Pull!

Estragon pulls, stumbles, falls. Long silence.

POZZO:

Help!

VLADIMIR:

We've arrived.

POZZO:

Who are you?

VLADIMIR:

We are men.

Silence.

ESTRAGON:

Sweet mother earth!

VLADIMIR:

Can you get up?

ESTRAGON:

I don't know.

VLADIMIR:

Try.

ESTRAGON:

Not now, not now.

Silence.

POZZO:

What happened?

VLADIMIR:

(violently). Will you stop it, you! Pest! He can think of nothing but himself!

ESTRAGON:

What about a little snooze?

VLADIMIR:

Did you hear him? He wants to know what happened!

ESTRAGON:

Don't mind him. Sleep.

Silence.

POZZO:

Pity! Pity!

ESTRAGON:

(with a start). What is it?

VLADIMIR:

Were you asleep?

ESTRAGON:

I must have been.

VLADIMIR:

It's this bastard Pozzo at it again.

ESTRAGON:

Make him stop it. Kick him in the crotch.

ESTRAGON:

What do we do now?

VLADIMIR:

Perhaps I could crawl to him.

ESTRAGON:

Don't leave me!

VLADIMIR:

Or I could call to him.

ESTRAGON:

Yes, call to him.

VLADIMIR:

Pozzo! (Silence.) Pozzo! (Silence.) No reply.

ESTRAGON:

Together.

VLADIMIR and

ESTRAGON:

Pozzo! Pozzo!

VLADIMIR:

He moved.

ESTRAGON:

Are you sure his name is Pozzo?

VLADIMIR:

(alarmed). Mr. Pozzo! Come back! We won't hurt you!
Silence.

ESTRAGON:

We might try him with other names.

VLADIMIR:

I'm afraid he's dying.

ESTRAGON:

It'd be amusing.

VLADIMIR:

What'd be amusing?

ESTRAGON:

To try him with other names, one after the other. It'd pass the time. And we'd be bound to hit on the right one sooner or later.

VLADIMIR:

I tell you his name is Pozzo.

ESTRAGON:

We'll soon see. (He reflects.) Abel! Abel!

POZZO:

Help!

ESTRAGON:

Got it in one!

VLADIMIR:

I begin to weary of this motif.

ESTRAGON:

Perhaps the other is called Cain. Cain! Cain!

POZZO:

Help!

ESTRAGON:

He's all humanity. (Silence.) Look at the little cloud.

VLADIMIR:

(raising his eyes). Where?

ESTRAGON:

There. In the zenith.

VLADIMIR:

Well? (Pause.) What is there so wonderful about it?

Silence.

ESTRAGON:

Let's pass on now to something else, do you mind?

VLADIMIR:

I was just going to suggest it.

ESTRAGON:

But to what?

VLADIMIR:

Ah!

Silence.

ESTRAGON:

Suppose we got up to begin with?

VLADIMIR:

No harm trying.

They get up.

ESTRAGON:

Child's play.

VLADIMIR:

Simple question of will-power.

ESTRAGON:

And now?

POZZO:

Help!

ESTRAGON:

Let's go.

VLADIMIR:

We can't.

ESTRAGON:

Why not?

VLADIMIR:

We're waiting for Godot.

ESTRAGON:

Ah! (Despairing.) What'll we do, what'll we do!

POZZO:

Help!

VLADIMIR:

What about helping him?

ESTRAGON:

What does he want?

VLADIMIR:

He wants to get up.

ESTRAGON:

Then why doesn't he?

VLADIMIR:

He wants us to help him get up.

ESTRAGON:

Then why don't we? What are we waiting for?

They help Pozzo to his feet, let him go. He falls.

VLADIMIR:

We must hold him. (They get him up again. Pozzo sags between them, his arms round their necks.)

Feeling better?

POZZO:

Who are you?

VLADIMIR:

Do you not recognize us?

POZZO:

I am blind.
Silence.

ESTRAGON:

Perhaps he can see into the future.

VLADIMIR:

Since when?

POZZO:

I used to have wonderful sight— but are you friends?

ESTRAGON:

(laughing noisily). He wants to know if we are friends!

VLADIMIR:

No, he means friends of his.

ESTRAGON:

Well?

VLADIMIR:

We've proved we are, by helping him.

ESTRAGON:

Exactly. Would we have helped him if we weren't his friends?

VLADIMIR:

Possibly.

ESTRAGON:

True.

VLADIMIR:

Don't let's quibble about that now.

POZZO:

You are not highwaymen?

ESTRAGON:

Highwaymen! Do we look like highwaymen?

VLADIMIR:

Damn it, can't you see the man is blind!

ESTRAGON:

Damn it, so he is. (Pause.) So he says.

POZZO:

Don't leave me!

VLADIMIR:

No question of it.

ESTRAGON:

For the moment.

POZZO:

What time is it?

VLADIMIR:

(inspecting the sky). Seven o'clock . . . eight o'clock . . .

ESTRAGON:

That depends what time of year it is.

POZZO:

Is it evening?

Silence. Vladimir and Estragon scrutinize the sunset.

ESTRAGON:

It's rising.

VLADIMIR:

Impossible.

ESTRAGON:

Perhaps it's the dawn.

VLADIMIR:

Don't be a fool. It's the west over there.

ESTRAGON:

How do you know?

POZZO:

(anguished). Is it evening?

VLADIMIR:

Anyway, it hasn't moved.

ESTRAGON:

I tell you it's rising.

POZZO:

Why don't you answer me?

ESTRAGON:

Give us a chance.

VLADIMIR:

(reassuring). It's evening, Sir, it's evening, night is drawing nigh. My friend here would have me doubt it and I must confess he shook me for a moment. But it is not for nothing I have lived through this long day and I can assure you it is very near the end of its repertory. (Pause.) How do you feel now?

ESTRAGON:

How much longer are we to cart him around? (They half release him, catch him again as he falls.) We are not caryatids!

VLADIMIR:

You were saying your sight used to be good, if I heard you right.

POZZO:

Wonderful! Wonderful, wonderful sight!

Silence.

ESTRAGON:

(irritably). Expand! Expand!

VLADIMIR:

Let him alone. Can't you see he's thinking of the days when he was happy. (Pause.) Memoriapraeteritorum bononrn— that must be unpleasant.

ESTRAGON:

We wouldn't know.

VLADIMIR:

And it came on you all of a sudden?

POZZO:

Quite wonderful!

VLADIMIR:

I'm asking you if it came on you all of a sudden.

POZZO:

I woke up one fine day as blind as Fortune. (Pause.) Sometimes I wonder if I'm not still asleep.

VLADIMIR:

And when was that?

POZZO:

I don't know.

VLADIMIR:

But no later than yesterday—

POZZO:

(violently). Don't question me! The blind have no notion of time. The things of time are hidden from them too.

VLADIMIR:

Well just fancy that! I could have sworn it was just the opposite.

ESTRAGON:

I'm going.

POZZO:

Where are we?

VLADIMIR:

I couldn't tell you.

POZZO:

It isn't by any chance the place known as the Board?

VLADIMIR:

Never heard of it.

POZZO:

What is it like?

VLADIMIR:

(looking round). It's indescribable. It's like nothing. There's nothing. There's a tree.

POZZO:

Then it's not the Board.

ESTRAGON:

(sagging). Some diversion!

POZZO:

Where is my menial?

VLADIMIR:

He's about somewhere.

POZZO:

Why doesn't he answer when I call?

VLADIMIR:

I don't know. He seems to be sleeping. Perhaps he's dead.

POZZO:

What happened, exactly?

ESTRAGON:

Exactly!

VLADIMIR:

The two of you slipped. (Pause.) And fell.

POZZO:

Go and see is he hurt.

VLADIMIR:

We can't leave you.

POZZO:

You needn't both go.

VLADIMIR:

(to Estragon). You go.

ESTRAGON:

After what he did to me? Never!

POZZO:

Yes yes, let your friend go, he stinks so. (Silence.) What is he waiting for?

VLADIMIR:

What are you waiting for?

ESTRAGON:

I'm waiting for Godot.

Silence.

VLADIMIR:

What exactly should he do?

POZZO:

Well to begin with he should pull on the rope, as hard as he likes so long as he doesn't strangle him. He usually responds to that. If not he should give him a taste of his boot, in the face and the privates as far as possible.

VLADIMIR:

(to Estragon). You see, you've nothing to be afraid of. It's even an opportunity to revenge yourself.

ESTRAGON:

And if he defends himself?

POZZO:

No no, he never defends himself.

VLADIMIR:

I'll come flying to the rescue.

ESTRAGON:

Don't take your eyes off me.

He goes towards Lucky.

VLADIMIR:

Make sure he's alive before you start. No point in exerting yourself if he's dead.

ESTRAGON:

(bending over Lucky). He's breathing.

VLADIMIR:

Then let him have it.

With sudden fury Estragon starts kicking Lucky, hurling abuse at him as he does so. But he hurts his foot and moves away, limping and groaning. Lucky stirs.

ESTRAGON:

Oh the brute!

He sits down on the mound and tries to take off his boot. But he soon desists and disposes himself for sleep, his arms on his knees and his head on his arms.

POZZO:

What's gone wrong now?

VLADIMIR:

My friend has hurt himself.

POZZO:

And Lucky?

VLADIMIR:

So it is he?

POZZO:

What?

VLADIMIR:

It is Lucky?

POZZO:

I don't understand.

VLADIMIR:

And you are Pozzo?

POZZO:

Certainly I am Pozzo.

VLADIMIR:

The same as yesterday?

POZZO:

Yesterday?

VLADIMIR:

We met yesterday. (Silence.) Do you not remember?

POZZO:

I don't remember having met anyone yesterday. But tomorrow I won't remember having met anyone today. So don't count on me to enlighten you.

VLADIMIR:

But—

POZZO:

Enough! Up pig!

VLADIMIR:

You were bringing him to the fair to sell him. You spoke to us. He danced. He thought. You had your sight.

POZZO:

As you please. Let me go! (Vladimir moves away.) Up!

Lucky gets up, gathers up his burdens.

VLADIMIR:

Where do you go from here?

POZZO:

On. (Lucky, laden down, takes his place before Pozzo.) Whip! (Lucky puts everything down, looks for whip, finds it, puts it into Pozzo's hand, takes up everything again.) Rope!

Lucky puts everything down, puts end of rope into Pozzo's hand, takes up everything again.

VLADIMIR:

What is there in the bag?

POZZO:

Sand. (He jerks the rope.) On!

VLADIMIR:

Don't go yet.

POZZO:

I'm going.

VLADIMIR:

What do you do when you fall far from help?

POZZO:

We wait till we can get up. Then we go on. On!

VLADIMIR:

Before you go tell him to sing.

POZZO:

Who?

VLADIMIR:

Lucky.

POZZO:

To sing?

VLADIMIR:

Yes. Or to think. Or to recite.

POZZO:

But he is dumb.

VLADIMIR:

Dumb!

POZZO:

Dumb. He can't even groan.

VLADIMIR:

Dumb! Since when?

POZZO:

(suddenly furious.) Have you not done tormenting me with your accursed time! It's abominable! When! When! One day, is that not enough for you, one day he went dumb, one day I went blind, one day we'll go deaf, one day we were born, one day we shall die, the same day, the same second, is that not enough for you? (Calmer.) They give birth astride of a grave, the light gleams an instant, then it's night once more. (He jerks the rope.) On!

Exeunt Pozzo and Lucky. Vladimir follows them to the edge of the stage, looks after them. The noise of falling, reinforced by mimic of Vladimir, announces that they are down again. Silence. Vladimir goes towards Estragon, contemplates him a moment, then shakes him awake.

ESTRAGON:

(wildgestures, incoherent words. Finally.) Why will you never let me sleep? **VLADIMIR:**

I felt lonely.

ESTRAGON:

I was dreaming I was happy.

VLADIMIR:

That passed the time.

ESTRAGON:

I was dreaming that—

VLADIMIR:

(violently). Don't tell me! (Silence.) I wonder is he really blind.

ESTRAGON:

Blind? Who?

VLADIMIR:

Pozzo.

ESTRAGON:

Blind?

VLADIMIR:

He told us he was blind.

ESTRAGON:

Well what about it?

VLADIMIR:

It seemed to me he saw us.

ESTRAGON:

You dreamt it. (Pause.) Let's go. We can't. Ah! (Pause.) Are you sure it wasn't him?

VLADIMIR:

Who?

ESTRAGON:

Godot.

VLADIMIR:

But who?

ESTRAGON:

Pozzo.

VLADIMIR:

Not at all !(Less sure.) Not at all! (Still less sure.) Not at all!

ESTRAGON:

I suppose I might as well get up. (He gets up painfully.) Ow! Didi!

VLADIMIR:

I don't know what to think any more.

ESTRAGON:

My feet! (He sits down again and tries to take off his boots.) Help me!

VLADIMIR:

Was I sleeping, while the others suffered? Am I sleeping now? Tomorrow, when I wake, or think I do, what shall I say of today? That with Estragon my friend, at this place, until the fall of night, I waited for Godot? That Pozzo passed, with his carrier, and that he spoke to us? Probably. But in all that what truth will there be?

(Estragon, having struggled with his boots in vain, is dozing off again. Vladimir looks at him.) He'll know nothing. He'll tell me about the blows he received and I'll give him a carrot. (Pause.) Astride of a grave and a difficult birth. Down in the hole, lingeringly, the grave digger puts on the forceps. We have time to grow old. The air is full of our cries. (He listens.) But habit is a great deadener. (He looks again at Estragon.) At me too someone is looking, of me too someone is saying, He is sleeping, he knows nothing, let him sleep on. (Pause.) I can't go on! (Pause.) What have I said?

He goes feverishly to and fro, halts finally at extreme left, broods. Enter Boy right.

He halts. Silence.

BOY:

Mister . . . (Vladimir turns.) Mister Albert. . .

VLADIMIR:

Off we go again. (Pause.) Do you not recognize me?

BOY:

No Sir.

VLADIMIR:

It wasn't you came yesterday.

BOY:

No Sir.

VLADIMIR:

This is your first time.

BOY:

Yes Sir.

Silence.

VLADIMIR:

You have a message from Mr. Godot.

BOY:

Yes Sir.

VLADIMIR:

He won't come this evening.

BOY:

No Sir.

VLADIMIR:

But he'll come tomorrow.

BOY:

Yes Sir.

VLADIMIR:

Without fail.

BOY:

Yes Sir.

Silence.

VLADIMIR:

Did you meet anyone?

BOY:

No Sir.

VLADIMIR:

Two other . . . (he hesitates). . . men?

BOY:

I didn't see anyone, Sir.

Silence.

VLADIMIR:

What does he do, Mr. Godot? (Silence.) Do you hear me?

BOY:

Yes Sir.

VLADIMIR:

Well?

BOY:

He does nothing, Sir.

Silence.

VLADIMIR:

How is your brother?

BOY:

He's sick, Sir.

VLADIMIR:

Perhaps it was he came yesterday.

BOY:

I don't know, Sir.

Silence.

VLADIMIR:

(softly). Has he a beard, Mr. Godot?

BOY:

Yes Sir.

VLADIMIR:

Fair or . . . (he hesitates)... or black?

BOY:

I think it's white, Sir.

Silence.

VLADIMIR:

Christ have mercy on us!

Silence.

BOY:

What am I to tell Mr. Godot, Sir?

VLADIMIR:

Tell him . . . (he hesitates). . . tell him you saw me and that. . . (he hesitates). . . that you saw me. (Pause. Vladimir advances, the Boy recoils. Vladimir halts, the Boy halts. With sudden violence.) You're sure you saw me, you won't come and tell me tomorrow that you never saw me!

Silence. Vladimir makes a sudden spring forward, the Boy avoids him and exits running. Silence. The sun sets, the moon rises. As in Act 1. Vladimir stands motionless and bowed. Estragon wakes, takes off his boots, gets up with one in each hand and goes and puts them down center front, then goes towards Vladimir.

ESTRAGON:

What's wrong with you?

VLADIMIR:

Nothing.

ESTRAGON:

I'm going.

VLADIMIR:

So am I.

ESTRAGON:

Was I long asleep?

VLADIMIR:

I don't know.

Silence.

ESTRAGON:

Where shall we go?

VLADIMIR:

Not far.

ESTRAGON:

Oh yes, let's go far away from here.

VLADIMIR:

We can't.

ESTRAGON:

Why not?

VLADIMIR:

We have to come back tomorrow.

ESTRAGON:

What for?

VLADIMIR:

To wait for Godot.

ESTRAGON:

Ah! (Silence.) He didn't come?

VLADIMIR:

No.

ESTRAGON:

And now it's too late.

VLADIMIR:

Yes, now it's night.

ESTRAGON:

And if we dropped him? (Pause.) If we dropped him?

VLADIMIR:

He'd punish us. (Silence. He looks at the tree.) Everything's dead but the tree.

ESTRAGON:

(looking at the tree). What is it?

VLADIMIR:

It's the tree.

ESTRAGON:

Yes, but what kind?

VLADIMIR:

I don't know. A willow.

Estragon draws Vladimir towards the tree. They stand motionless before it. Silence.

ESTRAGON:

Why don't we hang ourselves?

VLADIMIR:

With what?

ESTRAGON:

You haven't got a bit of rope?

VLADIMIR:

No.

ESTRAGON:

Then we can't.

Silence.

VLADIMIR:

Let's go.

ESTRAGON:

Wait, there's my belt.

VLADIMIR:

It's too short.

ESTRAGON:

You could hang onto my legs.

VLADIMIR:

And who'd hang onto mine?

ESTRAGON:

True.

VLADIMIR:

Show me all the same. (Estragon loosens the cord that holds up his trousers which, much too big for him, fall about his ankles. They look at the cord.) It might do in a pinch. But is it strong enough?

ESTRAGON:

We'll soon see. Here.

They each take an end of the cord and pull.

It breaks. They almost fall.

VLADIMIR:

Not worth a curse.

Silence.

ESTRAGON:

You say we have to come back tomorrow?

VLADIMIR:

Yes.

ESTRAGON:

Then we can bring a good bit of rope.

VLADIMIR:

Yes.

Silence.

ESTRAGON:

Didi?

VLADIMIR:

Yes.

ESTRAGON:

I can't go on like this.

VLADIMIR:

That's what you think.

ESTRAGON:

If we parted? That might be better for us.

VLADIMIR:

We'll hang ourselves tomorrow. (Pause.) Unless Godot comes.

ESTRAGON:

And if he comes?

www.ingramcontent.com/pod-product-compliance
Lightning Source LLC
Chambersburg PA
CBHW020211290326
41948CB00001B/11